PORSCHE

RS

PORSCHE

RS

Cover design by Danielle Farmer
Type set in Source Sans Pro/Bebes Neue

ISBN: 978-0-7643-6915-5
Printed in China

Published by Schiffer Publishing, Ltd.
4880 Lower Valley Road
Atglen, PA 19310
Phone: (610) 593-1777; Fax: (610) 593-2002
Email: Info@schifferbooks.com
Web: www.schifferbooks.com

For our complete selection of fine books on this and related subjects, please visit our website at www.schifferbooks.com. You may also write for a free catalog.

Schiffer Publishing's titles are available at special discounts for bulk purchases for sales promotions or premiums. Special editions, including personalized covers, corporate imprints, and excerpts, can be created in large quantities for special needs. For more information, contact the publisher.

We are always looking for people to write books on new and related subjects. If you have an idea for a book, please contact us at proposals@schifferbooks.com.

CONSTANTIN BERGANDER | FABIAN HOBERG | PETER BESSER

PORSCHE
RS

DEVELOPMENT, HISTORY, AND TECHNOLOGY

SCHIFFER PUBLISHING

4880 Lower Valley Road • Atglen, PA 19310

Contents

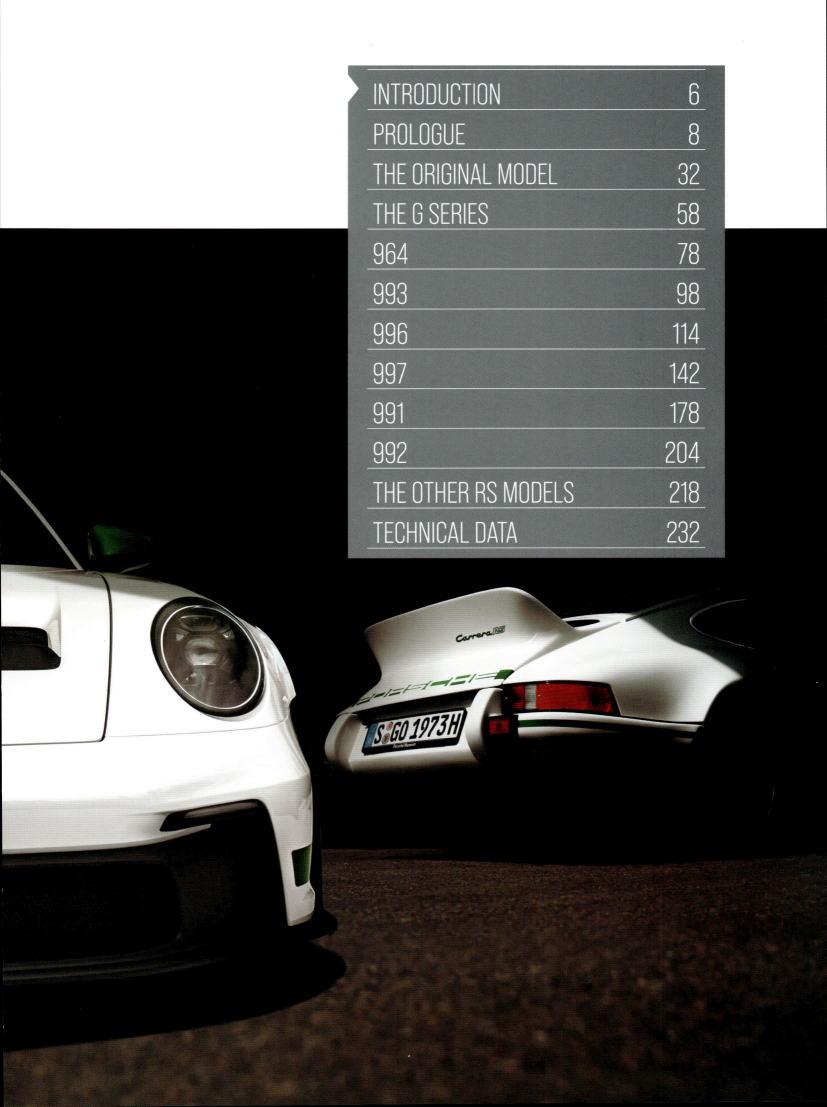

INTRODUCTION

Dear Porsche 911 drivers, fans, and admirers,

What "RS" means at Porsche can be experienced in many different ways. We think the most exciting (and probably the best) way is the following: with a racing driver at the wheel—preferably Walter Röhrl—a helmet on one's head, and a racetrack under the tires. As friends of dynamic locomotion, we are generally reluctant to give up the steering wheel but are happy to make an exception for professionals—especially since "the tall one" complements the RS experience fabulously with his unrivaled wealth of experience.

While conducting research for this book, we experienced the RS intensively with every fiber of our bodies. In the Porsche archive, we collected interesting and revealing material from seven decades to reconstruct history and communication as faithfully as possible. We also delved into contemporary magazines that categorized the cars precisely. We spent hours in telephone conversations with developers and designers who were part of the RS story. And of course, around and in the car—always unselfishly and exclusively out of scientific interest.

We particularly enjoyed speaking with those who were and are responsible for the RS at Porsche. They worked with so much enthusiasm and love for the car that, even decades later, they can still remember details, experiences, quotes, anecdotes, and work steps—and more than fifty years later, even the origin of the 911 Carrera RS 2.7 to the exact day.

In this book, we have collected all that has been passed on, preserved, conveyed, written, and experienced to provide a multifaceted insight into Porsche's 911 RS world. With its ascetic vehicles, the manufacturer has been setting the standard for dynamic road cars for decades.

We would like to take this opportunity to thank all those who made this possible, including Frank Jung and Jens Torner from the Porsche Archive; Astrid Böttinger, Kuno Werner, and Kai Roos from the Porsche Museum; Jonas Bierschneider from the Porsche press department; and the RS experts August Achleitner, Jürgen Barth, Hermann Burst, Tilman Brodbeck, Peter Falk, Harm Lagaaij, Walter Röhrl, Roland Kussmaul, and Andreas Preuninger. Without their support, this book would not have been possible.

We would also like to thank Peter Besser, Jonas Seidel, and Steven Raunheimer for their fabulous photos; Björn Tolksdorf, and Timo Friedmann for their fine-tuning of the text; and Sarah Schröder for her support. We hope this book provides you much reading enjoyment!

Fabian Hoberg & Constantin Bergander, Autumn 2022

Constantin Bergander

Fabian Hoberg

PROLOGUE

The idea for the 911 Carrera RS 2.7 was born when a 911 T proved too slow in curves: without a rear wing, the 911 produced a lot of lift. This was particularly tricky when cornering. Ernst Fuhrmann commissioned the development of optimizations in 1972 because he saw his 911 lose at the International DMV Cup race in Hockenheim.

Ernst Fuhrmann was having a bad day. When he traveled to the Hockenheimring on May 14, 1972, he was met by rain and cold. Only a few motorsport fans were at the track with him to experience the traditional "Hockenheim May Cup" live. Some stayed home because the event fell on Mother's Day. Others left early because it was simply too wet in the spectator areas.

Fuhrmann was not thinking of leaving, because he wanted to see his car win. The brand-new German Racing Championship (DRM), an early forerunner of the later DTM, was hosting its second race of the season. As management spokesman at Porsche, Fuhrmann was keeping a very close eye on how the Porsche 911 T performed on his employer's home track.

He experienced an exciting race. Hans-Joachim Stuck started in the pole position but missed the start. He and his Ford Capri RS 2600 had to work their way back up from third position. Klaus Fritzinger, a private racing driver in last year's Capri, was a tough opponent, but Stuck still managed to get back

to the front and won by a narrow margin—even though his six-cylinder engine was running on only five cylinders for the entire race.

None of that interested Fuhrmann, because, while three Ford teams finished on the podium, things went badly for Porsche. Entrepreneur and racing driver Hartmut Kautz managed only sixth place in his 911. The only 911 in the field lagged behind the crowd. It was an embarrassment. Fuhrmann knew that motorsport was the soul of Porsche. If the soul is suffering, then the body is usually not doing well either.

It is not known exactly how Fuhrmann reacted to the failure after the race, whether he shouted angrily at his employees or spoke to them calmly. But there was the power of the boardroom in his voice when he asked the Porsche engineers present: "What caused it?" They had no answer. Perplexed faces. And the air was thick in the pit lane.

INTERNATIONALES DMV MAI-POKAL-RENNEN
für Motorräder aller Klassen
Rennwagen Formel 3
und Deutsche Rennsportmeisterschaft
Division 1 und 2

14. MAI 1972

Conti TS Stahlgürtel
mit unübertroffener km-Leistung

MOTODROM HOCKENHEIM

Veranstalter: Badischer Motorsport-Club e. V./DMV Hockenheim
u. Rheydter Club für Motorsport e. V./DMV Rheydt
Offizielles Rennprogramm Preis DM 2,–

On May 14, 1972, Hockenheim hosted one of the rounds of the newly created German Racing Championship. Stuck dominated in the rain in a Ford; Porsche failed.

A WINNER EMERGES FROM DEFEAT

What we do know, however, is what happened next. Immediately after the disappointing race on Sunday, the development of a future legend began at Porsche. Fuhrmann initiated changes to the Porsche 911 to make the car competitive—and thus initiated the design and construction of the 911 Carrera RS 2.7.

He commissioned a specification sheet and a brief description for future modifications to the 911. In the weeks and months that followed, his developers devoted themselves to lightweight construction, aerodynamics, and performance enhancement.

These building blocks established a long-standing tradition in the 911 model series. From then on, the letters RS stood for very special 911s. For those derivatives that were closer to the track than to the road. For whom speed is more important than composure, who put lightness before luxury. RS stood for "Renn Sport," or racing sport in English.

October 2022 marked the fiftieth anniversary of this first 911 RS, with the eye-catching ducktail and Carrera lettering on the side. In the decades that followed, its successors continued to develop its legacy with the continuous pursuit of better driving performance. Not all of them adopted its teachings, but they did surpass themselves with each generation.

THE RS STORY

Long before Fuhrmann had the 911 developed into an RS, other Porsches bore those letters. The first was the 550 Spyder RS in 1953, a featherweight racer that achieved fame, and not only on the racetrack. It was followed in 1957 by the 718 RS. It was produced in various versions but was always easy to handle, light and powerful. These cars were victorious in several classes.

The Porsche brand celebrated its greatest motorsport successes with the 917, winning the World Sports Car Championship twice before the regulations ruled it out. An equal replacement was out of the question for financial reasons. Instead, Porsche sent the 911 to the racetrack. It first had to fail in customer sport before becoming immortal.

THE FIRST PORSCHE RS: PORSCHE 550 1500 RS SPYDER CARRERA

Porsche's RS history began long before the legendary two-seven. As early as October 1953, the manufacturer presented its first RS model at the Paris Motor Show. An open-top sports car, a Spyder, was displayed there. Porsche called it the 550 1500 RS Spyder Carrera. It would be the manufacturer's first sports car specially developed for racing that customers would also be able to drive on public roads. With the Porsche 356, it was the other way around. This special feature made the 550 1500 RS the blueprint for all future RS models.

Colloquially, this car lost its iconic nickname. In common parlance, it was simply called the Porsche 550, because it was the car manufacturer's 550th design. Anyone who

With the 550 Spyder, Porsche won the class in 1954 and achieved third place overall in the Carrera Panamericana against the larger-displacement competition.

talks about the car like a sober official will slur the 1500 (displacement in cubic centimeters), the RS (racing sport), the Spyder (open-top car), and the Carrera (borrowed from the Carrera Panamericana). In other words, everything that truly makes it special.

78 HP AT THE STARTING LINE

Initially, the Porsche 550 could hardly fulfill its promise of great sport for the road. It was fitted with a modified engine from the Porsche 356, which produced 78 hp, a modest figure even back then. Unlike in its donor car, it now sat in front of the rear axle, with the transmission behind it. The four-cylinder engine worked reliably, but it was not a high-revving, durable racing engine. It also lacked the power for motorsport. Engineer Dr. Ernst Fuhrmann, who later became the head of Porsche, was therefore given the task of developing a high-performance engine as early as 1952.

Fuhrmann was known as a man of rapid throttle changes and spontaneous engine characterization. The subject of his doctoral thesis at university was "Valve trains in high-speed combustion engines." What he developed ran wonderfully fast. His new engine, the Type 547, was put to the test for the first time on April 2, 1953. It produced 110 hp at 7,800 rpm.

RS STANDS FOR RACING SPORT

Just one year later, he installed the engine in racing cars. The 1.5-liter four-cylinder boxer engine had two camshafts per cylinder bank, driven by a king-shaft, with dual ignition, two ignition coils, and two distributors. It now produced 117 hp at 7,800 rpm. It was a thoroughbred racing engine that was too sophisticated for large-scale production cars. Nevertheless, it became the nucleus of Porsche's successes over the next decade.

However, the Porsche 550 made its racing debut with a different drive system. In the summer of 1953, it was the first car with a rear-mid engine to start in the 24 Hours of Le Mans. Equipped with a modified 1.5-liter VW engine, it was driven by Richard von Frankenberg and Paul Frère to a respectable fifteenth place. Directly behind them: racing legends Hans Herrmann and Helmut Glöckler, also in a Porsche. The cars even took first and second place in the classification up to 1,600 cc (97.6 cu. in.).

It was a first, hopeful success. In 1954, Porsche finally installed the Fuhrmann engine in the 550 Spyder. Four gears transmitted power to the rear wheels, while a limited slip differential ensured sufficient traction in curves. The lightweight runabout—weighing just 550 kilograms (1,213 lbs.)—was able to reach speeds of up to 220 kph (137 mph). The frame of the 550 Spyder consisted of welded tubes, the body of light metal in self-supporting composite construction. Production of the 550 Spyder totaled fourteen factory and seventy customer cars. Of these, thirty-three went to the USA. The price for a new car on the German market was 24,600 marks. This made the sports car almost twice as expensive as a Porsche 356, which in turn cost as much as two VW Beetles. For 1956, Porsche optimized the frame and drivetrain in the 550 A. That year, Porsche produced seven factory cars and thirty-three customer cars, seventeen of which went to the USA. According to Porsche's own information, only 124 units of the 550 Spyder were built by 1957. Other sources put the figure at 144 vehicles.

Among Porsche's victories with the 718 RS 60 Spyder was the 1960 Targa Florio.

THE 718 AND ITS SUCCESSORS

When Porsche replaced the 550 in 1957, only insiders were aware of it. Its successor, the 718 RSK, looked almost identical to its predecessor. However, it now featured significantly faster technology. It was lighter, better on the brakes, and more powerful on the accelerator. Once again, Fuhrmann's Carrera engine powered the wildest road-going Porsche of the year. At the start of production, the engine was given a slight power boost to 148 hp. In 1958, a larger displacement (1.6 liters or 97.6 cu. in.) and again more power (160 hp) followed.

During its five-year production period, the car evolved in line with FIA regulations. For 1960, the motorsport authorities demanded more everyday benefits; for example, improved range, more room, and better visibility. Porsche responded by enlarging the fuel tank, trunk, and windshield. From then on, an internal windshield wiper in the open car removed spray or condensation from the windshield. The performance remained the same, as did the focus on motorsport. But the look and name changed. At the start of the new decade, the car was called the 718 RS 60 Spyder.

Fifty-six years later, the German magazine *Auto Motor und Sport* described the 1960 model as "the perfect man-machine unit" because it carried no weight that was not absolutely necessary and because its passengers could nestle precisely between the tubular steel mesh and the upholstery. These were characteristics that helped the small, light, and maneuverable racing cars achieve success in motorsport. Porsche Spyders won the European hill climb championships between 1958 and 1961 and again between 1963 and 1965.

FURHMANN FINALE IN THE 904

The 718's successor, the 1963 904, was also powered by a modified Carrera engine, now with a displacement of 2 liters (122 cu. in.) and an output of 180 hp. After around ten years of evolution, the Fuhrmann engine reached its peak performance. How fitting, because the 904 was a powerful racing car with a top speed of over 250 kph (155 mph). Today, it is almost unimaginable that there was a slightly modified version of it sold under the name Carrera GTS with road approval.

The 904 was the logical further development of the RS concept—without using the famous nickname. It was also characterized by its low weight and high performance. The developers of the mid-engined GT sports car achieved the special lightness for the first time with a plastic body. Despite its high price of 29,700 deutsch marks, the one hundred units planned for homologation sold out immediately.

The 904 scored its first victory in 1964 at the legendary Targa Florio endurance race. A year later, Eugen Böhringer and Rolf Wütherich took second place in the Monte Carlo Rally in a 904. Wütherich shared a tragic fate that was associated with the Porsche brand. Ten years earlier, he had been sitting next to James Dean when the actor was killed in an accident in the USA in a 550 Spyder.

Hans Herrmann and his Porsche 550 Spyder at the Carrera Panamericana in 1954

The first mid-engine car at the 24 Hours of Le Mans: in 1953, Hans Herrmann's Porsche started the race on the Seine in the Porsche 550 Coupe.

In 1954, the 1.5-liter Fuhrmann engine in the Porsche 550 Spyder produced 110 hp. The car was capable of speeds of 220 kph.

The interior of the Porsche 550 Spyder: two narrow seats, a thin steering wheel, three round instruments, and little space

The Fuhrmann engine made its last appearance in the Porsche 904 (road version: Carrera GTS). It was too complicated for use in large-scale production.

The Porsche 904 Carrera GTS of 1963 was the logical further development of the RS concept. If you wanted one of the one hundred homologation examples, you had to be prepared to invest a good 30,000 deutsch marks in those days.

*Herbert Müller and Willy
Mairesse won the Targa
Florio in the Porsche 906
Carrera in 1966.*

*On the way to the Monte
Carlo rally: Eugen
Böhringer and Rolf
Wüterich with their
Porsche 904. Beside it are
Peter Falk and Herbert
Linke with their Porsche
911 2.0 Coupe.*

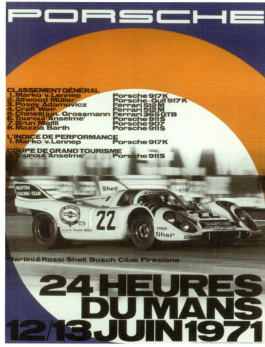

Demonstration of power: Helmut Marko and Gijs van Lennep won the 1971 24 Hours of Le Mans in a Porsche 917K with a two-lap lead over the runner-up, another Porsche 917 KH. The year before, Hans Herrmann and Richard Attwood in the 917 KH with starting number 23 secured the first triumph for the still-young Porsche company in the endurance classic on the Sarthe.

The 906/Carrera 6 was created in 1965 as the successor to the 904, powered by the racing version of the six-cylinder engine from the new 911. Porsche also fitted the sports car with an optional eight-cylinder boxer engine. It became a light, fast, and successful racing car with road approval. Only eighty units were built. Porsche stopped using the Carrera engine. After almost ten years, it was technically exhausted. Even in the first Porsche 911 presented in 1963, there was no place for the engine. Large-scale production would be too complex and expensive d. Due to the complex technology involved, Porsche only trusted a few specialists worldwide to carry out maintenance work on the racing engine.

PORSCHE EYES A NEW RACING SERIES

At the end of the 1960s, Porsche successfully competed in several classes. At enormous financial risk, the manufacturer even took part in the prestigious sports car championship. And it was a success. In 1970, the Porsche 917 mid-engined sports car achieved overall victory at Le Mans. It became one of the most successful racing sports cars of the 1970s. However, Porsche could no longer participate in the sports car championship with it after 1972. Henceforth, the FIA allowed a maximum displacement of 3 liters (183 cu. in.). The engines of the 917 were 4.9 liters (299 cu. in.) at that time.

Porsche therefore had to reposition itself strategically in motorsport. The 917 competed successfully in the North American CanAm series, which allowed large engines.

On the domestic market, the manufacturer wanted to get into broad-based customer sport and attract more private drivers. The best way to do this was in the German Automobile Circuit Championship (DARM). However, at that time it was dominated by the cars from Alfa Romeo, BMW, and Ford.

In 1972, the "Big Division," of up to 4-liter (244 cu. in.) displacement, began in the new German Racing Championship (DRM)—the most important racing series in Germany. All the greats of motorsport competed in Group 2 ("improved touring cars") or Group 4 ("sports cars," or beginning in 1970, "special

GT vehicles"). Several BMWs, Ford Capris, and Ford Escorts raced here. Porsche drivers competed with the 911. However, it could not keep up with the competition at higher speeds. On May 14, 1972, Ernst Fuhrmann realized this, too. And he acted. A few months later, the Porsche 911 Carrera RS 2.7 was created on his initiative.

For the FIA homologation of Group 4, Porsche had to build five hundred vehicles within twelve months and a total of a thousand units in the same period for Group 3 ("GT vehicles"). This would mean that the new Porsche 911 would not be a pure road racing car, but a sports car with road homologation that could also be used in racing.

The successor to the Porsche 356 was initially called the Porsche 901, and the example shown here is the last one that originally still had a zero in its name.

PORSCHE 911

In 1963, Porsche unveiled the successor to the 356 C. The Porsche 901 made its debut at the IAA in Frankfurt am Main. The 2+2-seater coupe outperformed its predecessor in almost all disciplines, especially in terms of size, room, and engine power. Production did not begin until September 1964 because the car had not yet been fully developed when it made its debut. In addition, the 904 racing car initially occupied Porsche's only assembly hall. At its market launch, the car was called the Porsche 911 because Peugeot owned the trademark rights to three-digit numbers with a zero in the middle.

The idea for the 911 went back to the mid-1950s. In 1957, Erwin Komenda, then chief designer of the body shop, sketched out a possible successor to the 356 together with Alexander Porsche. Porsche's four-seater design, designated 754 T7, was developed into a prototype.

Ferry Porsche wanted a larger interior for the new car but did not insist on full-size rear seats. He also included a larger trunk, a smoother-running engine, and cheaper maintenance into the specifications. All that remained of his son's proposal was the front end. The body was shorter, the rear narrower.

SIX-CYLINDER BOXER ENGINE FROM THE BEGINNING

Test manager Klaus von Rücker, together with Ferdinand Piëch and Hans Mezger, developed an air-cooled 2.0-liter six-cylinder boxer engine for the 911. The new unit was to be more powerful than the four-cylinder engines of the 356 but cost less than the eight-cylinder engines of the GT racing cars. As a result, it had overhead camshafts, seven crankshaft main bearings, chain drive for the valves, and dry sump lubrication—the 911 standard for several decades.

The new boxer engine delivered 130 hp at 6,100 rpm and could handle up to 7,100 rpm in series production. It pushed the 911 from 0 to 100 kph (0 to 62 mph) in 8.8 seconds and gave it a top speed of 211 kph (131 mph). Equipped with this drivetrain, the 911 cost 21,900 deutsch marks at launch.

THE MOTORSPORT CAREER OF THE PORSCHE 911

The 911 competed in motorsport for the first time In January 1965. At the wheel at the time was Peter Falk, later project manager of the 911 Carrera RS 2.7. At the Monte Carlo Rally, he and Herbert Lange took fifth place in a near-production 911. Only bucket seats, an engine souped up to 160 hp, and a shorter ratio gearbox made the difference from the production car. This was followed by several motorsport successes in rally and GT championships.

In 1967, Porsche launched the lightweight 911 R racing version. Hoods, doors, bumpers, and front fenders were all made of lightweight plastic. Front side panels made of thinner glass and rear windows made of plastic reduced the car's weight even further. The coupe weighed around 800 kilograms (1,764 lbs.) after the radical makeover. It was powered by a Carrera 6 boxer engine producing 210 hp. Only twenty-four vehicles were made, including the prototypes. This car prepared the Porsche teams mentally for a project that would only come to fruition five years later.

MORE DISPLACEMENT FOR IMPROVED PERFORMANCE

Beginning in the summer of 1969, Porsche increased the displacement of the 911 engines from 2.0 to 2.2 liters (122 to 134 cu. in.). For the road versions, this meant an output of up to 180 hp. With a displacement of 2,247 cubic centimeters (137 cu. in.), the racing engine of the 911

produced 230 hp. The car now started in the higher GT class up to 2.5 liters (153 cu. in.).

In 1971, the racing department opted for even larger cylinders. The engineers increased the displacement of the boxer engine to exactly 2,381 cubic centimeters (145 cu. in.) and drew around 250 hp from the engine at 7,800 rpm. At the 24 Hours of Le Mans, a 911 finished sixth overall and first in its class.

In 1972, the production vehicles followed suit. However, Porsche did not change the bore but installed a crankshaft with a longer stroke (70.4 instead of 66 millimeters, or 2.8 instead of 2.6 inches). The racing department used this shaft to build a new engine. It increased the bore to 86.7 millimeters (3.41 inches), resulting in a displacement of 2,494 cubic centimeters (152 cu. in.). With mechanical direct injection, the engine in the Porsche 911 S 2.5 delivered around 270 hp. The competition car, priced at 49,000 marks, was produced in a small series to compete against the powerful BMWs and Fords in the GT class.

It was only with the development of the Porsche 911 Carrera RS 2.7 that a competitive 911 was created that could consistently hold its own against other brands. "The 911 Carrera RS 2.7 was conceived as a homologation vehicle. It was designed to be a very light, fast sports car, without frippery and lots of electronics," recalled Peter Falk, former head of testing for production vehicles at Porsche.

The 1967 911 R weighed only 800 kilograms (1,765 pounds). Only 23 examples of the 210hp super Porsche were built.

*Two RS milestones: the Porsche 911
Carrera RS 2.7 of 1972 and the Porsche 550
1500 RS Spyder Carrera of 1954*

*Initially, only the sharpest
derivatives were allowed to bear
the name Carrera. Porsche later
changed the nomenclature.*

Over the next fifty years, Porsche developed the RS idea from an exceptional sports car to a sub-brand. Always in focus: more power, consistent lightweight construction, sophisticated aerodynamics, and racing technology. There is still no end in sight to this story.

CARRERA

The word "Carrera" is firmly associated with Porsche. Like the sports cars themselves, the term originates from motorsport. In the demanding Carrera Panamericana endurance race in Mexico, most manufacturers had relied on large engines in

heavy sports cars for many years. Porsche, on the other hand, favored small, high-revving engines in lightweight vehicles—a winning combination.

In the 1953 edition of the race, Porsche would start with two 550 Spyders. In addition, there were two 550 Spyders from the Automobile Club of Guatemala with drivers Jose Herrarte and Jaroslav Juhan. A total of ten of the 192 starters would be driving Porsches. Herrarte won the class up to 1,600 cubic centimeters (97.6 cu. in.) in this tough sports car world championship race, driving prototype number 2 of the 550 Spyder 1500 RS. He finished in thirty-second place overall.

One year later, Porsche wanted to prove its dominance once again. The 1954 Porsche 550 Spyder was fitted with the new Fuhrmann engine, which had previously been tested in terms of performance and durability for thousands of miles on the Nordschleife of the Nürburgring. Hans-Herrmann also won the class at the Mille Miglia with the new engine.

At the fifth and last edition of the Carrera Panamericana, after 3,077 kilometers (1,912 miles), Hans Herrmann ended up in third place. Jaroslaw Juhan was just thirty-six seconds behind him in fourth place in the overall standings—a double victory in the class up to 1,500 cubic centimeters (91.5 cu. in.). On the engine hood in the rear: the name Carrera.

PORSCHE AND CARRERA

To commemorate the race, the most powerful production cars were given the Carrera designation in the following years, just like the four-camshaft engine designed by Ernst Fuhrmann.

In the Porsche 550 A Spyder, the Carrera engine produced 135 hp; 1.6-liter versions produced 165 hp. The best-known owner is probably James Dean, who died in an accident in a 550 Spyder, named the "Little Bastard," in September 1955. Since then, the Spyder has been surrounded by the myth of the automotive bad boy in the USA.

In 1956, Umberto Maglioli won the Targa Florio for the first time for Porsche, after a distance of 720 kilometers and around seven thousand corners. He drove a Porsche 550 Spyder A RS 1500 International. Since then, vehicles with Carrera engines and RS in the name have rarely been beaten.

But it was precisely these customers whom Porsche wanted to continue to serve with cars such as the lightweight 1600 GS Carrera GT and the Porsche 2000 GS Carrera 2. For the 911, the designation returned with the Carrera RS 2.7—and that designation remains. In the meantime, the 911 and the name Carrera are inextricably linked.

PORSCHE 356 CARRERA

In 1955, Porsche decided to offer the Carrera engine in the 356. Beginning with the IAA in October 1955, all top Porsche models were called Carrera. The three body variants—coupe, convertible, and speedster—are equipped with the Fuhrmann engine. The 356 A Carrera 1500 GS produces 100 hp, more than twice as much as the 356 A 1300 with its 44 hp. The Carrera Coupe takes twelve seconds from 0 to 100 kph, and the top speed is 200 kph.

In addition to the engine, the 356 Carrera received wider tires, larger steering wheels, bucket seats, and a 250 kph speedometer. However, the engine demanded high revs and had enormous maintenance costs. Clearly, with the 356 Carrera, Porsche was building the first super sports car for the road. Then as now, such cars are exotic. Of the total of 21,045 356 As built, Porsche only sold around seven hundred Carrera models.

The 1960 motorsport season was extremely successful for Porsche overall. In addition to the overall victories in Sebring and at the Targa Florio (both rounds of the prestigious World Sports Car Championship), Herbert Linge and Paul-Ernst Strähle secured the first overall victory for Porsche in November with their 356 B 1600 GS Carrera GT Coupe at the 5th Tour de Corse on the demanding track on the Mediterranean island of Corsica.

THE MINDS BEHIND THE PORSCHE RS MODELS

Since the planning and development of the Porsche 911 Carrera RS 2.7, many engineers, test drivers, racing drivers, designers, and builders have worked on the RS models. Some of the most important are highlighted here.

PETER FALK

Auto mechanic and mechanical engineer Peter Falk joined Porsche as a test engineer in 1959, and he became head of racing car development in 1964. In 1965, he came fifth in the Monte Carlo Rally in a Porsche 911 as Herbert Linge's co-driver. Among other things, he supervised the 917, 959, and TAG-Turbo models. Falk was Porsche's man for very fast cars. He became head of testing in 1970, and in 1972, he was commissioned to "develop a road-legal but race-ready 911." The 911 Carrera RS 2.7, for which Falk was responsible as project manager, was first his company car and later became his favorite car. Falk retired in 1993. Even in 2022, he is still supporting Porsche with historical topics. Now almost ninety, he still has all the figures concerning his developments memorized.

HERMANN BURST

A graduate engineer and expert in aerodynamics, Hermann Burst arrived at Porsche's racing division in 1969 from the Research Institute for Automotive Engineering and Vehicle Engines Stuttgart (FKFS) at the University of Stuttgart. In 1971, he became a senior employee in the "Body testing of production vehicles." He was interested in passive safety, rust prevention, a pleasant interior climate, and aerodynamic optimization. Burst was instrumental in the development of the rear spoiler for the 911 Carrera RS 2.7. His professional highlights also include fully galvanized bodywork, studies with aluminum bodies, the integration of airbags, the aerodynamics of the 959, and the active airflow of the 964. Despite his departure from Porsche in 1992, he remains closely associated with the brand. He is very happy when, during classic car trips in his 356 Cabrio, he meets other Porsches with spoilers, especially "ducktail Porsches."

TILMANN BRODBECK

Tilmann Brodbeck has loved the Porsche brand ever since he met a 356 on his way to the Solitude racetrack—and its road-holding ability enchanted him. After school, Brodbeck studied mechanical and aeronautical engineering at the TH Darmstadt, specializing in aerodynamics, and then applied for a job at Porsche in Zuffenhausen. He was also interested in working at Porsche because his best friend worked there and visited him several times driving a blood-orange 911. Brodbeck applied proactively, and Burst and Falk hired him in October 1970. As a member of Hermann Burst's team, Brodbeck was one of the spiritual fathers of the 911's rear spoiler on the Carrera RS 2.7. When it debuted, Brodbeck was already working on other tasks, including development of the 924. After ten years of development work at Weissach, he moved to Zuffenhausen, becoming assistant in turn to chairmen of the board Fuhrmann, Schutz, Branitzki, Bohn, and Wiedeking. He retired in 2009.

HARM LAGAAIJ

Designer Harm Lagaaij (also spelled Lagaay) began working at Porsche in September 1971. Shortly afterward, he was given the task of designing a logo for a new, particularly sporty vehicle. He invented the "Carrera" between the wheel housings. Lagaaij worked on the 911 RS 2.7 until 1972. This was followed by vehicles such as the 911 G model and the Porsche 924. The designer and his colleagues also supervised the graphics for racing cars such as the 911 Carrera RSR and 936 in the elaborate Martini Racing look. In 1977, Lagaaij moved to Ford as a designer, then to BMW Technik GmbH as chief designer. He returned to Porsche in 1989, replaced his former boss Anatole Lapine as chief designer, and in the years that followed, developed the 968, 928 GTS, Boxster, Cayman, Carrera GT, and Cayenne, and the 911 models 993, 996, and 997. Harm Lagaaij worked as head of the Porsche design department at Weissach until 2004.

ERNST FUHRMANN

Dr. Ernst Fuhrmann is regarded as an ingenious engineer and engine designer. As a mechanical engineer with a PhD, he was responsible for the "M547" with vertical shaft, which became known as the Carrera engine or Fuhrmann engine. After taking a job change with a supplier, Fuhrmann returned to Porsche in 1971 and became Technical Managing Director. After the Porsche-Piëch family withdrew from active positions in the company, Fuhrmann became spokesman of the Management Board and Technical Managing Director of Porsche KG in March 1972. In August 1972, he became spokesman of the Executive Board of the new Porsche AG and later Chairman of the Executive Board. At that time, he considered the technology of the 911 to be almost exhausted, and pushed for its replacement by the 928, but was unable to prevail against the Porsche family. He remained head of Porsche until 1981, when he retired. Dr Ernst Fuhrmann died in February 1995.

HELMUTH BOTT

After completing an apprenticeship at Daimler-Benz and studying engineering at the University of Stuttgart, teacher and car mechanic Helmuth Bott joined Porsche as a plant assistant in 1952. After his time as an instructor and author of repair manuals, he became the responsible test engineer in 1955. The Porsche 911 was developed under his leadership. In 1979, Bott became Head of Research and Development. He energetically pushed ahead the development of all-wheel drive at Porsche. He was the driving force behind the 911 Turbo, the innovative 959, and the 964 Carrera 4. The development center in Weissach is also based on his initiative. In his honor, the most difficult section of the track is called the "Bott chicane." Bott remained with Porsche until 1988. After leaving the company, he continued to work as a consultant for Porsche. Bott died in May 1994.

FERDINAND PIËCH

A grandson of Ferdinand Porsche, after studying mechanical engineering, Ferdinand Piëch joined Porsche in 1963 as a clerk in the racing engine testing department. Two years later, he became head of the department, and beginning in 1965, he oversaw all development work. Under his leadership, a number of technical highlights were created, including the 917 racing car—one of the most successful racing cars of the twentieth century. With it, Porsche won the 24 Hours of Le Mans for the first time. In 1967, his Porsche 911 R heralded what the RS 2.7 would later perfect. In 1971, Piëch became Technical Managing Director of Porsche. However, he had to leave the post just one year later since the Porsche-Piëch family withdrew from active positions in the company. Ferdinand Piëch moved to Audi and later to VW, where he became an extremely memorable Chairman of the Board of Management. Born in Austria, he died in August 2019.

JÜRGEN BARTH

Jürgen Barth began his training at Porsche in 1963 as an automobile mechanic and industrial agent. In 1969, he became assistant to Huschke von Hanstein in the sports and press department. His task: organizing rally activities. Beginning in 1969, he was responsible for sports approval at Porsche and, in 1976, for the overall administrative organization of Porsche Motorsport. In 1982, he became head of Porsche customer sport and set up a new customer sport department in Weissach. Starting in 1968, Barth also raced on the side, not only on long-distance circuits but also in rallies and hill climbs. In the 1970s and 1980s, Barth was one of the world's best sports car drivers. He did not drive Porsche exclusively and won the 24 Hours of Le Mans (1977) and the 1,000 km on the Nürburgring (1981), among others.

HANS MEZGER

A native of Swabia, Hans Mezger began his career at Porsche in 1956 in the technical calculation department. There he was involved in the further development of the Carrera engine, the 1.5-liter eight-cylinder engine, and the Formula 1 engine in the Porsche 804. A formula he developed simplified the construction of camshafts. From 1965, he headed the racing development department and was responsible for the legendary twelve-cylinder engine of the Porsche 917 and the TAG turbo engine for McLaren, among other things. He is best known for developing the engine for the first Porsche 911, and the "Mezger engine" continues to power the 997 RS model series. Mezger retired at the end of 1993 after thirty-seven years at Porsche. He died in June 2020 at the age of ninety.

ROLAND KUSSMAUL

Mechanical engineering graduate Roland Kussmaul started at the Porsche Development Center in Weissach in 1969, initially as a developer for the Leopard tank. Peter Falk brought him into the racing department in 1974, where he initially worked on racing cars. Kussmaul was responsible for the rally use of the 911 SC RS in 1978 and later for the resulting small series. Kussmaul and Barth drove successfully in private rallies. In addition to internal development work, he had assignments as a development and racing engineer, including at the 24 Hours of Le Mans with the 956 and 962 racing cars. Beginning in 1990, Kussmaul developed cars for the newly created Porsche Carrera Cup and eventually became head of development for racing and special vehicles. He was also responsible for the 911 GT3 of the 996 series. Kussmaul retired in 2008.

AUGUST ACHLEITNER

As the son of the main department head at BMW, August Achleitner was familiar with expensive and fast vehicles from an early age. The mechanical engineer was impressed by the Porsche 911, but he thought it could be improved. He moved from Munich to Stuttgart and started working in Porsche chassis development in 1983. His goal: to make the 911 better, while retaining its basic concept. By 1989, he had worked his way up to the "Technical Product Development, Vehicle Concepts and Package" department. In 2001, he took over responsibility for the 911 model series. The 997, 991, and 992 model series were created under Achleitner's leadership. At the beginning of 2019, the enthusiastic motorcyclist and mountain biker handed over responsibility for the two-door sports cars to his colleague Frank Walliser and retired.

ANDREAS PREUNNINGER

In the 1990s, Andreas Preuninger took part in a three-hour tour of the Porsche Development Center in Weissach. Afterward, he knew that he wanted to work for Porsche. This desire motivated him during his studies. He improved his driving style while working as a freelance journalist for *Auto Motor und Sport* magazine. He frequently applied for jobs at Porsche, always on his own initiative, even while he was already working for a supplier in Spain. For a long time, the poor economic situation stood in the way of his employment, but in 1997, his wish came true. In October 2000, he became Head of GT Vehicles. He worked on the facelift of the 996 GT3 and brought the letters RS back onto the road with the 996 GT3 RS. From then on, he was responsible for all the manufacturer's RS models.

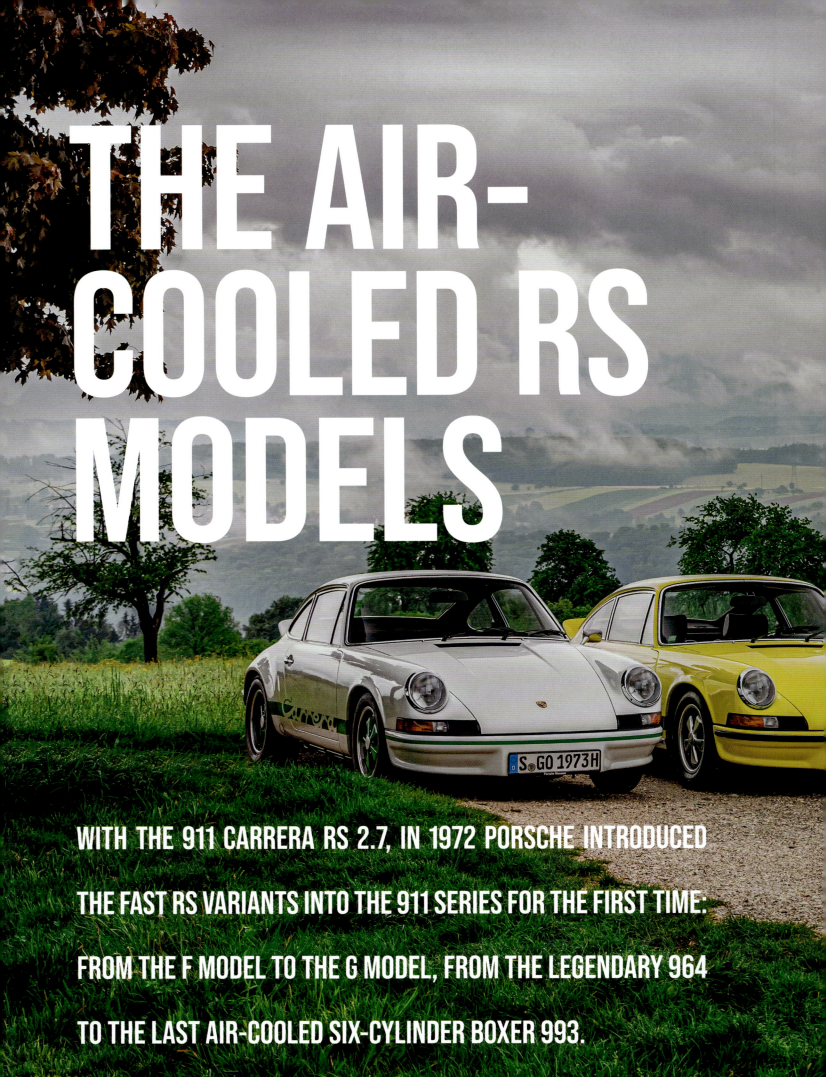

THE AIR-COOLED RS MODELS

WITH THE 911 CARRERA RS 2.7, IN 1972 PORSCHE INTRODUCED THE FAST RS VARIANTS INTO THE 911 SERIES FOR THE FIRST TIME: FROM THE F MODEL TO THE G MODEL, FROM THE LEGENDARY 964 TO THE LAST AIR-COOLED SIX-CYLINDER BOXER 993.

THE ORIGINAL MODEL

1972 WAS A DIFFICULT YEAR FOR PORSCHE. THE FIRST-GENERATION 911 WAS NEARING THE END OF ITS MODEL CYCLE. PORSCHE HAD BEEN MAKING THE SPORTS CAR AT ZUFFENHAUSEN FOR ALMOST EIGHT YEARS. OVER THE YEARS IT WAS GIVEN A FEW TECHNICAL IMPROVEMENTS, BUT NO MAJOR OVERHAUL.

Trendsetter: The Porsche 911 Carrera RS 2.7 was the first production car with a rear spoiler as standard equipment. Many soon followed its example.

To survive in the market, a completely new model was needed. The planned successor to the 911, the 928, was not yet ready; it would not appear until 1977. Porsche therefore urgently needed a new car—or a new variant that would cause a stir and attract customers—for financial reasons.

At the same time, another problem arose. The highest motorsport authority, the FIA, wanted to restrict the prototype class to just 3-liter displacement for the 1972 racing season. This would end the dominance of the 917 racing cars, because their engines were at least 4.5 liters. After winning the one-make world championship for sports cars in 1969, 1970, and 1971, Porsche was determined to continue racing successfully. To do so, however, the manufacturer needed a new racing car that met the new FIA requirements. For cost reasons, Dr. Ernst Fuhrmann was not planning a new racing car, but a production-based solution—a 911 for the racetrack.

THE BEGINNING

After Fuhrmann's visit to the Hockenheimring in May 1972, during which he saw his car lose, work began on the new project. The recent poor performance of the Porsche 911 was also due in part to the existing regulations. These only allowed the racing cars a little more displacement than was available in production cars. Porsche was allowed to start with a maximum displacement of 2.5 liters (152.6 cu. in.) because the 911 was available at the dealership with a 2.4-liter (146.5 cu. in.) engine. Porsche's competitors had larger engines. Ford was already using a 2.6-liter (159 cu. in.) engine in its Capri, while BMW had a 3.0-liter (183 cu. in.) engine. To bring a competitive model to the starting line, Porsche therefore also needed more displacement for the production car.

Fuhrmann gave the project to Porsche's head of development, Helmuth Bott. He summoned his employees Tilman Brodbeck and Hermann Burst, and Wolfgang Berger became project manager. "Helmuth Bott only said that Porsche customers with their 911 road cars on racetracks have major problems in competing against vehicles from BMW and Ford, especially when cornering. He suspected that the rear end was too light, and we were to think about and fix the problem,"

Tilman Brodbeck recalled. The order was placed, but not for a new vehicle, but instead for "some kind of component for retrofitting."

THE START OF DEVELOPMENT

In the back of the minds of all the engineers was Professor Ferry Porsche's favorite saying. When asked what made a Porsche, he replied, "The Porsche goes fast around the rear." That should be, no, it *had* to be true for the 911 on the racetrack. Together with Hermann Burst, Tilman Brodbeck considered a design that became a real trend in the coming decades: the rear spoiler.

But time was of the essence. Development work began in May, and the new model was due to make its debut at the Paris Motor Show in October. Before that, however, it had to be extensively tested and then homologated before it could be launched the following season. For homologation as a racing car, Porsche also needed to produce at least five hundred vehicles. The target group: private drivers who were looking for a light and fast automobile.

Project leader Wolfgang Berger had a free hand in development and was given permission to recruit workers from the various departments. He wrote the specification sheet and simultaneously concerned himself with subsequent

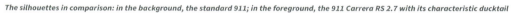

The silhouettes in comparison: in the background, the standard 911; in the foreground, the 911 Carrera RS 2.7 with its characteristic ducktail

The first variant of the Carrera side lettering was only used on early variants of the 911 Carrera RS 2.7. Later, the side sills retained the body color. Porsche positioned the C 1 centimeter behind the front door joint. Ferry Porsche generally did not like the lettering.

production and coordinating testing and production. About fifteen engineers developed the car in the following months. They were joined by additional employees from production.

The developers worked intensively on four aspects: weight, aerodynamics, the engine, and the suspension. "The project now depended not only on the experimental division, but also on the later production department, which supervised production of the small series," related Peter Falk. Developing a new car for a small production series was one thing. Reaching the production process was another thing. First and foremost, the 911 Carrera would be the perfect synthesis of weight, performance, aerodynamics, and handling.

THE BODY OF THE 911 CARRERA RS 2.7

Burst and Brodbeck were responsible for the body. Their primary objective was to reduce weight. The use of thin sheet-metal panels, thin windows, and plastic parts and the absence of insulation were intended to reduce the total vehicle weight to less than 900 kilograms (1,984 lbs.) so that the model could be homologated. At the same time, the aerodynamics were to be improved. Burst and Brodbeck wanted to minimize the lift typical of the 911 on the front and rear axles or eliminate it completely to achieve more neutral handling.

"I was young and had no idea at first, so the first thing I did was go the bodywork department and speak to the head mechanic and master craftsman about how to change which component," said Tilman Brodbeck. He remembered the car he had during his studies, a Fiat 850 Coupe. The first version of the Fiat had a smoothly sloping rear hood. The following model has a slight but striking upward curve at the end of the hood. At first, Brodbeck could not explain its function, but after conversing with his colleagues he understood: thanks to the upward curvature, the air flow changed and, at higher speeds, simultaneously pushed the rear end toward the road. This effect was achieved without increasing drag.

THE 911 LINES MUST REMAIN

The goal of the entire process was to retain the characteristic silhouette of the 911 and simultaneously to compensate for the disadvantage of the sloping rear end, using stylistically acceptable measures. This was to result in improved aerodynamics. Styling elements such as fenders, hood, roof, and rear end could not be changed in the process.

In the experiments, crude metal sheets and wide blocks on the engine hood initially served as prototypes for the later ducktail spoiler. "Turning the lift into downforce only came later with the RSR, but it had a much larger rear wing with a Maria Stuart collar," recalled Peter Falk. He was referring to the spoiler that ran across the entire rear end of the later racing version.

The developers mounted various shapes on the engine hood to see whether the basic character was retained and the lift decreased. Initially, they used a shape like that of a sloping board. Soon the design became more pleasing, so that the spoiler did not look so much like a foreign body.

"We made the first models for the 911 using welding rod and sheet metal and mounted them on the existing engine hood," said Brodbeck. Then they took a 911 and three different spoiler designs to the wind tunnel at the Technical University of Stuttgart. The head of the wind tunnel laughed at them in a friendly manner. Hermann Burst and Tilman Brodbeck were serious, however, for they could see the drag coefficient and lift values changing.

BALANCE IN THE 911

It is unimaginable today that lead was placed in the front bumpers of the first 911s to improve balance. The aerodynamics of the 911 were so poor that, even with a small spoiler, the lift on the rear axle was reduced by almost 50 percent. The engineers observed the air flow and turbulence in the wind tunnel by using smoke. They were thus able to see immediately the direct changes caused by the new airflow breakaway at the rear end.

As each axle was on a scale, they could directly read the changing lift values. An absolute prerequisite: the lift values on the front and rear axles had to be identical; otherwise the handling became critical. The drag coefficient should also

decrease. After three days in the wind tunnel with the three variants, the engineers decided on the spoiler's height and width. "That all happened very quickly," recalled Brodbeck.

The decision-making paths for the front spoiler, which was also developed in a wind tunnel and reduced the lift on the front axle by almost half, were short. When Ferdinand Piëch heard about it, he wanted to see the front spoiler in use as quickly as possible. A short time later, it was offered as a GRP (plastic reinforced by glass fibers) component—it would have taken two years to develop new tooling for a sheet metal front spoiler.

Once again, the decision was not long in coming. Helmuth Bott had the invention on the rear end shown to him and ordered practical trials. Günther Steckkönig, a Nordschleife specialist, test driver in road tests, and racing driver, took on the job and drove on the test track at Weissach with the new spoiler. He compared the handling with that of a 911 without spoiler—and the results were clear. He was able to drive faster and more safely with front and rear spoilers.

15 MILLIMETERS

The team around Wolfgang Berger, Herrmann Burst, and Tilman Brodbeck had further developed the aerodynamics in the wind tunnel at the Technical University of Stuttgart, but that was only half the job. "The wind tunnel was not the road; there is a great difference between them. We therefore went to Hockenheim for test drives, to see what and how much the spoiler brought," explained Peter Falk. Together with the developers, test driver Günther Steckkönig, and a photographer, they drove to the racetrack.

A designer from the styling department also joined them. He was there to see and understand what the technicians were looking for in the spoiler. They set up a test track for the electronic measurement of the car's maximum speed. The photographer stood about 15 meters (49 ft.) from the test track, and his job was to photograph the precise position of the car. From the photos, the developers could later see whether the front of the car was higher than the rear or vice versa. From this, they could determine the effect of the spoiler.

"We found that we could increase maximum speed with a higher spoiler, because drag was lower. We also repeatedly extended the airflow breakaway edge of the rear spoiler upward by millimeters, drove the car again, and extended it further. Not until we reached the reversal point, where the car became slower again, did we technically establish that height as the ducktail height, as it was to go into production," explained Peter Falk. Maximum speed was not everything, but it was extremely important.

But it was not always about the best result. The head of design did not like the spoiler. He reduced the height of the ducktail by 15 millimeters (0.6 in.). "That was like a slap in the face for us technicians, because we wanted the best technical

210 hp with a weight of just 960 kilograms (2, 115 lbs.). Even almost fifty years after its creation, the 911 Carrera RS 2.7 is still extremely sporty and fast.

solution. Even if the reduction cost only 2 to 3 kph, we were disappointed," brooded Peter Falk. Falk well remembers his first drive in the near-production vehicle, even after fifty years. "On the first drive, it took some getting used to. The car was very hard, because it was lighter and therefore had a less effective suspension, and was much louder. But the longer I drove the car, the more enthusiastic I became about its handling. It was light years ahead of the production car." Test drivers were also shocked in the beginning, but then they became enthusiastic about the reduced lift forces and the better traction, especially at high speeds. The roadworthy prototype was completed within three months, then production of the small series began.

TESTING AT EHRA-LESSEIN

Further road tests were scheduled at the VW test site at Ehra-Lessein during the major Porsche test trials in 1972. When Helmuth Bott was driving the ducktail 911 on the three-lane track at around 180 kph (112 mph), he spontaneously jerked the steering wheel to the right to provoke a yaw. "My heart was in my mouth, but after three oscillations, the Porsche immediately stabilized itself completely in a straight line and didn't rock," said his co-driver at the time, Tilman Brodbeck.

The new "ducktail" pushed the 911 Carrera RS 2.7 down at high speed and delivered additional cooling air to the rear-mounted engine. This effect was achieved without an increase in drag—on the contrary: the car's maximum speed rose by 4.5 kph (2.8

Important work in the wind tunnel with a measurable improvement: The "ducktail" reduced the drag coefficient of the 911 Carrera RS 2.7 from 0.409 to 3.97. The lift on the rear axle dropped from 145 to 42 kilograms.

The standard Porsche 911 had unfavorable aerodynamics. Because the spoiler significantly improved the drivability of the top-of-the-range model, it soon became available as a retrofit part.

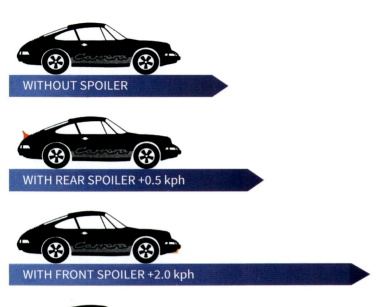

WITHOUT SPOILER

WITH REAR SPOILER +0.5 kph

WITH FRONT SPOILER +2.0 kph

WITH FRONT AND REAR SPOILERS (as on the production car) +4.5 kph

The influence of optimized air flow: the Porsche 911 was significantly faster with front and rear spoilers. The rear engine was also supplied with additional cooling air.

to the invention, this is achieved by the device forming a unit with the rear hood, extending over the substantial width of the latter and projecting over a considerable part of the rear hood in the longitudinal direction of the vehicle."

Wolfgang Berger and his team thus invented the rear spoiler as a production part for Porsche. And with the 911 Carrera RS 2.7, they created the first production vehicle with integral front and rear spoilers. This model soon unleashed the worldwide spoiler wave—it was a trendsetter.

"To me, the spoiler was just a solution to a technical problem. For a long time, I was unaware that in the process we had created an icon," Hermann Burst said later. On the other hand, the success of the new model did not surprise him. Porsche drivers were already sporty back then and immediately recognized the advantages of the aerodynamic package. With the new kit, the 911 was finally competitive. With the spoiler, Porsche achieved up to 69 percent less lift on the rear axle. A welcome side effect: taillight fouling was reduced enormously thanks to the effects of the airflow. Clean air was now directed around the rear lights.

The team was able to draw on experience with the 911 Turbo from 1973 onward. However, unlike the discreet, almost delicate RS spoiler, the "ducktail," the Turbo's rear spoiler was made wider and larger—and thus looked more martial. Since the 911 Carrera RS 2.7, sales teams have realized that a spoiler could be a sales booster.

TWO 2.7-LITER ENGINES

In the spring of 1972, in parallel with the Bergmann team, series development was working on a 2.7-liter (165 cu. in.) boxer engine for the 911 S. It was to supplement the existing 2.4-liter boxer in the 911 S and provide a variant with more displacement and improved performance. After the official homologation was set for 1973, it was determined that five hundred homologated cars had to be built—but not sold.

This loophole was a chance for Porsche to avoid a possible flop. The manufacturer could build the entire number and, if need be, after the numbers check and the classification as Group 4, rebuild them as 911 S 2.7s, again if sufficient buyers could not be found. Not all of Porsche's employees were convinced that the new variant with the rear spoiler would be a success.

mph). "After the first waggle test with the spoiler, the difference was clear. The Eleven was much smoother and more stable than without the spoiler. They were worlds apart," recalled Hermann Burst. With the aerodynamic component, he was able to carry out the waggle test at a significantly higher speed before the rear end swung. At the same time, the speedometer registered up to 270 kph (168 mph) instead of 255 or 260. "That finally made it clear to me that the spoiler was the right part for our Eleven. The test drivers from Weissach confirmed our experiences," said Burst. The speedometer scale even went as high as 280 kph (174 mph), and from March 1973 on, it went to 300 kph (186 mph).

Helmuth Bott was enthusiastic. He immediately saw it as a safety advantage and decided to put the spoiler into production. The front and rear spoilers were envisaged as a retrofit kit for 911 customers. However, at that time, improved safety was not a good selling point. Extreme sportiness and higher speeds in turns were better draws.

THE INVENTION OF THE REAR SPOILER

On August 5, 1972, patent application 2238704 was filed with the German Patent Office. It read, "The invention relates to a passenger car with a rear hood preferably mounted between side parts and an aerodynamic device provided in the rear for increasing the dynamic rear wheel pressure. The task underlying the invention is to create a highly effective aerodynamic device with which the rear axle pressure of a passenger car is increased or the lift around the rear axle is reduced when driving. However, this device should also be advantageously arranged in the rear of the car. According

The Federal Motor Transport Authority (KBA) refused to approve the rear spoiler. Consequently, Porsche had the cars individually approved by TÜV Süd in Stuttgart.

This is another reason why the 911 S with the 2.7-liter engine was only removed from the (planned) sales program after Ernst Fuhrmann put his foot down. He did not want to have two versions of the 2.7 in the portfolio. The 911 Carrera RS 2.7 was no further development of the 911 S; rather, it was a vehicle in its own right and the future top-of-the-line model ahead of the 911 S.

THE RS POWERPLANT

Engine developers Hans Mezger and Valentin Schäffer were working on a six-cylinder boxer engine. They increased displacement to 2.7 liters and built the units in their workshop. Increasing the bore to 90 millimeters (3.5 in.) was possible by using a thin Nikasil coating on the cylinders.

To maintain a high level of suitability for everyday use, the compression ratio, timing, and valve diameter remained identical to the 2.4-liter engine. In this way, the new engine was satisfied with normal gasoline. The 2.7-liter six-cylinder boxer with fuel injection delivered 210 hp at 6,300 rpm and developed 255 Newton meters (Nm) (ft.-lbs.) of torque at 5,100 rpm—and thus 20 hp and 40 Nm more than the 2.4 S. Full torque was available at 2,700 rpm instead of 4,000 rpm.

The engine enabled the RS version to accelerate from 0 to 100 kph (0 to 62 mph) in 5.8 seconds. The 911 Carrera RS 2.7 became the first production car to break the six-second mark in tests carried out by the German magazine *Auto Motor und Sport*. Maximum speed was greater than 245 kph (152 mph).

A newly developed five-speed transmission had longer ratio fourth (27/25 instead of 26/25) and fifth (29/21 instead of 29/22) gears. Further gear ratios were available as a special request for the racing version. The racing versions were also fitted with a forward oil pump to ensure better lubrication under extreme loads. Initially, Porsche was still considering a four-speed transmission, as well as the automatic transmission called the Sportomatic. However, they did not find their way into series production—apart from the vehicles for Peter Porsche and Luise Piëch. Both drove cars with the Sportomatic.

THE SUSPENSION

The performance, weight, and aerodynamic measures also required modifications to the car's suspension. Porsche had gained experience with wider rear tires in racing sport. The developer therefore tried them on the Carrera RS 2.7. "We wanted to improve traction and handling with wider tires on the rear axle, because the weight on the rear axle was the greatest. Although customer service initially opposed this on account of higher storage costs, we were able to prevail," said Peter Falk.

Porsche tested several variants of the rear spoiler . . .

. . . on the prototype of the 911 Carrera RSR (internal designation: E42).

For the first time at Porsche, a production vehicle had different-sized tires on the front and rear axles. In front were two Fuchs 6 x 15 forged wheels with 185/70VR15 tires, and in the rear, 7 x 15 wheels with 215/60VR15 tires. To accommodate the tires, Porsche widened the body in the rear by 42 millimeters (1.6 in.). "After that worked well in development, production, and use, this combination was used on all subsequent models," said Peter Falk.

All RS 2.7 models were fitted with a firmer and lighter Bilstein suspension instead of the standard Boge shock absorbers. The stabilizer bars measured 15 millimeters (0.6 in.) in diameter as standard (13 millimeters, or 0.5 in., for homologation). The supports on the front axle were made of forged aluminum, which saved around 2.5 kilograms (5.5 lbs.) in weight. Reinforced rear axle control arms and a cross-tube reinforcement were used at the rear. In addition to the torsion bar suspension, large coil springs did the work on the rear axle.

THE SALES DEPARTMENT DOESN'T WANT THE CAR

At the beginning of the 1970s, while Porsche sold sports cars for everyday use, it did not yet sell extreme sports cars for racetracks and everyday driving. This changed with the new model. Doing away with comfort was not welcomed everywhere, however. For example, instead of armrests on the doors, Porsche installed light door pull straps, like Fiat on its 600. The sales staff were correspondingly reserved in their reaction to the new model—they saw only limited sales opportunities. Many salespeople also did not want the spoiler on a standard 911, since they believed it disrupted the classic design, the original shape. Only a few employees recognized the advantages of the spoiler. Porsche boss Ernst Fuhrmann summoned his sales team in Weissach and discussed the new special model with them. "The sales staff were of the opinion that a car with such an ugly add-on part would be difficult to sell, perhaps a maximum of a hundred units worldwide," says Tilman Brodbeck.

One problem: it was not just the Porsche sales department that was responsible for sales, but the VW-Porsche-Vertriebsgesellschaft mbH, which was founded jointly with VW for the 914 project—and it was equally staffed so that half of the team were VW employees who had little or nothing to do with a high-powered lightweight sports car. "The sales department initially rejected the car because it was too simple and too loud for them," recalls Peter Falk.

FUHRMANN PUSHES THE RS THROUGH

Ernst Fuhrmann remained resolute. He was determined to bring the car onto the market and issued the order: either the sales department sells the RS or it doesn't get a single car. Fuhrmann got his way (and the car). Porsche planned to produce 500 units to homologate the 911 Carrera RS 2.7 for Group 4 ("special GT vehicles"). It would be a road-legal vehicle for customers who also wanted to take part in racing events.

The contemporary advertisement read, "The Porsche Carrera RS: only 500 men will drive it." On October 5, 1972, the new model was unveiled at the Porte de Versailles Motor Show in Paris. By the end of November, all five hundred vehicles had already been sold.

"It was only when the vehicles had been sold and a further one thousand units went to customers that we realized we had created a special model. You don't normally see such leaps in sales," said Peter Falk. Porsche also offered the front and rear spoilers as accessories for all 911 models—another success. "Together, they resulted in very good handling at higher speeds, which is why 911 drivers were happy to order them."

PROBLEMS WITH THE KBA

But until then, there were still problems. The Federal Motor Transport Authority (KBA) in Flensburg refused to accept the

Hans Mezger and Valentin Schäffer increased the displacement of the six-cylinder boxer, with a bore of 90 mm to 2.7 liters.

lightened and weighed, and then modified to RS (Sport) or RSL (Touring) standard according to customer requirements. After that, the actual vehicle weight was no longer decisive. The remaining vehicles outside the FIA homologation finally received approval from the Federal Motor Transport Authority. The car was then a little heavier—and there was a new KBA president.

DIFFERENCES BETWEEN THE VARIANTS

Internally, Porsche called the model the 911 SC, to accelerate type identification and reduce costs. This designation therefore appeared in the vehicle paperwork, while the sales name was 911 Carrera RS 2.7. Within the model, there were four different variants. The RSH, RS, and RL were technically almost identical, and only the RSR, a pure racing car, differed significantly from the production cars.

During production, especially after reaching a thousand vehicles for the second homologation, Porsche changed further details, such as the thickness of the sheet metal (0.88 instead of 0.8 millimeters), the windshield, and the subframe for the front axle. All thin sheet metal parts brought a weight advantage of 9.5 kilograms (21 lbs.). The first models were delivered to customers at the end of 1972. After the car had achieved homologation, the buyers

rear spoiler and would not approve it for road use. "We drove all the way from Stuttgart to Flensburg in a car, explained the spoiler to the staff, but unfortunately, we didn't get approval," said Peter Falk. He no longer knows the exact reasons but puts it down to pedestrian protection and the displeasure of the KBA president at the time, Dr. Parigger.

TÜV (Technical Inspection Agency) Stuttgart therefore inspected each of the five hundred vehicles individually and issued the vehicle approval. "We had already worked together with TÜV on previous conversions, and our experiences were good," said Falk. Individual approvals always worked, but they were time-consuming and expensive. The advantage was that every 911 Carrera RS 2.7 was precisely documented, weighed, and registered. This was important for FIA homologation.

Up to the 1,010th car (i.e., the achievement of Group 3 homologation), each vehicle was first elaborately produced, then

could request individual options. In spring 1973, Ferry Porsche ordered a 911 Carrera 911 RS in the "472" (RSL) Touring version with electric sunroof, Blaupunkt Radio Cologne, and a 2.9-liter engine from the testing department.

Today, there are more RS models on the road than were originally built. Many received the body kits or front and rear spoilers only later, and their engines are a larger displacement or the later 2.7 of the 911 S. Even if they are technically and visually almost identical to the originals, they are not part of the hard, genuine RS core.

THE DERIVATIVES OF THE CARRERA RS 2.7

Porsche was surprised by this success and, through July 1973, built three times as many cars as planned. A total of 1,580 vehicles were produced. Consequently, Porsche was

New Carrera lettering: the letters are framed in a contrasting color to the body paint, with a wide stripe in the same color running through them.

911 Carrera RSL: the touring version of Porsche's super sports car was still dynamic, but it was more comfortable—and thus heavier and somewhat slower.

also able to homologate the 911 Carrera RS 2.7 for Group 3 in addition to Group 4. It was the fastest German production automobile of its day.

For Porsche, the 911 Carrera RS 2.7 was first of all a basis for motorsport. The manufacturer built the first five hundred examples of the car for FIA homologation without unnecessary weight, in a basic version weighing 935 kilograms (2,061 lbs.). After the official weight taking, they went back to the factory and received any additional equipment ordered. Customers could choose between three options. These were:

RSH: Only seventeen vehicles retained their original homologation specification (conversion code 0). Porsche changed nothing after they were weighed. Just five of these vehicles came from the original homologation series of 500 vehicles.

- Front bumpers and spoiler made of plastic
- Rear bumpers and spoiler made of plastic
- Thin glass windows
- All decorative items deleted
- Front coat of arms deleted
- Lettering on engine hood deleted
- Rear lid lock omitted, replaced by two rubber hood holders
- Elimination of underbody protection
- Elimination of three gas springs
- Simplified door frames with pull straps
- Elimination of glove compartment lid
- Passenger seat backrest adjustment omitted
- Clothes hooks omitted
- Passenger sun visor omitted
- Elimination of emergency seats in rear
- Omission of clock
- Omission of sound insulation mats
- Luggage compartment lining omitted
- Elimination of cover for steering compartment
- Low-frequency fanfare
- Needle felt instead of carpet
- Recaro bucket seat with adjustable backrest
- 165VR15 tires on 6-inch rims at the front, 185VR15 tires on 6-inch rims at the rear

RS Sport M471: With the 911 Carrera RS 2.7 Sport, Porsche improved suitability for everyday use but limited this to what was absolutely necessary—the rear seats, floor carpets, clock, and armrests were still missing. Lightweight seat shells replaced heavier sports seats, and the Porsche emblem on the hood was only glued on. Compared to the more comfortable Touring model, the Sport weighed 115 kilograms (253 lbs.) less and had an empty weight of 960 kilograms (2,116 lbs.). Porsche built two hundred examples of the RS Sport. The price: 34,000 deutsch marks plus 700 for the "471 Conversion Set" (RS sports package for customer sport). It consisted of:

- Passenger bucket seat with adjustable backrest
- Gas struts for the engine hood and trunk lid
- Key strips for door panels,
- Glove compartment lid
- Clothes hooks
- 185/70VR15 tires on 6-inch rims at the front, 215/60VR15 tires on 7-inch rear rims in the rear
- Trunk trim
- Lid for steering compartment
- Partial underbody protection
- Front stabilizer bar with 15 millimeter diameter

RSL M472: Most RS buyers chose the Touring variant. The "472 Conversion Set" was added for more comfort for 2,500 deutsch marks. The car had the equipment of the 911 S and therefore weighed more than its purist sister and was somewhat slower. The Touring required 6.3 seconds to reach 100 kph (62 mph),

and its top speed was 240 kph (149 mph). A total of 1,308 vehicles were built with the RSL specification.

Although the RS was conceived as a lightweight sports car, buyers of the Touring readily accepted heavy options. For example, they ordered power windows (495 marks). Three customers even chose an electric sunroof for 1,230 marks. Sports drivers most frequently selected the M409 sports seats for 250 marks and the limited slip differential for 650 marks (M220). Koni shock absorbers (145 marks) and a roll bar (385 marks) were also popular. Customers who liked to show what kind of car they were driving chose the Carrera logos on the sides for 90 marks or the Porsche logos for 70 marks. The standard equipment was even more extensive:

- Sheet steel rear bumpers
- Trim moldings
- Rear hood lock
- Crest on the front
- Sound insulation mats
- Dual horns
- Complete door equipment
- Interior trim included
- Carpet like the 911 S
- Coat hooks, glove compartment lid
- Lighting for luggage compartment, glove compartment, ashtray
- Passenger sun visor
- Emergency seats

"Conversion Kit 491" for motorsport: The 911 Carrera RSR 2.8 had wider rear fenders, the brakes of the Porsche 917, and a displacement of 2.8 liters. This model also had plastic fenders, Plexiglas windows, and simpler headlights. It weighed a further 20 kilograms (44 lbs.) less than other RSRs.

Lightweight construction down to the last detail: a blind cover on the fifth instrument in the panel of the 911 Carrera RS 2.7 Sport. The touring version had a quartz clock in this position, an improved version of which was installed from the end of March 1973.

A bit of comfort: heavy seats in the 911 Carrera RS 2.7 Touring. Factory black brushstrokes around the door panels prevented the body color from showing through to the inside.

Lots of lateral support, low weight: the bucket seats in the 911 Carrera RS 2.7 Sport. There were a total of five different seats to choose from.

Part of the essentials: the lightweight Porsche 911 retained its interior heating. The US model has extensive labeling due to local laws.

As with the Fiat 600, the 911 Carrera RS 2.7 Sport used simple straps for closing the doors.

- Windows like the 911 S
- Clock
- Second battery
- Underbody protection
- Optional standard engine hood made of aluminum
- 185/70VR15 tires on 6-inch rims in front, 215/60VR15 tires on 6-inch rims in the rear

RSR: The RSR pure racing version ("491 Conversion Set") was added later. The price: 25,000 deutsch marks more than the basic car. In contrast to the other variants, the manufacturer conceived the car uncompromisingly for motorsport. Fifty-five racing cars were created within the Group 4 regulations, with five-centimeter-wider mudguards for 9-inch (front) and 11-inch (rear) rims, racing suspension, brake system of the 917 with two main brake cylinders, and ribbed brake calipers.

The biggest change, however, concerned the engine. Porsche increased the bore to 92 millimeters (3.6 in.), and the result was a 2.8-liter (170 cu. in.) six-cylinder. Higher compression (10.3:1), larger valve diameter and modified valve angle, dual ignition, camshafts with four bearings, engine oil cooler, and a different exhaust system resulted in 300 hp at 8,000 rpm and torque of 290 Nm (214 ft.-lbs.) at 6,300 rpm. The transmission received a limited slip differential and its own oil cooler. Options included a 120-liter (31.7-gal.) fuel tank, roll bar, and other gearbox ratios.

THE "CARRERA" LOGO

Porsche wanted the new top-of-the line Eleven to stand out clearly from the other models and therefore went looking for a new additional name to boost sales. As the most powerful model of the first generation, the 911 Carrera RS 2.7 was the first 911 to bear the nickname "Carrera"—still the crowning glory of the Porsche range today.

The lettering adorned the side view between the wheel arches. It originated from the Mexican endurance race Carrera Panamericana, in which Porsche achieved a class victory with the 550 RS Spyder in 1953 and came in third overall

1. Müller / van Lennep — Martini-Porsche *Carrera RSR*
2. Munari / Andruet — Lancia Stratos
3. Kinnunen / Haldi — Martini-Porsche *Carrera RSR*
4. McBoden / Moreschi — Chevron
5. Nicodemi / Moser — Lola
6. Steckkönig / Pucci — Martini-Porsche *Carrera RSR*

Shell

Bosch / Bilstein / Dunlop

1973 TARGA FLORIO WINNER

MARTINI RACING PORSCHE

An important victory: Herbert Müller and Gijs van Lennep won the 1973 Targa Florio in the 911 Carrera RSR.

In the spring of 1973, Porsche exhibited the 911 Carrera RS 2.7 at the Autosalon in Ghent. The car had previously made its debut in Paris in October 1972.

TOTAL NUMBERS

a year later. The Spanish word also means "race" in German, and RS stands for "Renn Sport" (racing sport).

According to the press release at the time, the term Carrera is also understood as a "quality predicate for a technical delicacy that has proven itself on racetracks and rally courses." In short: an ideal name for the top-of-the-range 911 model. "We wanted to assign the already famous and well-known name 'Carrera' to a production model and thought about how we could best represent this," recalled Harm Lagaaij, a designer at Porsche at the time. Maybe just write it on? Until then, Porsche had only occasionally used side lettering on racing cars, with the name "Porsche" between the front and rear wheel arches.

Original drawings no longer exist. But Harm Lagaaij remembers that two versions of the lettering were created. In the first, it sits in a contrasting color to the body paint at the bottom of the sill, framed by light shading. "With dark paintwork, however, the name would have been very difficult to read," explained the former Porsche designer. In addition, the sticker on the wavy stone guard of the side sills made an unclean impression. This design can be found only on the first prototypes and the first vehicles delivered—and in contemporary brochures.

Harm Lagaaij and his team developed a second proposal for the series. For the typography, the design team drew on the existing variants, slightly adjusting only the height and length of the lettering. The letters of the Carrera logo are framed in a

Models	Version	Number
911 Carrera RS 2.7	Touring (M472)	1.308
911 Carrera RS 2.7	Sport (M471)	200
911 Carrera RS 2.7	Basis (0)	17
911 Carrera RS 2.7	RSR (M491)	55

In addition to the approximately ten different prototypes, there were also the following models:

contrasting color to the body paint, interspersed with a wide stripe in the same color. "As the 911 RS 2.7 was usually only sold in light paint colors, the lettering is very easy to read," he said.

WIDE CHOICE OF COLORS

Porsche offered a total of twenty-nine modern and eye-catching colors for the 911 Carrera RS 2.7. Only twenty-seven of these were sprayed on the body by the manufacturer. Most popular with customers were pale yellow (296), GP white and blue (205), GP white and red (185), light ivory (160), and blood orange (126). Bush green (2), strawberry (4), olive (4), signal orange (5), and GP white (7) were rarities. There were no requests for beige gray and ivory.

Upon request, the cars could be fitted with colored Fuchs five-spoke wheels. Within the 911 series, white was reserved exclusively for the RS. The only exception was a Targa E for

Different body widths: the 911 Carrera 2.7 (in the background) with slim bodywork and the 911 Carrera RSR with wide fenders. Both cars were built on the same production line. Before the marriage, however, Porsche removed the RSR from regular production and completed it in the motorsport department.

the Porsche family. Porsche avoided metallic finishes, since the additional coats of paint would mean an added five kilograms of weight. Again, the only exceptions were cars for the Porsche family.

Even in the seventies, the colors and combinations on offer were still rather bold and unusual for a sports car. Anatole Lapine, head of Porsche Design at the time, gave his team plenty of creative leeway. "It was more than just a finger exercise. The shape and color scheme of the logo had to match the character and the overall statement of the model," explained Harm Lagaaij.

The second variant was easier to produce and stick onto the bodywork. Using the two-layer principle, Porsche employees in production applied the double sticker to the side above the stone guard and then peeled off the top layer—pure manual work. Other distinguishing features of the top-of-the-range 911 included the inverse "Porsche" lettering across the width of the rear lid, "Carrera RS" on the underside of the side panel, and the "2.7" in chrome— still a particularly attractive detail today.

FIRST RACING SUCCESS

The old sales slogan "Win on Sunday, sell on Monday" was still true in the 1970s. Racing successes were always important to

Exclusive color: within the series, Porsche only painted the Carrera RS 2.7 in Grand Prix White. Carrera lettering in green, red, or blue (to match the rims) was only available for this paint finish.

Porsche developed twenty-nine new modern and eye-catching colors, of which only twenty-seven were used on cars. Particularly popular: light yellow, Grand Prix white/blue, Grand Prix white/ red, light ivory, and blood orange. Colored Fuchs five-spoke wheels were also available on request. Black was always dipped; green, red, and blue were painted by hand.

Porsche Museum

Porsche. In June 1972, a forerunner of the 911 Carrera RS 2.7 took part in a race on the Austria Ring in the prototype class. To keep it a secret, the car was entered by a private racing team. The car hit the track with widened fenders and two types of rear spoilers. It was powered by a more powerful 2.8-liter boxer engine, a forerunner of the later RSR racing engine. Günter Steckkönig drove the camouflaged prototype straight to tenth place overall.

Porsche focused on the circuit. Nevertheless, the sportiest 911 started at the East African Rally—albeit with a small team and a small budget.

Important success: the winning car in the 1973 Targa Florio with the starting number 8, driven by Herbert Müller and Gijs von Lennep, secured the eleventh Porsche triumph in the traditional endurance race in Sicily.

Fast not only on the circuit: Leo Kinnunen and Claude Haldi completed the podium of the '73 Targa with a third-place finish behind the factory Lancia Stratos of Munari/Andruet.

Following the racing debut of a 911 Carrera RSR with a significantly widened body at the Tour de Corse in November 1972, Porsche decided to extend the 911's racing success story in 1973. Porsche wanted to enter a works team in the 1973 one-make world championship, including top drivers Herbert Müller and Gijs van Lennep.

At the beginning of February 1973, an RSR driven by Peter Gregg and Hurley Haywood crossed the finish line twenty-two laps ahead of the field at the 24 Hours of Daytona—a brilliant start to the new season. Herbert Müller and Gijs van Lennep won the Targa Florio in May 1973. "The victory was important for us because it showed that the RSR with the larger rear wing is very fast on circuits and rally tracks," recalled Peter Falk.

The Targa Florio doesn't have the scree, but it does have the topography and course of a rally. In its first season, the 911 Carrera RSR won three international and seven national championships—and thus established the 911's success for decades to come. At the International Race of Champions (IROC) in October 1973, Roger Penske from the USA entered twelve identical 911 Carrera RS 2.7s in which drivers from different racing classes competed against each other.

In addition to the works team, many private drivers and teams relied on the 911 RSR and achieved numerous victories in national and international events over the next few years. For the 1974 season, Porsche increased the engine capacity to 3.0 liters and achieved an output of 330 hp.

Porsche also used the 911 in rallying. The East African Safari in April 1973 and the 1,000 Lakes Rally in August 1973 were regarded as test runs for future events. Perfectly prepared, Porsche entered two 911 RS models in the East African Rally in April 1974. After 5,000 kilometers (3,107 miles), Björn Waldegård and Hans Thorszelius finished second overall in the rally, which was both energy- and material-intensive. In the end, Porsche only missed out on a well-deserved victory due to the cancellation of one stage.

FROM RACING CAR TO INVESTMENT PROPERTY

With the 911 Carrera RS 2.7, Porsche developed a vehicle that customers could use every day and in races. Drive to races and then home again? With the new model that was not a problem.

"The 911 RS 2.7 would be the only historic Porsche vehicle that I would like to own today. Then it was beyond my means, and at that time, I drove a 914 2.0. But I was fortunate to be able to work on this fantastic project, to decisively pave the way for better handling, and also for the look, which is strongly characterized by spoilers," Tilman Brodbeck said later.

On July 10, 1973, Porsche completed the last 911 Carrera RS 2.7 at its factory in Zuffenhausen. Fifty years after its debut, good examples currently cost more than a million euros.

"You have to be very fast to drive Germany's fastest car." In 1972, Porsche advertised the small planned number of the 911 Carrera RS 2.7—and its speed. In other advertisements, the manufacturer ran the headlines "Germany's fastest rarity: Edition of 500" and "The Porsche Carrera RS: Only 500 men will drive it."

THE G SERIES
PORSCHE 911 CARRERA RS 3.0

TEN YEARS AFTER THE PREMIERE OF THE 911, PORSCHE GAVE THE SPORTS CAR A THOROUGH BUT EVOLUTIONARY MAKEOVER—THE SILHOUETTE WAS NOT TO BE WATERED DOWN UNDER ANY CIRCUMSTANCES. WITH THE 1973 MODEL YEAR, SERIES PRODUCTION OF THE NEW 911, KNOWN INTERNALLY AS THE G SERIES, BEGAN. FOR THE FIRST TIME, PORSCHE SIGNIFICANTLY CHANGED THE BODYWORK.

With the 911 Carrera RSR 3.0, Porsche was back on the racetrack with the most powerful version of the G model.

The car was made longer for the new model year. It now measured 4,291 millimeters (169 in.) in total. New plastic bumpers met the strict US crash regulations. Porsche offered the Coupe, Targa (from 1973), Convertible (from 1983), and Speedster (from 1988) variants. With the introduction of the 911 SC, Porsche widened the body for all models beginning in 1977. The G series and the 911 were produced with this body for twelve years until mid-1989 (the end of the K program).

The G model inherited its classic shape from its predecessor, the F model. The ducktail was now available as an optional extra for all derivatives. Henceforth, every 911 would also have an engine with a displacement of 2.7 liters. What was once special was now almost standard. It was little consolation that Porsche used the engine in various power levels from 150 to 210 hp.

The market launch of the G series took place at an unfavorable time. The oil price crisis in the fall of 1973 hit Porsche hard. In 1974, orders at Porsche fell by 40 percent, and the entire German car market collapsed. Orders for the 911 were 30 percent down from the previous year. The German government enforced the 100kph speed limit on highways and car-free Sundays. But Porsche had long been developing sports cars for the whole world, including for countries where the oil crisis had not hit so hard.

PORSCHE 911 CARRERA RS 3.0

Just two years after the introduction of the 911 Carrera RS 2.7, its almost new drive system was no longer in the premier league. Its 210 hp was still a lot on the road in 1974, but on the racetrack, the performance level developed faster. The big boxer was no longer powerful enough for motorsport. Porsche therefore made plans for a new super sports car in the summer of 1973.

The successor to the 911 Carrera RS 2.7 was to be a sporty lightweight version of the new 911 and would be produced as a small series, in order to be able to race and win. After all, Porsche had the title of European GT champion to defend.

The main aim of development was to improve the car's strengths—engine, aerodynamics, weight, and traction. The specifications included more power, a more effective rear spoiler, a larger wheel/tire combination, and a dry weight of 900 kilograms (1,984 lbs.). With these specifications, the engineers developed a Carrera RS (Group 3, series GT) and a Carrera RS + M491 (Group 4 racing package).

Porsche described the models internally as follows: "The basic type represents the further developed Carrera RS in G version. The vehicle has a 3.0-liter engine for road use and can be registered for road traffic. However, the model will only be available in limited numbers and is ideally suited for Group 3 competition. With a few exceptions, the chassis is a real 'racing chassis,' uncompromisingly hard, direct, and offering little comfort."

The M491 racing package included a further developed 3.0-liter racing engine, 9-inch spoked wheels at the front, and 12-inch spoked wheels at the rear, with central locking and matching fender extensions. Both models were fitted with an improved rear spoiler.

FURTHER DEVELOPMENT FOR MOTORSPORT

"For homologation reasons, we had to come up with something for the 911 RS 3.0. Like our competitors, we used a wider body to gain more traction through a wider track and wider tires," recalled Jürgen Barth. He had been responsible for sports homologation at Porsche since 1969. The manufacturer did not want to develop a new car, because, as always, money was tight.

The engineers therefore limited themselves to an evolution of the Carrera

911 RS 2.7, eliminating the need to type an entire vehicle. This was a series production modification, a so-called post-homologation. In other words, it was a comprehensive update.

The new car was powered by a boxer engine with a displacement of 3.0 liters. This actually made a new FIA homologation necessary. However, Jürgen Barth's team used a trick to reduce the number of new cars that needed to be produced. "According to the FIA regulations, we had to build a hundred cars. However, we were able to count the RSR with the 3.0-liter engine, which was built fifty times in the same year, because we were able to credibly explain to the commissioners that the new model was an evolution. The 3.0 RSR became the 3.0 RS," said Barth in retrospect.

This reduced costs. Porsche quickly obtained homologation for the RS 3.0. The small number of units eliminated the need for large-scale production. Porsche built the small number of sporty derivatives by hand.

Some Italian FIA commissioners initially objected because they did not accept the reinforcement of the G model on the rear axle—although this was present in all production cars and was therefore permitted in motorsport. "They didn't want to understand it or didn't understand it. That is why I wrote a whole page as an addendum for the FIA homologation to

The RSR was a pure race car; therefore, it had only the driver's seat and limited equipment.

The larger rear wing provided more downforce, while the wider track with wider tires provided more traction.

explain this reinforcement," says Barth. After that, there are no more problems.

MOST POWERFUL GERMAN SPORTS CAR

Porsche unveiled the 911 Carrera RS 3.0 in 1974. The successor to the 911 Carrera RS 2.7 weighed 1,060 kilograms (2,337 lbs.) in roadworthy condition. Empty weight for homologation was 900 kilograms. Its new 3-liter six-cylinder boxer engine produced 230 hp. It was thus the most powerful German automobile in production when it hit the market.

However, with a price of almost 65,000 DM, it cost almost as much as a Ferrari 365 GTB or a Maserati Bora. Both were even more powerful. Nevertheless, after the success of the 911 Carrera RS 2.7, Porsche was confident that the car would quickly attract buyers.

In a 1974 press release, Porsche wrote, "The new model is designed as an optimal Group 3 car for competition purposes, but is also suitable for road use. For pure racing purposes, this even more powerful and promising Carrera RS is available on request in the racing version (improved as per Group 4) to defend its dominant position in the international GT championships."

At first, orders trickled in slowly. The reasons were the spike in oil prices in October 1973 and a speed limit on the autobahns. However, when the federal authorities declared the crisis over, there was a noticeable uptick in sales of the super sports car. This confirmed the manufacturer's theory that the RS philosophy was a real sales argument.

LIGHTWEIGHT CONSTRUCTION

To save weight, Porsche made the roof outer skin, door outer skins, seat recesses, and switch panel from thin sheet metal. Reinforcements and supports in the area of the spring strut bearings, rear stabilizer bar bearings, and the footrests ensured stability. Porsche modified the rear cross members and the front wheel arches to allow the use of additional coil springs.

They offered a more precise response and therefore better handling than the standard torsion bars. According to homologation, these modifications were permitted if they supplemented rather than replaced the original springs, a trick that other manufacturers also used. The original spring was made weaker, and the additional coil spring took over the work.

As usual, the interior was spartan: a naked interior without floor carpeting and soundproofing material, but with black felt on the seats. The glove compartment flap, door pockets, and armrests on the doors were missing. Instead, Fiat 600–type straps were again used to pull the doors shut. The clock was omitted as it had been on the previous model.

Instead of sport seats, thin-walled Recaro lightweight shells accommodated the two passengers. While the driver's seat could be reclined, the front passenger's seat remained fixed. Four-point seat belts secured both occupants firmly in the car. A lightweight lid support for the hood replaced the heavy gas pressure damper.

While the front windshield was made of 4.2-millimeter-thick (0.165 in.) production glass, Porsche installed windows made of thin glass in the rear and sides. The side rear windows were permanently installed and could not be opened. To achieve a particularly sporty look, Porsche anodized the window surrounds, exterior mirrors, and headlight trim rings in black.

Success at Daytona in 1975: Peter Gregg and Hurley Haywood won the 24-hour race. Other Porsche 911 Carrera RSRs finished in positions 2 to 6.

The 911 RS only achieved homologation as the result of a trick—Porsche added the RSR to the list and thus achieved the required number of units. With 330 hp, the racing car from 1974 could reach speeds of up to 280 kph.

REAL DOWNFORCE FOR THE FIRST TIME

A further-developed spoiler made of fiberglass-reinforced plastic (GFK) with a polyurethane border was fitted in the rear. The aerodynamicists reached a significant milestone in the first evolutionary stage. With a width increased by 6 centimeters (2.36 in.) and extensive rubber beading, the spoiler now provided real downforce. The previous models had only reduced uplift.

Its effect was not to be underestimated: the new spoiler looked powerful and gave the rear end a beefy note—as well as a selling point. However, the spoiler was so prominent that Porsche again feared problems gaining approval, based on experience from production of the previous model. To avoid the problem prophylactically, the TÜV in Stuttgart carried out an individual inspection of the component on every car. Better safe than sorry.

Porsche offered the rear spoiler with the all-round rubber strip in two versions: as a racing spoiler and as a road spoiler, which was fitted only upon delivery to the local dealer. Porsche decided not to install a front spoiler like the one on the previous version. Instead, the manufacturer integrated a wide oil cooler and two air shafts for the front disc brakes in the front end, which was made of GFK. The effect was close to that of the previous front spoiler.

A BIGGER ENGINE

For the 911, the model change meant a major expansion of the top-of-the-line engine. A displacement of 2.7 liters was now standard, from the base model to the 911 Carrera. To delineate the sporty top end, Porsche worked on the standard engine according to the now-proven RS tactic: in its sportiest form, the six-cylinder would be larger, more refined, and more powerful.

The engineers increased the cylinder bore from 90 to 95 millimeters (3.5 to 3.7 in.), resulting in a total volume of 2,993 cubic centimeters (182.6 cu. in.). Larger intake and exhaust valves with diameters of 49 and 41.5 millimeters (1.9 and 1.6 in.), respectively, increased the gas flow rate. Compression rose significantly, from 8.85:1 to 9.8:1. In addition, a lightweight flywheel improved the unit's "revability."

The measures meant constructive changes to the engine. Instead of magnesium, Porsche made the crankcase from durable aluminum. The reason: according to calculations, the original material would not withstand the pressure generated by the 3.0-liter engine and would crack.

The boxer achieved its maximum output of 230 hp at 6,200 rpm, while maximum torque of 274 Nm (202 ft.-lbs.) was reached at 5,000 rpm. Although the Carrera RS 3.0 was one of the most powerful production Porsches of this time, it did not reach its mechanical load limit. The engines of the pure racing cars produced about 330 hp. Porsche left sufficient reserves even for the fastest production sports cars.

Racing cars like the 911 RSR 3.0 ended up with collectors all over the world after retiring from racing. In 2016, the eye-catching Jägermeister returned to Germany.

The five-speed gearbox adopted from the 911 Carrera RS 2.7 featured splash lubrication and an oil pump, as well as oil cooling by means of a cooling pipe coil in the front left wheel arch for greater durability under extreme loads. A Fichtel & Sachs series clutch with increased pressure transferred the engine power to the transmission. A limited slip differential with an 80 percent locking factor provided more traction when cornering.

FAST, BUT NOT FASTER

The Porsche was capable of 0 to 100 kph (0 to 62 mph) in 5.5 seconds, and it took 23.6 seconds to reach 200 kph (124 mph). Its maximum speed was 250 kph (155 mph) at 6,400 rpm. This was slightly superior to its predecessor—a tribute to its big spoiler.

Auto tester, racing driver, and journalist Paul Frère commented, "The current car was a mile per hour slower than the 911 Carrera RS 2.7, although its acceleration remained almost the same. Nevertheless, this is one of the fastest road cars we have ever measured. It reached a speed of 100 kph in a breathtaking 5.2 seconds, thanks to its outstanding rear wheel traction, and it covered the quarter mile in fourteen seconds."

What mattered most to Porsche was the dynamics, up to 180 kph (112 mph). Contemporary testers were impressed by the car's power and acceleration, comparing it to a rocket launch. Only at speeds above 180 kph did the acceleration diminish somewhat, as the professionals at *Auto Motor und Sport* magazine noted. Unusual for a sports car engine: drivers could drive the 911 without shifting gears. In fifth gear, the boxer exhibited good behavior from 2,000 to over 7,000 rpm.

CONVERSIONS FOR MOTOR SPORTS

With the racing package for Group 4, engine output was 330 hp with the same displacement. Engine compression was increased from 9.8:1 to 10.3:1, and the tachometer scale went to 10,000 rpm. Instead of six individual throttle valves, the racing version had one flat slide valve per cylinder bank, and a dual ignition replaced the single ignition. Two single-pipe systems combined the exhaust gases in one exhaust. Power was transmitted to the transmission via a stable racing clutch from Fichtel & Sachs.

To ensure that the engine received sufficient fuel at full throttle, two fuel pumps supplied it with fuel from the 110-liter (29-gal.) tank. For FIA approval, Porsche installed a fire extinguishing system, roll bar, and Recaro racing seats with six-point harnesses as standard in the racing car.

Full steam ahead through the Green Hell: Swiss driver Herbert Müller, together with Gijs van Lennep (NL), drove a Porsche 911 Carrera RSR 2.1 Turbo to sixth place in the 1,000 km race at the Nürburgring in 1974, ahead of teammates Manfred Schurti (FL) and Helmuth Koinigg (A).

A masterpiece of lightweight construction: with up to 500 hp at 1.5 bar boost pressure, the 911 Carrera RSR Turbo 2.1, weighing just 825 kilograms, accelerated to 200 kph in 8.8 seconds. For optimum weight distribution, the fuel tank was located where the passenger seat would be. The chassis worked with wishbones all round, while the half-shafts, wheels, and brakes came from the tried-and-tested 917.

MODIFICATIONS TO THE SUSPENSION

Porsche did not risk any experiments with the suspension. The engineers used the setup from the 911 Carrera RSR 2.8 but reinforced it in many places. They installed aluminum auxiliary struts on the front axle, as well as control arms and shock absorbers from Bilstein. Porsche used production parts for the steering bearings. On the rear axle, the engineers reinforced the short steel control arms but again used production parts for the bearings. With a diameter of 18 millimeters (0.70 in.), the elements of the torsion bar suspension were thicker than the preceding components, likewise the stabilizer bars with the same diameter. It was adjustable in the racing version. The result was a significant improvement in handling. The road holding, handling, and performance of the new Carrera were superior to those of its predecessor.

"In hairpin turns, because of the limited slip differential there was an increased tendency to push the front straight ahead, unless you got into the curve fast enough with the gas pedal and swung the rear around with power," wrote Paul Frère about the car's handling.

MORE TRACTION IN THE RS

Wider tires also fit under the widened fenders of the new model. In front, Porsche installed 215/60VR15 tires on eight-spoke rims; in the rear, 235/60VR15s on nine-spoke rims. Rather unusual today for a factory racing car: spacers widened the track of the production car. They measured 7 millimeters (0.27 in.) at the front and 21 millimeters (0.82 in.) at the rear axle. Rims with a different offset would probably have been more expensive.

With the sports package, more exact bearings ensured more precise steering behavior. Porsche adapted the wheels of the 917, as these could be changed using a quick-release fastener. At the front and rear, the bumpers were adapted to the GRP fender extensions to accommodate the wide tires to some extent.

The car's brakes came from the luxury sports class. The engineers adopted the system from the Porsche 917 Turbo short-tail racing car with more than 1,000 hp. It pressed its pads with four fixed pistons per cross-ribbed brake caliper against the perforated and internally ventilated discs. The front pistons had a diameter of 43 millimeters, the rear ones 38 millimeters—compared to its predecessor, this represents an increase in braking surface area from 7,600 to 11,800 square millimeters (11.8 to 18.3 sq. in.). For finer metering, the brake force distribution could be adjusted by means of a balance beam installed in front of the master brake cylinder. Drivers could individually adjust the brake balance between the front and rear axles—the finest racing technology in a standard model. The brake system of the 917 cost as much as a mid-range car at that time and showed that Porsche did not simply give the Carrera RS 3.0 a lackluster makeover, but designed a serious sports machine for the racetrack. Even after hard braking maneuvers in competition, there was no fading.

"If you switch from the gas pedal to the brakes in the Carrera RS, you can bask in the reassuring feeling that you're using a system that can also take on the 1,000-plus horses of the Turbo 917. The pedal forces required for effective braking are relatively high, but there is no question of the braking effect diminishing even under extreme conditions," wrote journalist Klaus Westrup in *Auto Motor und Sport* after testing the new Porsche.

SMALL PRODUCTION SERIES FROM THE FALL OF 1973

Porsche began production of the planned vehicles in the fall of 1973 to achieve homologation for April 1974. The new Carrera RS cost 64,980 Marks, around 25,000 Marks more than the 210 hp 911 Carrera (39,950 Marks) and almost twice as much as its predecessor, the 911 Carrera RS 2.7 (34,000 Marks). Another 15,000 Marks were added for the conversion to a pure racing car—Porsche quickly realized that the lightweight versions sold well. A total of 109 vehicles were built, fifty of which were pure RSRs for the racetrack. Other sources report fifty-three or even fifty-six vehicles. At the International Race of Champions (IROC) in October 1973, Roger Penske from the USA entered twelve identical 911 Carrera RSR 3.0s in which drivers from different racing classes competed against each other. Other sources even speak of fifteen vehicles.

The RSR 3.0's fender extensions, extremely wide tires, and air intakes were particularly striking.

The RS 3.0 was driven mainly by customer teams, not the factory. Until the end of the 1970s, the model was popular in circuit races and rallies. The supply of spare parts remained reliable, as the production vehicles continued to be built unchanged. At the end of the decade, some sports drivers only struggled with the performance.

With the 911 SC Carrera RS, Porsche refreshed the homologation in 1983 so that the vehicles could continue to compete in international rallies.

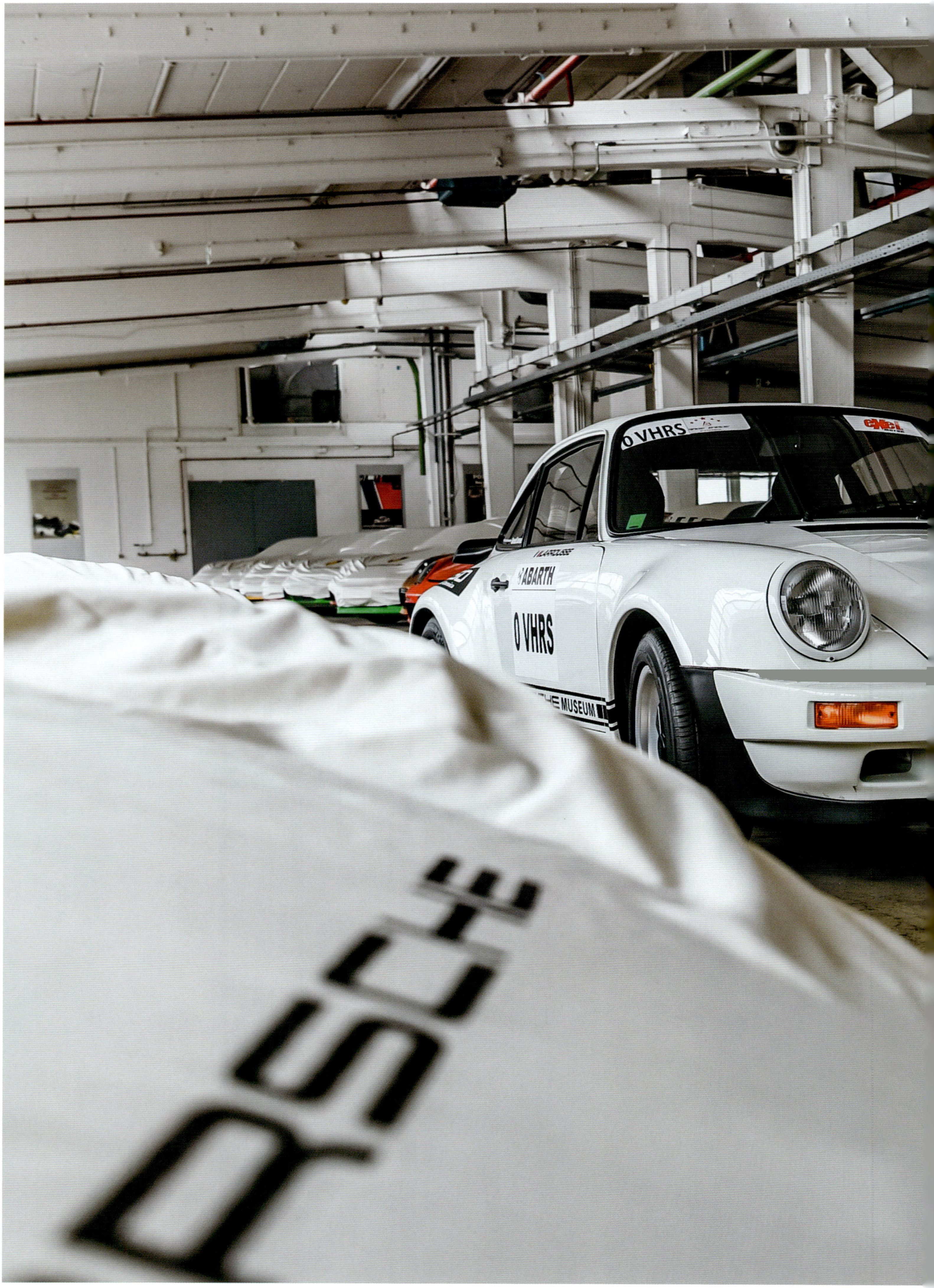
0 VHRS
ABARTH
0 VHRS
MUSEUM

Porsche calls the external storage area of its museum the "sacred hall," the "treasure chamber," the "vault," or simply the "depot." More than three hundred of the fast vehicles from its long history, such as the 911 SC RS, are parked there.

From the specifications: "Based on the 911 SC vehicle, a street-legal competition vehicle is to be developed as an evolution series."

For FIA approval, the 911 SC Carrera RS required a fire extinguisher on board.

permission of our bosses, I drove the Monte Carlo Rally together with Roland Kussmaul in the 911 SC so that we could stay in business, keep in touch with customers, and see what happened in practice," recalled Jürgen Barth. It was the last year in which the 911 could be used in accordance with the FIA guidelines. Barth and Kussmaul finished eleventh in the overall standings.

"It was clear to us that we could not jeopardize further rally entries, and we were able to convince the management to build at least twenty-five racing cars," said Jürgen Barth. At least twenty vehicles were required to maintain a valid homologation and continue using the cars in rallying in accordance with FIA regulations. Otherwise, 911s would no longer be able to compete. "So, we had managed to ensure that the 911 could compete in international competitions for another five years."

The competition in the World Rally Championship was already very stiff back then. Turbo engines, four-wheel drive, and lightweight bodies turned the vehicles into projectiles on gravel, mud, and sand. By then, the 911 SC was already a thing of the past. Nevertheless, Porsche gave it a try.

PORSCHE 911 SC CARRERA RS

At the end of the 1970s, Porsche was doing badly economically. Racing cars were barely selling. "Vehicles such as the 934, 935, and 936 were in demand, less so a 911 for Group 3," recalled Jürgen Barth, "but some customers wanted to continue rallying with the 911, so we had to homologate a new model."

The problem: FIA homologation automatically expired five years after the end of a model's production. This meant that the 911 Carrera RS 3.0 would no longer be able to compete in official races. The last time Porsche competed with it was at the East African Safari in 1978, where the cars did not reach the finish line but still took second place. In the following years, only private teams entered the 911 in rallies. "In 1983, with the

A PORSCHE 911 FOR GROUP B

On April 24, 1983, Porsche presented the specifications for the 911 SC Carrera RS, internally the Type 954. Porsche boss Helmuth Bott approved development of the new, lightweight super sports car on June 23, 1983. The description: "Based on the 911 SC vehicle, a road-legal competition vehicle is to be developed as an evolutionary series. This vehicle serves as a basic type for sports purposes. The homologation requirements for evolution series of Group B vehicles must be taken into account."

Since 1982, Group B had been a very special class of Gran Turismo vehicles in rally motorsport, which was used in the World Rally Championships until 1986. Statutes of the automobile sport authority FIA allowed light, powerful, and very fast rally cars that only a few top drivers could master. The best-known cars of this era included the Audi Sport Quattro S1, Lancia Delta S4, Peugeot 205 Turbo 16 E2, and Ford RS200. Drivers like Walter Röhrl piloted cars with almost 600 hp through forests and along deep ravines.

Following its successes on the circuit, such as at the 24 Hours of Le Mans, Porsche wanted to get involved in the increasingly popular rally scene in 1983. The 911 SC Carrera RS was the first step in this direction, allowing the company to venture into this world cautiously and, above all, cost-effectively.

The rally project ended in the Super-Porsche 959, which was built between 1986 and 1989. It arrived too late for its deployment in Group B.

THE FIRST RS WITH A TURBO BODY

According to the specifications, the 911 SC RS should reach speeds of 255 kph (158 mph) and accelerate from 0 to 100 kph in 5.3 seconds. It was to be capable of completing the sprint over one kilometer (0.62 mi.) in 24.5 seconds. The calculations were correct. After eleven seconds, the 911 SC RS reached 160 kph and thus accelerated better than a 911 Turbo. In a test, *Auto Motor und Sport* even recorded a time of 5.0 seconds to accelerate to 100 kph—the best value to date for a standard, street-legal sports car.

Porsche was not reinventing the wheel and the car but was drawing on many tried-and-tested components, including those from the first Carrera RS 2.7, Turbo, and SC. The engineers planned with a typing weight of 960 kilograms (2,116 lbs.), but handwritten notes increased the value to 980 kilograms (2,160 lbs.). The note stated, "Over 200 kilograms (441 lbs.) lighter than series SC, turbo look." With a full tank, the street model weighed 1,057 kilograms (2,330 lbs.), while the 911 Turbo weighed 1,290 kilograms (2,844 lbs.).

The effort was rewarded. Porsche won the Middle East Championship in 1984 and 1985. Henri Toivonen won with the 911 SC RS on the Costa Smeralda and at the 24 Hours of Ypres in Belgium. "We recognized the opportunity to extend homologation with just a few cars and therefore little financial outlay—and we seized this opportunity. We were able to build an affordable and competitive racing car without having to carry out any new development work," said Jürgen Barth, confirming the clever strategy.

Except for the missing clock, the cockpit was the same as that of the production vehicle.

For better support, the pilot and co-pilot sat in racing shells with safety harnesses.

The six-cylinder produced 250 hp at 7,000 rpm and its maximum torque of 250 Nm at 6,500 rpm.

At 7,000 rpm, the six-cylinder produced 250 hp, and 250 Nm (184 ft.-lbs.) of torque was achieved at 6,500 rpm. Porsche set the maximum rpm at 7,600, with 8,000 rpm for sport purposes. The tachometer was again scaled at 10,000 rpm. By comparison: the production boxer engine of the SC produced 204 hp at 5,900 rpm.

To make the engine stable, the mechanics went into detail. The crankshaft and flywheel were still from the production vehicle. However, the connecting rods were partially polished, and the forged pistons were new. The engineers fit race-proven cylinder heads from the 935 onto the cylinders.

ENGINE AND TRANSMISSION

The engineers improved the 3-liter boxer of the 911 SC in detail. This included a conversion of the modern K-Jetronic to the tried-and-tested mechanical intake manifold injection system from Bosch/Kugelfischer, including secondary air injection in the RdW (Rest of the World) version.

Hollow and thus lighter valves with forged spring retainers were able to withstand the high speeds. They could be adjusted using adjusting caps. Camshafts with a larger stroke ensured a longer gas flow. The compression ratio rose from

9.8:1 to 10.3:1. Finnish rally professional Henri Toivonen, who drove in several European Championship rallies in the 911 SC RC, said of the engine, "I have never driven a car with such a wide usable rev range."

PRODUCTION PARTS FOR THE SPORT ENGINE

In the extreme range, a modified oil pump adopted from the 911 Turbo ensured sufficient lubrication. Two oil coolers in the front wheel arches (in the competition version) and a modified ratio of the engine cooling fan kept the six-cylinder engine within the optimum temperature window.

In addition to using the Kugelfischer injection system, Porsche relied on modified or new fuel lines, intake filters, and throttle bodies for mixture preparation. These triple-throttle bodies were similar to those of the 911 Carrera RS 2.7 and ensured fast response under load, among other things.

The ignition system came from the 3.0-liter series engine; only the ignition distributor was adapted. The exhaust gases flowed to the outside via separate exhaust ducts on the left and right at the rear. The standard exhaust came from the Carrera RS 2.7, while the competition vehicles used that of the 911 R, which ensured a better gas flow.

TRANSMISSION WITH DETAIL IMPROVEMENTS

The 911 SC Carrera RS 3.0's five-speed transmission came from the 911 Carrera 3.2 and had an adapted transmission ratio, special synchronization with two retaining rings, and a separate oil pump plus oil cooler. This kept the oil within a comfortable temperature range under extreme loads. The bevel gear and crown wheel were the same as those of the production car, while the drive bearing was smaller. The limited slip differential had a locking factor of 40 percent as standard.

Porsche offered two different transmissions. The standard transmission was optimized for the racetrack. Upon request, customers could obtain a shorter gear ratio for rally use. Both versions were homologated. While first gear matched the standard gearbox of the 911 Carrera 3.2, Porsche downgraded second gear to 15/30 or 16/35 (rally), third gear to 21/29 or 20/32, fourth gear to 25/24 or 23/29, and fifth gear to 27/24 or 26/26.

To enable drivers to change gears quickly and safely, Porsche relied on a new clutch pressure plate with increased contact pressure, which originated from the 911 2.8 RSR. The steel spring clutch disk was fitted with modified dampers, and the release bearing was standard. A new gearshift bracket also reduced shift travel by 20 percent—ideal for fast gear changes during hard racing in competition.

The luggage compartment was also close to that of the production car.

PARTS KIT FOR THE RS SUSPENSION

To always get the extra power onto the road, the 911 RS SC was fitted with the suspension and brakes from the 911 Turbo—the 917 solution was too expensive and too complex, especially since the racing car had not been actively used by the factory for years. To ensure that the sports car was stable on the brakes, the model from the 1974 RS took over the brake master cylinders with the balance beam. The hydraulics apply pressure reliably, albeit with great effort without a brake booster on the brake pistons and brake discs of the 930 Turbo. The front axle came with, among other things, fender extensions, additional springs, and stabilization as on the 1973 model. The wishbones for the stabilizer bar suspension also corresponded to those of the RS model from 1973, while the wheel bearings were from the current series. For the front stabilizer bars, Porsche relied on a diameter of 18 millimeters (0.70 in.) as on the predecessor, the diameter being the same as that of the suspension joint.

On the rear axle, Porsche installed standard components from the 911 Turbo with additional springs. The torsion bar came from the 911 SC, wheel bearings from the 930, likewise the steering shafts and the settings. The rear stabilizer bar had a diameter of 18 millimeters.

Porsche also reached into the shelf for tires and took those from the 930 with widths of 7 and 8 inches. The manufacturer mounted 205/55VR16 tires in front, and 225/50VR16s in the rear. Porsche painted the rim stars Grand prix White (M348) to match the exterior paint. Upon special request, a narrow spare tire with compressor could be fitted in the front trunk at no extra charge.

BODY

The turbo body had to be modified at the front for the stabilizer bar mounts. New attachment points for the Matter roll cage were also required. To absorb the lateral forces during fast racetrack driving, Porsche reinforced the suspension strut mount, shock absorber mount and rear axle cross tube. For homologation reasons, additional openings and cut-outs were required in the bodywork—for example, for the master brake cylinder.

Porsche made the front fenders, doors, and front hood out of lightweight aluminum. To further reduce weight, the engineers installed windshield, door windows, side windows, and a rear window made of thin glass. In front, Porsche fitted flashing lights in the GFK fairing, while in the rear, the taillights and license plate light were installed in the GFK bumper.

The attachments with baffle tubes were made of aluminum. Porsche dispensed with side indicators and sill panels as well as PVC underbody protection, insulating mats, melting foils, and cavity preservation. Even the door panels and the cover for the door storage as well as the center console and the rear side paneling were sacrificed to reduce weight. Where else could you get so little car for so much money?

Electric windows, electric exterior mirrors, trunk lighting, automatic temperature control, rear fog light, auxiliary heater fan, and engine compartment lighting also fall victim to the diet. This made necessary a new wiring harness that weighed less.

Typical RS: there was no clock. The car adopted the speedometer from the 911 Turbo and the indicator lights from tamer models. Drivers could recline the racing seats and fasten themselves in with harness safety belts. Rear seats were also unnecessary ballast and therefore not suitable for the RS.

Instead of the heavy and large heat exchanger in the rear, Porsche installed a stand-alone gasoline heater. A lightweight electric fan was used in rally trim. This was because the lines to the oil cooler at the front were in the sills, where the warm air flowed from the engine into the interior in standard vehicles. In the rally version, three aluminum plates protected the underbody and the technology.

Porsche won the Middle East Championship with the 911 SC Carrera RS in 1984 and 1985, while Henri Toivonen was victorious at the Costa Smerelda and at the 24 Hours of Ypres in Belgium.

Two oil coolers in the front wheel arches (in the competition version) and a modified ratio of the engine cooling fan kept the six-cylinder engine within the optimum temperature window.

The exhaust gases flowed outward via separate guides on the left and right of the rear end.

To keep the center of gravity as low as possible, the engineers lowered the body by 25 millimeters (0.98 in.) at the front and 30 millimeters (1.18 in.) at the rear compared to the standard SC. Anyone who still did not recognize from the outside that this was a very special car could look at the rear. The lettering identified the car as the 911 SC RS.

PRODUCTION

Porsche hurried with development and production. Everything was to go quickly, so that the car would be finished and could be homologated for the next season. Porsche wanted to build one car per day for six days and two cars per day for another seven days. This made a total of twenty cars in thirteen production days.

Except for production of the prototype, Porsche did all the work in Zuffenhausen. Body shell construction, body shell modification, engine assembly, and overall assembly took place at the headquarters. The transmission was assembled at ZWN (Zahnradwerke Neuenstein), like that of the production car.

Porsche asked 188,100 Marks for the sports car. It was thus the most expensive Porsche to date that was licensed for the road. Remember: ten years earlier the 911 RS 3.0 had cost 65,000 Marks. But that was not all. For use in rally competition, Porsche demanded an additional 25,000 Marks. For this, customers got a durable, more powerful 280hp engine.

Finally, twenty-one vehicles were made for good friends of the brand. According to information provided by Jürgen Barth, ten of the white-painted cars went to sponsor Rothmans (some sources say six), two to Switzerland, two to the Porsche family, and the rest to private customers, most of them in the USA. Rothmans entered the 911 SC in the European Rally Championship, also including world championship races. The SC RS won the rally title in Belgium in 1984.

THE END OF GROUP B

With its concept of rear engine and lightweight construction, the Porsche 911 SC RS was no match for thoroughbred rally competition cars such as the Audi Sport Quattro, Lancia 037, or Peugeot 205 T16. Several tragic accidents in Group B brought about the end of the highest international rally series.

Henri Toivonen and Attilio Bettega died in a Lancia at the Corsica Rally. A Ford RS200 crashed into a crowd at the Portugal Rally, killing three spectators, and Marc Surer was involved in a serious accident at the Hesse Rally in his Ford RS200 in which his co-driver was killed. The FIA organizers canceled the remaining competitions and banned Group B in 1986.

The completely developed Porsche 959 was only entered in the Paris to Dakar Desert Rally in Egypt and at the Mille Piste Rally in France, but not in rally world championship races. The 959 technology demonstrator was only built until 1988. It was not until 1991 that the 911 RS 3.6 of the 964 model was followed by another successor in the RS line of ancestors.

964

SOMETHING LIKE THIS IS HARDLY IMAGINABLE TODAY—IT TOOK SIXTEEN YEARS FOR PORSCHE TO COMPLETELY MODERNIZE THE 911. MEANWHILE, THE UPDATE WAS ABSOLUTELY NECESSARY BECAUSE SALES WERE FALLING, NOT ONLY OF THE 911 BUT OF THE PREVIOUSLY POPULAR 944 AS WELL.

The Porsche 911 RS 3.6 continued Porsche's good old RS tradition: light, powerful, fast.

Porsche was in a deep crisis. The heavily revised 911 had to win more customers from 1989 onward and bring Porsche out of the red. To achieve this, the 911, known internally as the 964, was to become more modern, more suitable for everyday use, and easier to drive. Less than ever before, the focus was on the fun of purist sports drivers. The car had to be suitable for everyday drivers. To this end, Porsche integrated power steering and ABS. An automatic gearbox became available in 1990. Modern McPherson struts at the front and coil springs on semi-trailing arms at the rear replaced the torsion bar springs of the predecessor.

The base model of the new 911 was now called the Carrera 2, with a newly developed 3.6-liter six-cylinder boxer engine with 250 hp, dual ignition, knock control, and a three-way catalytic converter in the rear. For the first time, Porsche offered an all-wheel-drive version (Carrera 4) alongside the 911 with rear-wheel drive, as a simplified version of the 959 super sports car with all-wheel drive. The Turbo had a displacement of 3.3 liters for 320 hp, a small series 3.6 liters for 360 hp. Even though the body was like that of its predecessor, the 964 was a new design. Under the bodywork, Porsche developed almost 85 percent of all parts in the 964 from scratch. This is particularly noticeable in the beefy front end and the modified sill trims. Typical of Porsche's attention to detail: of course, the rain gutters on the car have also been optimized. The drag coefficient was now 0.32, making the new 911 the most streamlined 911 to date. Probably the most remarkable element: the newly developed rear spoiler blended seamlessly into the silhouette of the 964. It extended from a speed of 80 kph, broke up the lift, provided downforce, and improved engine cooling. The driving force behind its development was once again Hermann Burst, who was already jointly responsible for the aerodynamics of the 911 Carrera RS 2.7 and was again filing patents for the invention.

PORSCHE 911 CARRERA RS 3.6

Porsche in fact wanted to continue its long RS tradition with the 911 RS 3.6 of the Type 964, but because Group C ended in 1989, there was no suitable competition for production cars. Not on the circuit and not in rallies. "So, we founded our own racing series for Europe and defined a new car for it—the 911 RS 3.6," explained Jürgen Barth.

A new 911 Carrera RS was already under discussion at the end of 1988, before the launch of the new 964 generation, when Jürgen Barth, former racing driver and project manager as well as manager of customer sport, suggested to his motorsport boss Peter Falk that two or three racing cars should be built based on the new 964 Carrera 2. Barth wanted to enter them in the 24-hour race on the Nürburgring.

This position represented an interesting turn of events. After the first Carrera RS 2.7 was designed for the racetrack, Porsche drivers—including Jürgen Barth—liked to use the RS successors of the G model in rallies. The new 964 RS was set to cause a sensation on the racetrack again.

Barth was a well-known part of Porsche's RS story. He drove the prototypes of the Carrera RS 2.7, RSR 2.8, and RSR 3.0. Porsche knew the effect that wins had on sales. Peter Falk therefore approved development of the long-distance car—the 964 RS.

As tradition demanded, the new RS was to be lighter, nimbler, and more powerful than former production vehicles and again be good for racing use.

Jürgen Barth developed the new vehicle. And with it, he wrote the specification sheet for his own homologation: he was one of the initiators of the new BPR racing series (BPR for Jürgen Barth, Patrick Peter, Stéphane Ratel) for GT racing cars. "I was familiar with it, knew the Group 4 regulations from 1974, and knew what a good racing car had to be capable of," he said, looking back.

The series was a success. Seven manufacturers took part until 1996. From it, there later developed the ADAC GT Cup, the FIA GT Championship, and the ADAC GT Masters. "First we needed a few races to promote the cars, but then we were able to sell more of them," said Jürgen Barth. This tactic had long-term success: from the RS 3.6 later came the RS 3.8 and the RSR—and subsequently the first 911 GT2.

SEVERAL MOTORSPORTS PROJECTS

Porsche worked at several construction sites in parallel. In addition to the Nürburgring car, Jürgen Barth was also working on another project—a lightweight version based on the Carrera 4. Twenty-one examples of the 911 Carrera 4 Lightweight were made in 1990 and 1991. The all-wheel-drive racing car combined 265 hp with a weight of 1,105 kilograms

Porsche had been developing the lightweight version of the 964 RS since 1988 to once again have a production racing car for customer sport in its portfolio.

(2,204 lbs.). Porsche initially sold it for 225,000 marks and later for 285,000. The small series was very lucrative. Meanwhile, developers Roland Kussmaul and Helmut Flegl built a 964 Cup racing car based on the Carrera 2. It competed internally with the 964 RS but had little to do with it. The cars were used in the new Porsche Carrera Cup. They therefore lacked the co-driver's seat, soundproofing material, and servo linkage. Instead of on aluminum wheels, the racecar ran on 18-in. wheels made of magnesium. The engineers pushed the 3.6-liter boxer to 265 hp and 310 Nm (228 ft.-lbs.) of torque. A roll cage; short-ratio gears in the third, fourth, and fifth gears of the manual transmission; and a lowered body were also included.

For the 1992 model year, the 964 Cup was based on the body of the 964 RS, which is why it is mentioned in this list. The six-cylinder boxer engine was pushed to 275 hp at 6,100 rpm and 314 Nm (231 ft.-lbs.) of torque at 4,800 rpm. The ABS could be switched off on the 1,120 kilogram (2,469-lb.) lightweight racing car. It was a pure competition car for the racetrack—and promoted the idea of a thoroughbred sports car for the road.

SAME FORMULA FOR RS MODELS

This idea was now to be taken up by a production car. The Carrera RS 3.6 was intended to replicate the success of the small series in larger numbers. In this way, Porsche hoped to attract more sports car drivers. In September 1990, the manufacturer unveiled a new version of the 911 Carrera RS at the Birmingham Motor Show. Production began in the summer of 1991.

The RS had to polish up Porsche's tarnished motorsport image. In Formula 1, Porsche was unable to achieve any success as an engine supplier with a 3.5-liter V12 for Arrows. Sales of the 911 continued to be sluggish. With the RS, the Stuttgart-based company was hoping for a change toward more sportiness—all in the interest of better sales.

Porsche retained the recipe of the RS vehicles for the 964 model. This meant a powerful engine combined with the lowest possible weight. Technically, the 911 Carrera RS remained a close relative of the Carrera 2 used in the Carrera Cup, but the RS weighed between 1,225 and 1,250 kilograms (2,700 to 2,755 lbs.) depending on the equipment. Its base model was up to 175 kilograms (385 lbs.) heavier. Marketing feared that the new, purist RS, with its rattling gearbox and single-mass flywheel, would sell poorly. "They said they needed a more decent car," recalled Roland Kussmaul. Like the variants of the 911 Carrera RS 2.7 from 1972, Porsche also offered the new RS in various versions—including a comfortable touring model.

LIGHTWEIGHT CONSTRUCTION IN THE NEW RS

In the RS version of the 911 Carrera type 964, passengers cranked the side windows up and down by hand. Except for the front windows, thin glass panes were used. Thinner and strongly contoured bucket seats upholstered in leather replaced the Carrera sports seats. On the doors, Porsche installed slimmed-down panels with pull handles and strap openers instead of door handles.

Under the direction of developers Roland Kussmaul and Helmut Flegl, the 964 Carrera 2 was used as the basis for the cars for the newly created Porsche Carrera Cup, which from 1990 onward competed mostly in the supporting program of the popular DTM. The first champion was Olaf Manthey, who later took over development work for Porsche Motorsport with his Manthey-Racing GmbH team and won the 24-hour race at the Nürburgring seven times.

In the 1982 season, the cars of the Porsche Carrera Cup were based on the 964 RS.

Instead of the automatically extending rear spoiler of the normal Carrera models and the RS, there was an optional large fixed rear spoiler for even more downforce.

VARIANTS OF THE 964 CARRERA RS

Porsche built a total of 2,382 examples of the 964 Carrera RS, broken down as follows:

- 1,916 in the Sport version, including 72 with right-hand drive. This was the basic version. It did not have an M number for special specifications. The Sport version included a rigid sintered driving plate, a lightened flywheel, six-point seat belts, an emergency battery switch, and the absence of noise insulation and roof trim.

- Seventy-six in the Touring version, including fourteen with right-hand drive (M002). This more comfortable version featured full underbody protection with long-term warranty, height-adjustable sports seats, electric windows, and the more comfortable dual-mass flywheel of the Carrera 2.

- 290 in the N/GT racing sport version with road approval (M003). This version included a stripped-out interior, roll cage, an emergency stop switch on the outside, and preparations for racing.

- There were also 112 Cup Carreras (M001). This was the Cup vehicle with a similar body. However, Porsche did not count these as part of the total RS production figures.

Porsche also built the 964 as a Club Sport CS version—but only once. It had firm suspension, but not quite as hard as the RS. Its equipment included 20 millimeters lowering, the standard 250-hp engine, and less weight. As with the RS, Porsche dispensed with airbags, rear seats, insulating material, and electric windows in the one-off model. It is not known why just one was built.

There was no underbody protection, and the noise insulation was kept to a minimum. Instead of the standard fog lights, there were transparent plastic covers in the front spoiler. For greater rigidity, employees in production re-welded some areas of the body by hand. Drivers gripped a small 360 four-spoke leather steering wheel, optionally with a hub that was 30 millimeters (1.2 in.) longer, but without servo assistance. Central locking, alarm system, rear seats, airbags, and electric seat adjustment were also missing. There was no trim in the trunk. To further reduce weight, Porsche installed a front hood made of lightweight aluminum, manually adjustable Turbo exterior mirrors, and a 115-amp alternator. Technically,

this was not a problem, since dispensing with consumers of electricity reduced the power requirement. This resulted in a smaller wiring harness. In addition, one shaft could now drive the fan wheel and alternator at the same time—this saved the V-belt. This work in the depths of the engine shows how seriously the engineers took weight reduction.

As with its predecessors, the Touring version was to offer at least a little comfort. Porsche therefore installed electric windows and even a radio with eight speakers. Optional extras included heated seats, headlight cleaning system, air conditioning, sunroof, Symphony radio, and light alloy bumpers with front

A front hood made of lightweight aluminum was used to reduce the weight of the 964 RS.

Powerplant under the hood with the electrically extendable rear spoiler: the six-cylinder boxer engine with two valves per combustion chamber was a new development.

and rear impact absorbers. A clear windshield could also be fitted in place of the tinted one.

For left-hand-drive vehicles, Porsche offered power steering in the Touring version. Depending on the equipment, the RS weighed up to 1,320 kg (2,910 lbs.); it deliberately forewent one of its greatest strengths. The heavy catalytic converter could be ordered for some countries, but not for France. The 95-octane version delivered 10 hp more than the base engine and achieved 260 hp at 6,100 rpm and 314 Nm (231 ft-lbs.) of torque at 5,000 rpm. Instead of the hydraulic engine mounts used in the base vehicle, stiffer rubber mounts were used in the Carrera RS. Porsche also adopted the dual-mass flywheel on the Touring and the torque-controlled limited slip differential from the base model. The single-mass flywheel on the RS Sport saved 7 kg (15 lbs.) of weight.

LIGHTER AND STRONGER

The six-cylinder boxer engine newly developed for the 964, with two valves per combustion chamber, served as the drive. Compared to its predecessor, it had a larger bore of 100 millimeters (4 in.). The crankshaft—with a stroke of 76.4 millimeters (3 in.) and an additional torsional vibration dampener—increased the displacement of the RS to exactly 3,600 cubic centimeters (220 cu. in.). Porsche manufactured the housing for the duplex tracks from lightweight magnesium, and there were two spark plugs in each cylinder. In the RS,

pistons and cylinder liners were specially selected. Modified engine electronics ensured suitable valve timing. The boxer now refueled with 98 instead of 95 octane but produced 10 hp more than the base engine and reached 260 hp at 6,100 rpm and 314 Newton meters at 5,000 rpm. Instead of the hydraulic engine mounts used in the base vehicle, stiffer rubber mounts were used in the Carrera RS. Porsche also adopted the dual-mass flywheel in the Touring and the drive-torque-controlled limited-slip differential from the base. The single-mass flywheel in the RS Sport saved 7 kg (15 lbs.) in weight.

GOOD REVIEWS DESPITE LITTLE ADVANCE

The RS sprinted from 0 to 100 kph (62 mph) in 5.4 seconds and could reach speeds of up to 260 kph (161 mph). A Carrera 2 took 5.7 seconds and reached a maximum speed of 255 kph (158 mph), the 911 Turbo 5.0 seconds and 270 kph (168 mph). The magazine *Auto Motor und Sport* even drove the RS to 100 kph in 5.2 seconds and up to 263 kph (163 mph). "The top speed of 263 kph is identical, because it is not the power but the rev limiter that puts an end to it," wrote journalist Götz Leyrer in *Auto Motor und Sport* in 1991. "The engine ensures an immediate and impressive power delivery from 2,000 revolutions. And the RS unleashes it like a raging beast, with an almost relentless thrust and an engine roar whose aggressive pitch can only be matched by the air-cooled Porsche six-cylinder."

The new six-cylinder produced 260 hp at 6,100 rpm and 210 Nm of torque at 5,000 rpm.

Gears were changed via a manual five-speed gearbox, with a hydraulic clutch. An extended first and second gear were used in the transmission to avoid having to shift gears more frequently at low speeds during a race. The ZF limited slip differential locked at 20 percent when pulling and 100 percent when pushing. Even if the increase in power of 10 hp did not appear large on paper, the performance characteristics of the engine changed significantly, and it resembled a high-revving racing engine.

SENSITIVE SUSPENSION AND POWER-FUL BRAKES

Up front, the RS adopted the internally ventilated and perforated brake discs with a diameter of 322 millimeters (12.7 in.) from the 911 Turbo, including the four-piston fixed calipers made of light alloy. In the rear, Porsche installed the brake system from the Cup Carrera. This system ensured stable deceleration. Porsche tuned the ABS to be more precise.

Stabilizer bars at the front and rear and an automatically controlled rear spoiler improved running smoothness, as on the Carrera models. Porsche mounted 7.5 x 17 wheels with 205/50ZR17 tires in front and 9 x 17 wheels with 255/40ZR17 tires in the rear. The rims in the Cup design were made of lightweight magnesium. This reduced the weight of the unsprung mass by 10 kg (22 lbs.). In addition to optimum traction, the size of the wheels offered a further advantage. Slicks could be fitted for racing in Group N/GT, but only on standard rims. This reduced costs for the manufacturers. The aerodynamically optimized body, 40 millimeter (1.6 in.) lowering, and the smooth underbody also ensured a lift value close to 0. The engineers also fine-tuned the suspension. "To simply describe it with the word 'hard' would be a bit of a whitewash—the characterization that was once invented at Morgan in England is more apt—namely that the driver can feel whether the coin they have just driven over was heads or tails up," said Götz Leyrer about the handling of the RS.

Extremely high cornering speeds were a result of all this work. And Porsche fans loved it. Pure trans-sport use was limited. There was no more purist sports car with a license plate.

Light and spartan. In the interior, occupants cranked the side windows up and down by hand. Porsche installed opener loops on the doors.

THE 964 RS IS A SUCCESS

For homologation for the FIA N/GT Group in the 1992 season, Porsche had to build at least a thousand vehicles by the end of 1991. As many as two thousand units were planned. In the end, there would be even more. The press release stated, "This means that the numerous active sports drivers among Porsche's customers will once again have a promising racing car in the Gran Turismo class." Porsche sold more than 70 percent of the RS cars in the first year, followed by 15 percent in the second. Porsche completely abolished the originally planned limitation in the late 1992 model year to support sales of the 911 model series. The RS thus lost its exclusivity during its production period.

Color range: black, navy blue, Indian red, star ruby, and grand prix white

Optional: polar silver metallic, midnight blue metallic, and amethyst metallic, cobalt blue, horizon blue, polar silver, oak green, violet blue, amazon green, slate, Wimbledon green, and raspberry red, pearl color effect.

Interior: carpeting and headlining in black, seat center panels in combinations depending on exterior color:

- Black, violet, star ruby, gray violet (NV) for the paintwork in black, star ruby, and amethyst metallic

- Black, dark blue, navy blue, light blue (NS) for the black, navy blue, and midnight blue metallic paintwork

- Black, dark gray, pearl gray, light gray (NR) for the paintwork in black, Indian red, Grand Prix white, and night blue metallic

It is the details that make the difference: thinner and strongly contoured bucket seats replaced the Carrera's sports seats, and the clock was eliminated.

Porsche charged 30,000 marks more for the 964 RS than for the Carrera 2, making a total of 145,450 deutsch marks. Porsche charged 160,000 marks for the 964 RS N/GT, which was designed for circuit racing.

In order to boost sales in the USA, Porsche put the 964 RS America on wheels. It was more of a trim level than a racer.

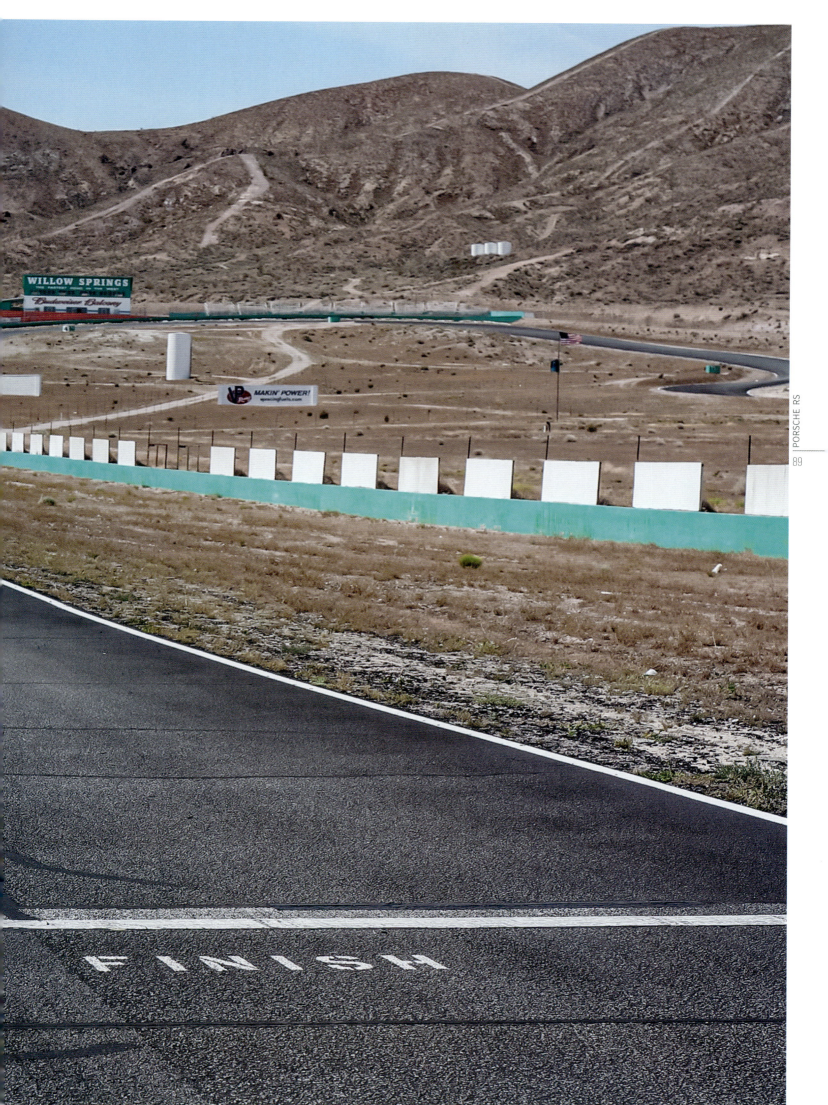

Between 1992 and 1994,
Porsche built 702 examples
of the 911 RS America.

PORSCHE 911 CARRERA RS AMERICA

Porsche did not launch the RS in the important US market because the necessary requirements for homologation and the lack of airbags could not be reconciled with that country's emission laws and safety regulations. Porsche therefore developed the RS America for the USA. The model made its debut in January 1992 and went on sale for the 1993 model year. It became a pure equipment variant without any motorsport reference.

Porsche wanted to stop its financial downturn in the USA. The manufacturer sold only 4,380 cars in 1991, and the trend was downward. In December, only 271 vehicles were sold. A year earlier, there were still 9,122 Porsches in the USA. The internal brochure "Report 1/92" states, "We expect these special vehicles to stimulate demand in the currently stagnating American market and wish our US colleagues every success."

This tactic was old hat at Porsche. As early as 1952, the manufacturer presented the 356 America Roadster for North America. Thanks to an aluminum body, it was lighter than a normal Porsche 356, more spartanly equipped, and thus ideally suited for the steadily growing motorsport community in the USA. Its 1.5-liter four-cylinder boxer engine delivered 70 hp and it was soon feared on the racetracks. Thanks to its low weight, it accelerated particularly quickly out of corners.

A good forty years later, Porsche took up the idea again, relying on its long history and, of course, on the 911 Carrera RS 2.7 with its ducktail in its advertising. The 964 RS America was based on the Carrera 2, with a 3.6-liter boxer engine, but in the US version it only produced 247 hp instead of 250 hp.

Other features of the car: 17in. magnesium wheels (M403), a sporty special

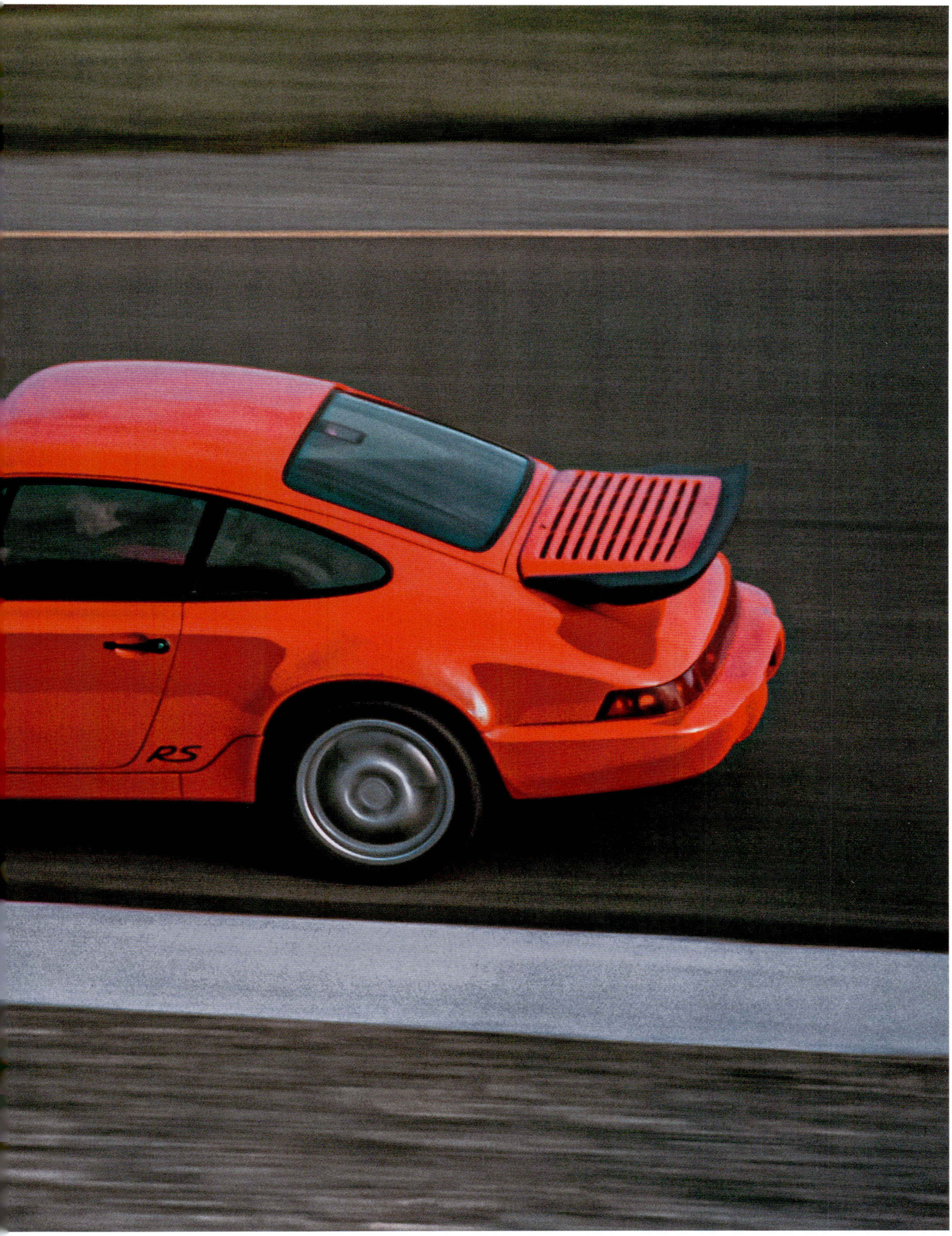
RS

suspension (M030) with progressive turbo springs at the rear, turbo shock absorbers at the front, and two millimeter thicker anti-roll bars now with a diameter of 22 millimeters (0.9 in.). The most striking component is the fixed, large rear spoiler with a rubber strip running all the way around. The lettering "RS America" ran along the rear end.

A MORE COMFORTABLE RS FOR THE USA

Instead of heavy all-leather seats, the standard sports seats with "Recaro Cord" fabric were used, as well as the door panels familiar from the European RS. Porsche did not install power steering. To compensate for the leverage forces, the sports steering wheel measured 380 millimeters (15 in.) in diameter. Unlike the purist RS for the domestic market, the RS America had electric windows, central locking, an alarm system, and a luggage rack in the rear—concessions to the comfort-conscious American customer. Instead of the lightweight aluminum front hood, the US model had a hood made of galvanized sheet steel. Porsche offered extras such as air conditioning, an electric steel sunroof, the 40 percent differential lock, and a radio with CD changer. Customers could also order a console for a Fujitsu cell phone. Porsche offered black, Indian red, and

Grand Prix white as standard colors, with polar silver metallic and night blue metallic as options.

With a weight of 1,340 kilograms (2,954 lbs.), the US version accelerated from 0 to 96 kph (60 mph) in 5.3 seconds. Thanks to its lavish equipment, the RS America weighed only 10 kg (22 lbs.) less than a basic Carrera. The model is more of a hybrid and certainly not a purist RS.

Compared to the expensive 964 RS models, the RS America cost $53,900 US and was therefore cheaper than the 911 Carrera 2. Nevertheless, only 617 US customers opted for this model in 1993, compared to eighty-four customers in 1994. In total, only 702 RS America models were produced between 1992 and 1994.

Between 1993 and 1994, Porsche created the 911 RS 3.8 and the 911 RSR 3.8.

PORSCHE 911 CARRERA RS 3.8

The Porsche racing department in Weissach modernized the RS for Europe in 1993. The 964 RS 3.8 was a road-legal racing car that was built by hand as a small series. Compared to its predecessor, the 3.8 had a larger displacement, an increase in power, the eye-catching rear spoiler, and a revised chassis.

Basing the 3.8 on the wide body of the 911 Turbo, the engineers added additional spoiler corners to the front and a large, wide double spoiler to the rear engine hood. This could be adjusted to six different positions depending on the intended use and racetrack.

Porsche made the front hood and the doors of light aluminum. For the side and rear windows, the engineers replaced the standard glass with thin glass. An additional front spoiler increased the downforce on the front axle. Two air intakes supplied the two oil coolers. In communications with those involved in motor sports, Porsche no longer called the car the 911, instead referring to it only as the Carrera RS 3.8. Only in official communications with the press was the car called the 911 Carrera RS 3.8.

In the interior, the RS followed the standard of its predecessor: no airbags, no radio, no air conditioning system, no electrically adjustable seats, and no rear seats—all to avoid unnecessary weight. Porsche even eliminated the paneling in the rear. Lightweight door panels were used in front. In the front, narrow leather-covered bucket seats held the occupants firmly in place.

Porsche did not offer a sliding sunroof, but the manufacturer knew that radio, airbag, and the Clubsport Package with roll bar, fire extinguisher, belts, and simplified interior equipment were interesting options. In total the RS weighed just 1,210 kilograms (2,667 lbs.), or 1,140 kilograms (2,513 lbs.) without fuel. That was exactly 140 kilograms (308 lbs.) less compared to the Carrera 2.

Depending on the racetrack, the rear wing could be adjusted to six different positions. The doors and hood were made of lightweight aluminum.

Porsche squeezed at least 300 hp and 360 Nm out of the 3.8-liter six-cylinder boxer engine; the Turbo wing was part of the RS package and provided sufficient engine cooling as well as downforce.

A NEW ENGINE FOR 1993

The Motor Sport Division in Weissach changed the drivetrain considerably in 1993. They increased the bore of the six-cylinder boxer to 102 millimeters. With the stroke unchanged at 76.4 millimeters, this resulted in a displacement of 3.8 liters. Lighter pistons, lighter rocker arms, new valves, and a new exhaust system ensured a fast gas flow.

An airflow with six individual throttle valves and sequential injection now provided each cylinder with the best possible supply of fuel. The racing mechanics relied on hot-film technology for the mass air flow sensor. A double oil cooler ensured that the oil was cooled under extreme loads.

The boxer delivered 300 hp at 6,500 rpm. The comparable figure for the Carrera 2 was 250 hp at 6,100 rpm. The maximum torque of 360 Nm was achieved at 5,250 rpm—an increase of 50 Nm compared to the basic model.

Compared to the red line of 6,700 rpm for the 3.6-liter engine, for the new RS engine the figure was 7,100 rpm. New engine electronics from Bosch controlled fuel regulation and ignition. Active knock control enabled more precise tuning and therefore greater power delivery. Two metal catalytic converters filtered the exhaust gases with little back pressure.

CLEARLY IMPROVED PERFORMANCE FIGURES

The RS 3.8 sprinted from 0 to 100 kph (0–62 mph) in 4.9 seconds and reached 200 kph (124 mph) in 16.6 seconds. Its maximum speed was 270 kph (168 mph). A single-disc dry sports clutch transmitted the power between the engine and the five-speed manual transmission. The short shift travel came from the RS 3.6.

To transfer the power to the road, Porsche installed a differential with 40 percent locking effect and fit 235/40ZR18 and 285/35ZR18 tires on 9 and 11-inch rims. Sufficient deceleration was provided by brakes from the 911 Turbo 3.6 at the front end and the Cup Carrera RS 3.6 at the rear. All brake calipers were coated in red.

Compared to the 964 RS 3.6, the engineers dispensed with a rock-hard chassis and gave the 3.8 RS some residual comfort. A modified spring rate and shock absorbers from Bilstein ensured precise response on the racetrack, but also a little comfort on longer journeys.

The forward stabilizer bar, with a diameter of 24 millimeters (0.94 in.), could be adjusted in five positions, while the strut brace between the shock mounts ensured greater stability in extreme driving situations. A stabilizer bar with a diameter of 21 millimeters (0.83 in.) and three adjustment options were used on the rear axle.

The Carrera RS 3.8, which cost 225,000 marks, was sold exclusively by the Porsche Motor Sport Division and not by local dealers or establishments. Porsche offered neither a right-hand-drive variant nor a vehicle for the American market.

Porsche delivered the first vehicles in April 1993. Just fifty-five examples were made, plus forty-five RSR 3.8s. The manufacturer painted them in the colors Indian Red, Grand Prix White, Navy Blue, Black, and Speed Yellow. By comparison, Porsche produced exactly 63,750 examples of the 964 series of vehicles. The 911 Carrera RS 3.8 was unquestionably the technical apex of the 964 series.

In the RS 3.8, Porsche dispensed with rear seats, airbags, radio, air conditioning, trim, and electric seat adjustment—for purist driving pleasure.

Shortly before production of the Type 964 ended, Porsche built the 911 Carrera RSR 3.8 racing car based on the 911 Carrera RS 3.8. It weighed just 1,120 kilograms and delivered 350 hp. Porsche delivered one example with road approval. All others were used on the racetrack.

PORSCHE 911 CARRERA RSR 3.8

With the RS's increase in displacement, Porsche improved its racing cars for the 1994 model year. Roland Kussmaul and his team experimented with further improvements to the RS in the wind tunnel and on the road. He wanted another dedicated racer for the racetracks. He envisaged that professional racing teams would be his customers. Jürgen Barth was finally able to sell Porsche's marketing strategists on the idea that a car for motor sports was exactly the right means with which to launch an effective advertising program.

Like its predecessor, the 964 Carrera RS 3.8 was based on the 964 Carrera RS. It was used as a pure racing car without road homologation for sprint and long-distance racing, including in the ADAC GT Cup. One customer insisted, however, on a street registration—and got it. It was the only RSR 3.8 to come with factory road approval.

The engineers further reduced the weight of the race car. The adjustable rear spoiler was made of plastic, and the interior was completely gutted. Racing seats, a roll-over cage, six-point belts, fire extinguishing system, battery master switch, and hood locks improved safety. The trunk hood and the doors continued to be made of aluminum. The rear sidelights were missing, as was the license plate light on the rear bumper. A racing fuel filler cap shortened pit stops. It was accessible from the trunk at the front, not in the front left fender as on the Carrera.

After all these measures, the RSR 3.8 weighed just 1,120 kilograms (2,469 lbs.). In the rear was a more powerful 3.8-liter (232 cu. in.) boxer, which now produced 350 hp at 6,900 rpm. In keeping with regulations in the ADAC GT Cup, however, engine power

was restricted to 325 hp, and the vehicle weight increased to 1,300 kilograms (2,866 lbs.). On delivery, the five-speed manual transmission was geared for a top speed of 265 kph (165 mph). However, with different gearing a maximum speed of up to 280 kph (174 mph) was possible. Like the Carrera RS 3.8, the locking effect of the differential was 40 percent.

Instead of a sports suspension, a special racing suspension with Uniball ball joints and Bilstein shock absorbers was used in the racing car. The suspension had adjustable stabilizers. Reliable deceleration was again ensured by the brakes of the 911 Turbo S, with racing pads and an ABS system tailored to racing use. Speedline rims measuring 9 x 18 inches in front and 11 x 18 inches in the rear were mounted in the wide wheel arches.

Depending on the regulations and the type of race—sprint or endurance—Porsche offered two fuel tank sizes with capacities of 43 or 120 liters (11.4 or 31.7 gal.). The 911 Carrera RSR 3.8 could therefore compete in the 24-hour races at the Nürburgring, Spa, or Le Mans. The RSR 3.8 could also compete in the Veedol Endurance Cup as a Procar and as an ADAC GT car. In addition, it was also able to compete in the Italian, Japanese, and American IMSA GT championships.

An air lifting system, central locks, and additional brake cooling were available as options. As with the Carrera RS 3.8, the body could be painted in Indian Red, Grand Prix White, Maritime Blue, Black, or Speed Yellow. Porsche was asking 270,000 marks for the sports car plus delivery charge. Depending on the source, between thirty-five and ninety vehicles were sold. In the fall of 1993, Porsche unveiled the new generation of the 911, internally known as the 993, at the IAA in Frankfurt. This marked the end of the 964 RS and RSR. However, Porsche was still convinced of the success of future super sports cars and lightweight competition vehicles—and was already planning its next coup.

993

PORSCHE WAS ON THE VERGE OF ADOPTING LIQUID COOLING. WHEN THE 993 SERIES WAS LAUNCHED IN 1993, THE AIR-COOLED BOXER ENGINE EXPERIENCED A FINAL, SIX-YEAR HURRAH.

The Clubsport package (M003) stood out because of its large front and rear spoilers. This increased downforce, even in wet conditions.

Conservative fans of the brand considered it to be "the last true Porsche 911"—an inflationary description that was already used for the original model and the G series before the 993 and would later be used for many other models, a bit like "the one true love."

The 993 model started out as the successor to the 964, with subtle but striking modifications. It remained true to the basic character of the sports car concept. The roof and trunk were from the predecessor; the interior remained almost unchanged. However, the front and rear sections were more elegant. Porsche had made its front fenders wider and flatter, and the headlights were less vertical.

Porsche invested around 400 million marks and four years of development work in the new 911. The brand was risking a lot of money because it urgently needed a top seller. Business was poor, and there was a lack of customers worldwide. This is why Porsche focused on a broad customer base when designing the new 911 and not just on Porsche enthusiasts, as had previously been the case with the 964.

In doing so, the manufacturer resorted to unusual means: the adapted "Weissach rear axle" from the 928, with its multi-link design, was intended to improve comfort as well as handling characteristics. The engine range stretched from 272 to 450 hp. New was the 911 GT2, a dynamic car based on the 911 Turbo. It exerted great pressure on the Carrera RS.

Visually discrete like a 911 Turbo, but clearly lighter at around 1,300 kilograms, the 993 Carrera RS was more agile in corners than the Turbo.

PORSCHE 911 CARRERA RS

PORSCHE 911 CARRERA RS

With the change to the 993 generation, the Porsche 911 changed noticeably. It opened itself up to a wider audience and became downright approachable, its character less pointed. Nevertheless, Porsche continued to offer vehicles that appealed to fans of its previous impetuous cars, first and foremost the new 911 Carrera RS. It followed the example of its predecessors with lightweight construction and plenty of power: 300 hp met 1,270 kilograms (2,800 lbs.). The sports car made its debut at the Amsterdam Motor Show in January 1995.

THE LAST OF ITS KIND

An internal market analysis positioned the car. According to Porsche, "The 911 Carrera RS is intended to demonstrate the technical superiority of the 911 Type 993 and thus strengthen Porsche's brand positioning as an 'innovative specialist.' In addition, the 911 Carrera RS is intended to convey the Porsche legend built up through numerous racing victories among the general public, in keeping with the motto 'our contribution to popular motorsport.' Porsche's claim to leadership in the sports sector must be clearly reactivated by the 911 Carrera RS."

The 993 RS was the first RS model not to be built according to any international homologation. This meant that the 993 RS could only compete in national popular sports such as Porsche Clubsport.

However, the 911 Carrera RS did not achieve the aforementioned victories in the international arena. Contrary to tradition, it was not the basis for the 911 competition car used worldwide. "Another model, the new 911 GT2, was a better fit for the GT group. It was created in the repair workshop in Weissach and was homologated there by the customer sports department. The RS, on the other hand, was created in series development," recalled Jürgen Barth, racing driver and Porsche race director at the time.

A CARRERA RS FOR NATIONAL RACING SERIES

This left the new 911 Carrera RS only for national mass sports—such as Porsche Clubsport. "There was no homologation for an international racing series for the Carrera RS 993. This

Porsche configured the 993 RS uncompromisingly for sport: bucket seats, roll cage, sports steering wheel, and harness belts. Many electrical aids were omitted.

meant it could not race against competitors. That sets it apart from its predecessors," continued Jürgen Barth. This made it the first RS model in the 911 series that was not explicitly developed as an international motorsport variant. Porsche planned this role for the 911 GT2 from the outset. So, would the Carrera RS be purely an equipment and model variant? After its participation on the circuit and in rallies, that would be something new for Porsche.

Nevertheless, the 911 Carrera RS of the Type 993 came at just the right time, because 1995 was an important year for Porsche. After three lean years, sales were finally on the rise again. In May, after its debut, the first customers were delighted with the new RS model. What they did not know at the time: their car would be the most powerful, standard, air-cooled 911 with a naturally aspirated engine and road approval.

To be able to homologate a suitable sports car for the national Group N/GT, Porsche needed to sell at least 1,000 vehicles, but only 1,200 vehicles of this type worldwide. Production began in January 1995, initially only as a particularly sporty Clubsport variant (M003), to secure supplies for the 1995 motorsport season.

Porsche began deliveries of the RS base version (M002) in May 1995. Curiously, strictly speaking there was no version for the domestic market. Porsche only produced it in the so-called RdW version short for "rest of the world." The new 911 Carrera RS was thus homologated only for the countries of Switzerland, Belgium, Luxembourg, the Netherlands (all with left-hand steering), and South Africa (right-hand steering). Customers from Germany, Austria, and England had to import the model privately with a special permit. Porsche originally planned a price of 145,000 marks for the new 911 Carrera RS. This would have made it 450 marks

cheaper than its predecessor. However, the vehicle went on sale for 147,900 marks. This means it costs almost 20,000 marks more than the basic 911 Carrera model. The sportier Clubsport version was priced at 164,700 marks.

LIGHTWEIGHT CONSTRUCTION IN THE 911 CARRERA RS

Dispensing with anything superfluous was part and parcel of the RS family. The interior of the new 911 Carrera RS was correspondingly sparse: instead of wide door panels, Porsche installed thin ones with straps as door openers. The electric adjustment of the exterior mirrors was omitted; thin glass panes on the sides and rear replaced the standard windows. Even the defroster wires in the rear window had to go. The work on the glass resulted in a total weight saving of five kilograms (11 lbs.).

Rear seats, power windows, central locking, headlight cleaning system, antenna support, speakers, interval switch for the windshield wipers, light distance regulation, instrument dimmer, and interior light all were eliminated.

For countries in which an immobilizer was mandatory, Porsche installed a system without the usually coupled central locking system, which weighed around 1.5 kilograms (3.3 lbs.). The developers even streamlined the wiring harness. The starter battery stored only thirty-six ampere hours.

A lightweight front hood made of aluminum replaced the standard steel part. Instead of gas pressure dampers for the trunk lid, lightweight aluminum retaining rods were used, eliminating another 7.5 kilograms (16.5 lbs.). With this consistent asceticism, it seems incongruous that the Japanese version (M007) offered electric windows and generally more comfort features.

100 KILOGRAMS LIGHTER

Special seat shells painted in the body color and upholstered in leather weighed 30 kilograms (66 lbs.) less than the seats of the 911 Carrera. Porsche only applied a thin layer of underbody protection. Because full protection against rust was no longer provided, the manufacturer reduced the usual ten-year long-term warranty against rusting through to three years. The engine compartment of the RS was still lined with insulating material—at least to some extent. The result of these efforts: at 1,270 kilograms (2,800 lbs.) the RS weighed precisely 100 kilograms (220 lbs.) less than the basic 993 Carrera, but still 50 kilograms (110 lbs.) more than the 964 RS.

Unnecessary luxury negatively affected the power-to-weight ratio. Anything that was not absolutely necessary for driving was not fitted to the car ex works. Nevertheless, many extras were available for an extra charge. These included airbags for the driver and front passenger (M562), windshield with green sun strip (M567), electric power windows, and the Düsseldorf radio with radio upgrade and two door speakers (M336 and M451), as well as racing shells from the 964 Speedster, with thin leather upholstery and a strut brace.

The 92-liter (24-gal.) fuel tank that was an option for the 911 Carrera was standard equipment on the 911 Carrera RS. It otherwise cost 590 marks. The tank of the right-hand-drive vehicle held only 73.5 liters (19.4 gal.) of gasoline due to the modified steering column guide. Instead of the 6.5-liter (1.7-gal.) washer fluid tank, 1.2 liters (0.3 gal.) had to suffice for the right-hand-drive model.

DESIGN CHANGES ON THE 911 CARRERA RS

The RS models of the Porsche 911 were never about simply omitting heavy parts, but about taking a holistic approach. Porsche therefore added additional reinforcements to the body of the 993 series to be able to accommodate the 18-inch wheels. A few connections between body parts were additionally machined or reinforced. This increased the rigidity of the body by 20 percent compared to its predecessor, the 964 RS.

Newly shaped sill trims in conjunction with the front and rear spoilers ensured improved aerodynamics. While a neutral lift value was achieved at the front axle, the airflow at the rear axle provided downforce at higher speeds. To achieve this, the engineers took their cue from the car's predecessor. They removed the automatically extending spoiler of the 993 and fitted a large, fixed surface instead. At the front of the RS, a centrally split front spoiler with rounded corners was added. All this made the 911 Carrera RS look almost like a racing car that had strayed onto the road.

Porsche sprayed five solid colors and two metallic paints on the optimized body ex works. There was a choice of black, Indian red, Grand Prix white, Riviera blue, speed yellow, polar silver metallic, and night blue metallic. The Clubsport version was only available in solid colors. In the interior, Porsche matched the color of the seat belts, door opening straps, RS lettering, and carpet trim on the rear wall to the exterior color. They were black, Indian red, Riviera blue, or speed yellow. The seats were always upholstered in black and dark gray perforated leather.

A POWERFUL ASPIRATOR FOR THE 993

As with its predecessor, the engine of the 993 RS was based on that of the Carrera models. The engineers enlarged the bore of the 3.6-liter block from 100 to 102 millimeters (3.93 to 4.01 in.) and thus increased the displacement to 3.8 liters (231.9 cu. in.). The exact figure is 3,746 cc, as in the previous RS 964.

The RS featured larger intake and exhaust valves with hydraulic valve lash adjustment for rapid throttle changes. The intake valves now measured 51.5 (2.03 in.) instead of 49 millimeters (1.93 in.) in diameter. Porsche had enlarged the exhaust valves from 42.5 to 43 millimeters (1.67 to 1.69 in.). In conjunction with a new camshaft, they provided increased throughput of the air-fuel mixture. To prevent the exhaust gases from transferring the higher temperatures to the cylinder heads, the exhaust valves had a ceramic coating.

With the 3.8-liter six-cylinder engine, Porsche developed the most powerful naturally aspirated engine in the model series. Initially, the engine produced 272 hp, later 300 hp.

The 911 Carrera RS cost at least 147,900 marks in 1995. Porsche built 1,014 units of the fast road sports car, which produced 300 hp and was capable of 277 kph.

VARIORAM: THE NEW ASPIRATOR

From the 1996 model year, Porsche installed a switchable resonance intake system with variable intake manifold lengths, known as Varioram, in the 993 Carrera. The engineers adapted it to the special features of the 3.8-liter boxer. With this technology, the engine generates more torque at low revs and more power at higher revs.

It worked like this: at low and medium engine speeds, the intake air flowed through a long intake manifold. From an engine speed of more than 5,000 rpm, the system halved the length of the intake manifold. The intake manifold was split in two for this function. One part was permanently connected to the cylinder head; the other could be moved variably. Two vacuum-controlled displacement parts adjusted the length of the intake manifold of each cylinder bank, depending on the engine speed.

As a further improvement on the 964 RS, Porsche also lightened the engine's crankshaft drive. Thanks to wider cheeks, the shaft was more resistant to bending and torsion than that of the 964 RS. These measures reduced the weight by a total of 800 grams (28 oz.). Thanks to the low oscillating masses, Porsche was able to dispense with a vibration damper.

Porsche also installed a different engine management system with a hot-film sensor as a mass air flow sensor, and a twin-pipe exhaust system with two catalytic converters. The compression ratio was now 11.3:1, and the dual ignition shortened the flame path by 17 percent compared to the 964 RS.

COMFORT AND LIGHTWEIGHT CONSTRUCTION

Instead of the light single-mass flywheel of the 964 RS, which was rough and rumbled when idling, the 993 had a dual-mass flywheel. This prevented the transmission of vibrations from the crankshaft to the gearbox, so that the latter operated more quietly. The dual-mass flywheel was only not used in the M003 Clubsport version, to be prepared for extreme loads. Instead, here Porsche relied on steel spring dampers.

These extensive measures increased the output of the 3.8-liter boxer engine from 272 to 300 hp at 6,500 rpm and 355 Nm (262 ft.-lbs.) of torque at 5,400 rpm. The engine was redlined at about 7,000 rpm and propelled the 911 Carrera RS from 0 to 100 kph in just five seconds. Its maximum speed was 277 kph (172 mph). For these impressive figures, the engine operated near the knock limit. It relied on knock control with vibration sensors. These reacted sensitively to the knocking of each individual cylinder and could regulate the ignition individually.

The engine itself also contributed to lightweight construction. Porsche manufactured highly stressed housing parts from aluminum, less stressed parts from plastic or magnesium. Only the camshaft, rocker arm, and intermediate shaft gear were made of gray cast iron. The cooling air fan, oil pump housing, intake system, and chain housing were made of magnesium.

Steel was used for the crankshaft, connecting rods, intermediate shaft,

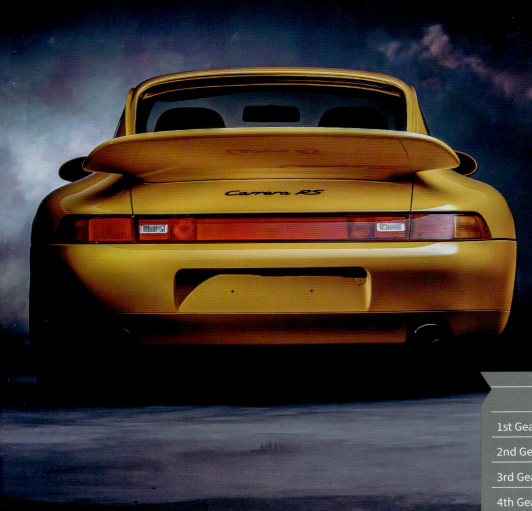

Starting with the 1996 model year, the 993 RS drew 300 hp at 6,500 rpm from 3.8 liters of displacement.

	Carrera RS	Carrera RS Clubsport (M 003)
1st Gear	3.154	3.154
2nd Gear	2.000	2.000
3rd Gear	1.517	1.517
4th Gear	1.242	1.241
5th Gear	1.024	1.031
6th Gear	0.821	0.821

The 3.8-liter engine worked right up to the knock limit. This enabled the 993 RS to race from 0 to 100 kph in five seconds and reach speeds of up to 277 kph.

valves, valve discs, valve springs, valve seat rings, sprockets, pulley, paneling, and exhaust system, as well as the oil tank and its lines. The vacuum tank, cooling air duct, heating air duct, valve cover, air filter housing, clamping, and slide rails were made of lightweight plastic. The engineers opted for aluminum for the crankcase, pistons, cylinder liners, cylinder heads and camshaft housings, brackets, oil coolers, and oil lines.

Lightweight construction meant sacrificing comfort, even in terms of noise. "However, you have to put up with an extremely throaty noise level, because of course the omission of insulating material is also part of the weight-reducing measures in the RS model," wrote Götz Leyrer in *Auto Motor und Sport*.

Despite the immense changes, the powerplant did not mutate into a high-maintenance racing engine but remained suitable for everyday use with long maintenance intervals. The oil was changed every 20,000 kilometers (12,427 mi.), as were the air filters. Spark plugs, fuel filters, and oil filters should be replaced every 40,000 kilometers (24,855 mi.).

PRECISION WORK IN THE TRANSMISSION

A new feature of the RS was its close-ratio, six-speed manual transmission (G50/31). Porsche improved shift comfort by means of a new double-cone synchronization of the first and second gears. This reduced shifting forces by 30 to 40 percent—a significant advantage in long-distance races.

Thanks to the ball-bearing sleeves of the internal gearshift and the virtually backlash-free design of the parts between the external and internal gearshifts, the manual transmission operated more precisely and smoothly. In the Clubsport version, Porsche also used steel synchronizer rings. In addition, the bevel gear, ring gear, and gear wheels were optimized to make the transmission quieter.

Compared to the Carrera, Porsche had made the first three gears of the RS and the Clubsport version longer to cover the speed spectrum on the racetrack. However, the transmission ratio was different in the Clubsport version, even if only in fourth and fifth gears. A new locking system consisting of two components provided more traction—the automatic brake differential (ABD) and the mechanical rear axle transverse lock with locking values for traction/thrust of 40 and 65 percent, respectively. For comparison, those of the Carrera were 26/65 and the Carrera 4 25/40. The values for the 964 RS were 20/100. This allowed drivers to change loads safely and quickly when cornering and to maintain cornering radius even under load.

A SOFTER SUSPENSION

Porsche retuned the dampers and springs on the RS. The suspension was adjustable at the front and rear axles. The front support bearings could be positioned differently and could even be finely adjusted from above in the reversed racing position.

In the 993, Porsche used a new double wishbone rear axle. About 42 percent of all components were made of aluminum. The suspension specialists further optimized the suspension for the RS. The 911 Carrera RS was 30 millimeters (1.2 in.) lower at the front and as much as 40 millimeters (1.57 in.) at the rear. In addition, there were stiffer suspension stanchions and steering bearings. This improved the elasto-kinematics and made wheel guidance more precise in all areas. The stabilizers on the front and rear axles could be adjusted in five different stages at the front and three at the rear.

But the chassis was still not really comfortable. Götz Leyrer, editor at *Auto Motor und Sport*, mockingly wrote after a test, "There's not much in the way of ride comfort, partly because of the lowered body and the hard-tuned suspension. But nobody expects that from a dyed-in-the-wool sports car that is made for driving under extreme conditions."

With minimal changes to the camber, Porsche increased the possible lateral forces. This promised higher cornering speeds. Porsche also opted for a more direct steering ratio. The manufacturer used the steering gear of the 964 (built in 1991) but used power steering for the first time in the RS, so that the drivers had to apply less force. This resulted in the car being 7 kg (15.4 lbs.) heavier. Nevertheless, compared to the Carrera, higher steering forces were still required. "Trying this out on a closed track is undoubtedly a pleasure, because the RS is a gifted cornering artist that sets standards in lateral acceleration and handling—not to mention its powerful brakes that can cope with even the toughest demands," said Götz Leyrer.

45 PERCENT MORE BRAKING SURFACE

The modified chassis also included three-piece 18-inch Speedline wheels with a tire combination of 225/40ZR18s in

The front spoiler's side lips ensured better airflow around the vehicle and minimized lift on the front axle.

front and 265/35ZR18s in the rear. The wide wheels ensured even more spontaneous turning and better traction than those on the Carrera, which came with 16-inch wheels as standard.

The internally ventilated and perforated disc brakes with four-piston fixed calipers on the Carrera RS came from the 911 Turbo. Porsche painted the brake calipers red to better distinguish them from those of the production car. Compared to the 964 RS, the new model offered 45 percent more braking surface. Discs measuring 322 millimeters (12.7 in.) were used all around.

The 993 RS brakes significantly better than the 964 RS or the 993 Carrera. It comes to a standstill from 100 kph (62 mph) in 2.7 seconds. This is due in part to the newly tuned four-channel ABS and a larger master brake cylinder with hydraulic brake booster. Thanks to the fresh air supply from the front end, the brake system is well ventilated and cooled even under intensive use.

MISSING THE TARGET

Porsche failed to reach its target of 1,200 units, however. Only 1,014 cars were produced in total. The problem: die-hard RS fans, in particular, missed the rock-hard chassis of its predecessors, which made the RS unbeatable on the racetrack. Porsche also offered a 285hp performance kit for the Carrera 2, which narrowed the gap to the RS.

Doubters were likely to have been annoyed shortly afterward. With the introduction of the 996 and its liquid cooling, the era of the air-cooled standard boxer was finally over. Moreover, it initially seemed as if the RS abbreviation would disappear from the Porsche portfolio. Götz Leyrer's conclusion in *Auto Motor und Sport*: "So it's a tough guy for the fanatics; everyone else had better wait and see. Because as of the coming model year, all versions of the Carrera will have a 285 hp engine."

The Clubsport package (M003) stood out because of its large front and rear spoilers. This increased downforce, even in wet conditions.

In contrast to the standard 993 RS, the front spoiler of the Clubsport version has side lips and a continuous front end.

PORSCHE 911 CARRERA RS CLUBSPORT

Parallel to the Carrera RS, Porsche built the RS with the Clubsport package (M003)—a masterpiece for the racetrack. From the outside, the Clubsport version could be easily recognized by its aerodynamic components. A rolled-up lip was used at the front and a large spoiler at the rear, which could be adjusted depending on the application. Porsche integrated channels for the engine intake and cooling air into the variable add-on part with wide fins on the sides. Unlike the basic RS with its side lips, the front spoiler offered a continuous lip. The large spoiler package could also be ordered for the basic RS as option M471. It is an abbreviation with a history, because in the 911 Carrera RS 2.7, from 1972 that was the code for the sports version. The engine and chassis of the Clubsport are the same as those of the regular 993 RS. A welded-in roll cage ensures greater safety in races, and a strut brace for stiffer handling in extreme cornering. Special Recaro bucket seats

(the pair weighed 18 kilograms, or 40 lbs.) accommodated a six-point seat belt system. The battery main switch cut off all the car's power if required. A fire extinguishing system helped in the event of a fire. The insulation material was completely removed from the interior and engine compartment. Those wanting an airbag had to order it separately—but who needs an airbag in a racing car with six-point seat belts and a cage? The Clubsport version of the RS weighed 1,270 kilograms (2,800 lbs.). It sprinted from 0 to 200 kph (124 mph) in eighteen seconds and reached speeds of up to 280 kph (174 mph). "The way in which the RS achieves this is fascinating. With its promising power-to-weight ratio of 4.2 kilograms (9.25 lbs.) per hp, the new Carrera RS even moves through the twisting and tangled urban undergrowth with such aplomb, as if it were its very own terrain," wrote Horst von Saurma in *Sport Auto.* 227 customers chose the Clubsport package when ordering an RS. It is and remains an engineer's car, an uncompromising representative of a great sports car.

The opulent rear spoiler was available not only in the Clubsport version with the internal code M003, but also as an option for the basic RS.

Instead of 16-inch wheels, the 993 RS used three-piece 18-inch wheels with a tire combination of 225/40ZR18 at the front and 265/35ZR18 at the rear.

Passengers had to be agile to wriggle behind the side struts of the roll cage into the narrow sports seats.

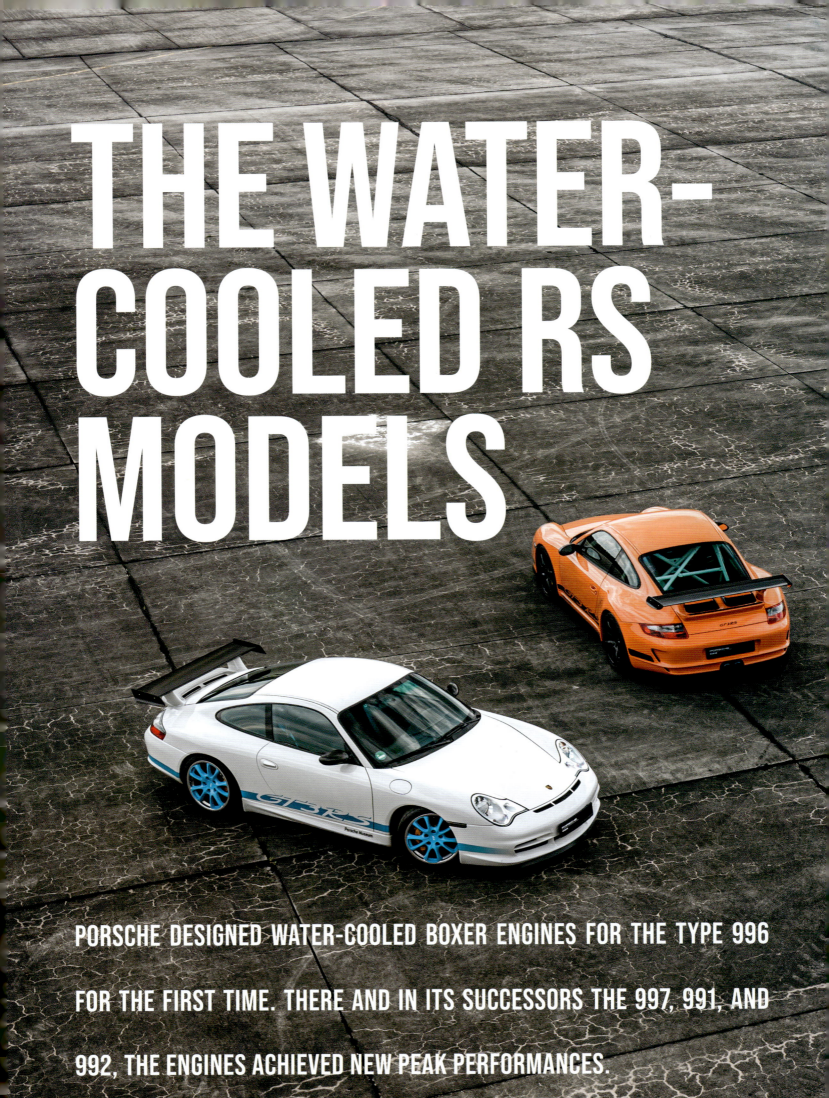

THE WATER-COOLED RS MODELS

PORSCHE DESIGNED WATER-COOLED BOXER ENGINES FOR THE TYPE 996 FOR THE FIRST TIME. THERE AND IN ITS SUCCESSORS THE 997, 991, AND 992, THE ENGINES ACHIEVED NEW PEAK PERFORMANCES.

996

TRADITION ONLY REMAINS ALIVE AS LONG AS IT HAS ROOM FOR DEVELOPMENT. EVEN A MANUFACTURER LIKE PORSCHE, WHICH ATTACHES GREAT IMPORTANCE TO ITS NOT-SO-LONG HISTORY, MUST NOT STAGNATE AND MERELY REPEAT WHAT HAS GONE BEFORE.

As of 1999, the Porsche 911 GT3 was "the legitimate successor to the RS model," as Porsche itself wrote in a press release. With it, the manufacturer homologated the GT3 race car.

After German reunification, Porsche was doing badly economically. *Der Spiegel* described the situation in 1993 as a crisis and predicted a hostile takeover by a large car manufacturer. Only innovation and courage brought about a turnaround. Modern production methods and new production planning, in which little was built to stockpile, reduced fixed costs.

Additional models appealed to more customers. And a common parts strategy, in which the number of individually developed components per model was reduced, cut costs in development and the supply chain. But Porsche's courage also meant questioning the inviolable, even the sacred air cooling system. After all, the 911 had to comply not only with a new strategy, but also with future emissions and noise requirements. For the first time since its introduction in 1963, Porsche was fundamentally changing the 911. It was based on a new platform that enabled parallel development with the previously introduced Boxster. From then on, a liquid circuit cooled the boxer engine. With the model change, the car also grew and offered significantly more space. And to underline all this, the 911 even swapped its famous googly eyes for new headlights in a fried egg design, which were controversial in fan circles.

Strictly speaking, identical parts with the predecessor were still present, but hardly worth mentioning. Porsche adopted the emblem on the hood, the hub covers of the rims, the steering wheel, and the airbags from the 993 series. Everything else on the 996 was new apart from basic things such as the vehicle layout and assembly process. This radical change of direction ultimately saved the manufacturer.

PORSCHE 911 GT3

Motorsport changed in the 1990s. The sports car world championship organized by the FIA became financially unattractive for most manufacturers due to excessively restrictive requirements. It ended in 1992, and in 1995 the international GT1 and GT2 classes were established instead. They were held for the first time in the new BPR Global GT Series. Porsche took part with the 911 derivatives of the same name.

SUCCESSOR WITH NO CARRERA AND RS

Porsche had been thinking about a motorsport commitment outside these classes since the days of air cooling. The name for the corresponding model was derived from the categories of the BPR series; in addtion to the GT1 and GT2 classes, there was a but therefore financially attractive GT3. However, there was no real championship here. Only with the start of the ACO GT in 1999 and the comparable FIA N-GT a year later was there a stage for GT3 vehicles. Porsche designed a GT3 racing car and the homologation model with road approval, the 911 GT3. The

manufacturer wrote in a press release on December 17, 1998, "The 911 GT3 is the legitimate successor to the RS model." At the time, nobody knew that Porsche would be producing genuine RS models again in the future.

A NEW SUSPENSION FOR THE 911 GT3

Roland Kussmaul, Head of Development for Racing and Special Vehicles, and Hartmut Kristen, Head of Customer Sport, were responsible for the car. They familiarized themselves with the regulations, obtained a 911 Carrera, and determined the necessary changes to the car. These mainly concerned the suspension. A 911 GT3 as a racing car had to have adjustment options that a 911 Carrera did not offer. The homologation model was therefore fitted with Bilstein shock absorbers with spring plates that could be adjusted in height. Unlike with its predecessors, this option was no longer available in the 996. The tie rods were fitted in such a way that a change in ground clearance did not have a negative effect on handling.

Uniball dome bearings and split wishbones were also used. The latter allowed more camber than the standard parts—an important detail for racing cars. Modified subframe bolting and adjustable anti-roll bars with a larger diameter and greater

What already was and what would come: the Porsche 911 GT3 of 1999 next to the Porsche 911 GT3 RS of 2003.

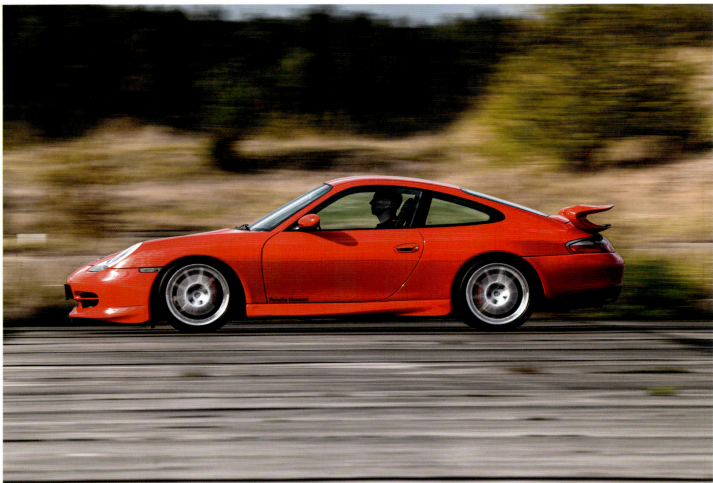

wall thickness than in the 911 Carrera further improved handling. The brakes came from the 911 Turbo, which was unveiled later, but without its ventilation system. The optional aero kit available for all 911s, consisting of a front bumper and rear wing, compensated for the lift on the rear axle.

When the first prototypes of the road car were driven, their proximity to real racing cars became clear. Porsche works driver Herbert Linge tested an early version of the 911 GT3 on the then catastrophically bad roads between Weissach and Mönsheim. He broke off the five-kilometer (3-mile) route prematurely, drove back, and told Kussmaul that it would be nice if the car had a suspension.

The 911 GT3 had little visual originality. Exclusive rims and aero kit were available for every 911; the brakes came from the 911 Turbo. However, the engine, chassis, and seats clearly distinguished the homologation model from the 911 Carrera.

TEST DRIVES ON THE ROAD

Kussmaul agreed. "The GT3 wasn't supposed to be a race car and a tooth-breaker," he recalled of the development phase. Its chassis had to be suitable for homologation of the racing version, but also feel comfortable enough for everyday use in a road car. He decided how this compromise should feel himself, in his free time. And he did so on "THE test track par excellence."

In the days of the 996, Kussmaul could still take test vehicles home spontaneously and without red tape. He used his drives from Weissach to Hemmingen and Eberdingen to tune the chassis. In the evening, he drove over known bumps and level crossings on his way home and evaluated the car's reaction. The next day, he had the components adjusted accordingly. This saved development time, he noted pragmatically.

There was not enough time or resources for "real" tests on the test tracks at Ehra-Lessien or Nardo. Instead, the engineers

There was a lack of time and budget for test drives on the large test tracks. The engineers carried out high-speed tests with the 911 GT3 on the A5 motorway leading to Basel.

The 911 GT3 took its rear apron and exhaust system from the 911 Carrera.

carried out many high-speed tests at night on the A5 autobahn in the direction of Basel. There they checked whether the transmission needed an additional radiator (no) and how quickly the car accelerated to 100 kph (4.8 seconds). The police were in the know. Occasionally, during a break in the parking lot, the law enforcement officers asked whether everything was going well during the test drives.

A WATER-COOLED MEZGER ENGINE

Engine professional Hans-Georg Breuer was responsible for the powerplant of the first 911 GT3. He did not use the new, water-cooled boxer from the 911 Carrera. Instead, for reasons of stability, he built something like a best-of Porsche engine. In the prototype, he combined cylinder heads from the 959, the crankshaft and crankcase from the 911 Turbo of the 964 series, and the cylinder blocks from the 911 GT1, with small parts from many other units. The oil reservoir was located outside the engine.

To ensure that heads and blocks fit together, Breuer had to machine the cooling channels in a complex process. He also added the Variocam camshaft adjustment system on the intake side and titanium connecting rods. The latter allow particularly

high engine speeds in the racing car. Even in the road version, the engine revved to 7,800 rpm. In the standard engine, the modified elements become independent components with corresponding 996 part numbers. Occasionally, however, parts with 964 identification numbers are found in the vehicles.

In the press release from December 1998, Porsche celebrated the motorsport genesis—and falsely suggested that the engine of the 911 GT3 was based on that of the 911 Carrera of the Type 996: "The engineers at Porsche Motorsport have increased the displacement of the water-cooled engine from 3.4 liters to 3.6 liters (207.5 to 220 cu. in.). Thanks to numerous modifications and the use of components from the GT1 engine and the transmission from the 911 GT2, the 911 GT3 delivers 360 hp (265 kW)," according to the document. However, apart from the number of cylinders and cylinder spacing, the 911 Carrera and 911 GT3 engines had nothing in common.

OFFICIAL SUCCESSOR TO THE 911 CARRERA RS

The official classification of the 911 GT3 as the successor to the Carrera RS combined the new nomenclature based on the motorsport classes with the vibrant RS history. At that time, the abbreviation GT3 was unknown in the portfolio, whereas

A wing from the shelf: Porsche did not develop a new rear spoiler for the first 911 GT3 but made do with an existing component.

In the interior of the 911 GT3, Porsche combined the dashboard of the Carrera models with sporty bucket seats.

No rear seat: for weight reasons, the 911 GT3 came from the factory with just two seats.

the letter sequence RS was established. Its use on a production car was not planned for the 996 generation. Starting in 2001, it was at least used on the corresponding racing car.

The road car proved its talent on the world's toughest racetrack. With Walter Röhrl at the wheel, it lapped the Nordschleife of the Nürburgring in 7:56.33 minutes. No production car before had broken the eight-minute mark. Röhrl, himself involved in the development of the car, had declared that he would set this milestone prior to the record-setting lap.

Sport Auto saw the new nomenclature as a "departure from RS-asceticism" and praised the car's suitability for everyday use: "In view of the dynamic driving class, which actually has professional traits, the ride comfort is perfectly acceptable." Even air conditioning and an audio system would fit into the concept. Only the tendency to understeer was not very popular because it cost time on the racetrack in Hockenheim.

The British magazine *Autocar* raved after the test, "Listening to this car, you could never doubt that there is a direct link between the legendary 1971 Carrera 2.7 RS and Porsche's new GT3, despite the switch from air to liquid cooling." Jürgen Schramek stated in *Rally Racing,* "The GT3 guarantees the Porsche feeling of the old RS days."

Swiss journalist Jürg Wick complained that the lowered suspension and spoiler "can't console real 911 fans for the fact that the new edition launched in 1997 has been softened up." The car is "no longer a real challenge for the driver. That's why people are waiting all the more impatiently for a genuine sports version like the legendary RS versions."

Despite lightweight construction measures such as the absence of a rear seat, the 911 GT3 weighed 32 kilograms (70 lbs.) more than a 911 Carrera. Unlike its predecessors, it improved its performance despite the extra weight. Additional power from the heavier engine, larger brakes, reinforcements in the bodywork, and a new air flow system ensured faster lap times.

The 911 GT3 was only optionally spartan and truly "motorsporty." Porsche equipped it with the Clubsport package (optional equipment M003) at no extra charge. This included a bolted roll cage, FIA-approved fire-retardant seat covers, a battery master switch, fire extinguisher, red seat belts (or a six-point seat belt for the driver), and a lighter single-mass flywheel. The side airbags were omitted.

Porsche had to build 1,400 units of the 911 GT3 to achieve FIA homologation. A total of 1,868 vehicles were produced in two model years. The manufacturer did not offer the car in the USA because the strict emissions regulations could not be met. Porsche fans from the New World complained in internet forums and by email. Porsche did not begin serving this market until the second series of the 911 GT3.

The red zone of the tachometer in the 911 GT3 began at 7,500 rpm. Its Mezger engine was capable of 7,800 rpm.

From 2003 onward, the 911 GT3 clearly set itself apart from the weaker Carrera models. However, the legendary abbreviation "RS" was still missing from its name.

PORSCHE 911 GT3

A new man was in charge of Porsche's young GT department. Andreas Preuninger, engineer and devoted car enthusiast, began his career at Porsche in 1997. Beginning in October 2000, he was responsible for GT vehicles. From then on, he was the brains behind all the particularly wild models, supported by his mentor Roland Kussmaul. His first project: to redesign the successor to the RS, the 911 GT3. It would not become an RS, but it would be faster and better.

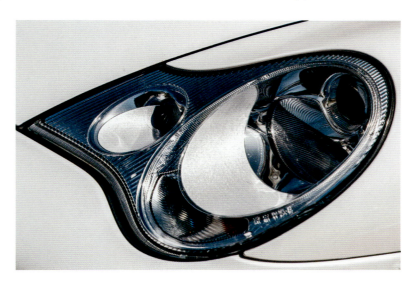

More visually appealing: Porsche modified the headlights of the 911 as part of the facelift.

DETAIL IMPROVEMENTS

Preuninger knew the 911 GT3 from his time as an instructor at the Porsche sports driving school. The color stuck in his mind: in retrospect, he described the car's orange-red color as "Mettwurst Metallic," which was not very positive. On the other hand, he had fond memories of the car itself. After all, the GT3 ensured that journalists and testers perceived the polarizing 996 as a genuine Porsche 911. At the time, *Auto Bild* ran the headline, "The 911 is back." Nevertheless, there were things that Preuninger wanted to improve, starting with the appearance. A car of this caliber had to be unique, he believed. And the first 911 GT3 was not. With Porsche Exclusive rims, aero kit, gentle lowering, and brakes from the 911 Turbo, a 911 Carrera almost looks like a 911 GT3. The feeling of an "off-the-shelf car," which—apart from the engine, chassis, and seats—only made use of the available parts, bothered Preuninger.

UNIQUE APPEARANCE

Preuninger took over management of the project when important details about its appearance had already been decided. These included the

The new rear wing reduced lift and, at the same time, reduced the drag of the 911 GT3.

More revolutions: the revised GT3 engine revved to a maximum of 8,200 rpm.

Similar but different: as of 2003, the 911 GT3 felt sportier, as confirmed by a number of journalists.

During the facelift, Porsche optimized the aerodynamics, performance, and autonomy of the 911 GT3.

Nordschleife. Porsche had also made the brake system larger than before. Instead of the four-piston calipers with 330 mm (13 in.) discs of the previous model, six-piston calipers with 350 mm (13.8 in.) discs were used on the front axle. At the rear, the dimensions remained 330 x 28 millimeters with four-piston fixed calipers.

For the first time, Porsche was fitting ceramic brakes as an option in the new 911 GT3. The system—with the sales name PCCB (Porsche Ceramic Composite Brake)—reduced brake fading thanks to its heat resistance. In addition, the brake discs weigh 18 kilograms (39 lbs.) less than steel discs. *Sport Auto* attested to its "very high and, above all, very constant friction values right from the start."

rear spoiler, which did not yet meet Preuninger's expectations after the facelift. This still annoyed him years later. However, his car was given important details that were missing from its predecessor—such as hub caps with GT3 lettering. It was the first change initiated by Preuninger.

Porsche's new GT man worked his way through all the details. He gave his first car special rims, a revised chassis, and a more powerful, more rev-happy engine. When it was finished, the new GT3 was no longer a "shelf car." Instead, it was one with many exclusive parts and revised aerodynamics. From then on, the 911 GT3 could no longer simply be replicated from a 911 Carrera.

However, it was not just about differentiation, but above all about function. A new spoiler lip reduced the airflow under the car. The revised front apron directed the airflow to the water coolers and on to the front axle brakes. In this way, the aerodynamics engineers reduced lift and improved braking performance.

FIRST USE OF CERAMIC BRAKES

Porsche had Michelin and Pirelli produce special tires for the facelift model. Up front, the new 911 GT3 was fitted with 235/40 tires on 8 x 18-inch rims (previously 225/40), and 295/30 tires on 11 x 18-inch rims in the rear (previously 285/30 tires on 10 x 18-inch rims). *Sport Auto* described the Pirelli P Zero Rosso as quieter than the Michelin tire at high speeds on the

MORE POWER FROM THE WATER-COOLED MEZGER ENGINE

Hans-Georg Breuer once again took care of the engine. He overhauled the intake and exhaust system, lightened the pistons, fitted new bucket tappets, and installed the VarioCam Plus continuously variable adjustment system. Instead of the previous 7,800 rpm, the 3.6-liter boxer engine now revved to a maximum of 8,200 rpm. Output rose from 360 to 381 hp.

Additional improvements concerned the gearbox. Gears 5 and 6 were now slightly shorter to improve traction at high speeds. The new gearbox also had an integrated oil pump and an externally mounted heat exchanger to better withstand high loads. Supplier Getrag provided stable steel synchronizer rings for clean gear changes.

The effort was worth it. Looking at the rear-mounted engine, Richard Hammond, host of the British car show *Top Gear*, said, "The GT3 proves that evolution works." His colleague and constant 911 critic Jeremy Clarkson even described the 911 GT3 as the best car he had driven in 2003. The editors of *Sport Auto* lapped the Nürburgring in the new edition nine seconds faster than four years earlier in the first 911 GT3. The testers clocked a time of 7:54 minutes.

British journalist Chris Harris noted that the revised 911 GT3 felt completely different from its predecessor and that its engine was noticeably more powerful. A total of 2,589 units of the improved 911 GT3 were produced in three model years.

Inspired by the original: the lettering on the flanks of the 911 GT3 RS honored the original model of 1972.

PORSCHE 911 GT3 RS

After two 911 GT3 models, the issue of homologation for motorsport was in fact over for Porsche. But a request from the racing department changed this status quo. Roland Kussmaul, then Head of Development for Racing and Special Vehicles, turned to Andreas Preuninger, Head of GT Vehicles. His 911 GT3 RS racing cars were wearing out their front tires too quickly, he complained. He needed a different, better chassis geometry.

THE RETURN OF THE RS

The geometry of the Porsche racing cars at that time, with their significantly lowered suspension, had such an unfavorable effect on the dynamic wheel camber that the cars put a disproportionately high load on their front wheels and had to come into the pits to change wheels long before the competition.

The solution was a new design with a modified pivot point for the wishbones on the wheel carrier. However, this was a modification that was relevant to homologation according to FIA rules. This meant that, for motorsport, 200 production

The year 2003 saw the launch of the Porsche 911 GT3 RS—it was also the first RS model with water cooling in the Zuffenhausen-based company's portfolio.

The sales department was initially less than enthusiastic about the 911 GT3 RS. They found the car obscene and feared sales of just under two hundred units worldwide. History shows that these worries were unfounded.

Homologation vehicle for a better axle design: the 911 GT3 RS was created because the competition versions had to contend with excessive tire wear due to the standard axle geometry—a race-critical disadvantage.

cars with the same components had to be put on the road. Kussmaul proposed simply delivering 200 Porsche 911 GT3s with modified axles to customers. According to the regulations, that would be enough.

A CAR FOR A WHEEL MOUNT

Preuninger recognized the opportunity to design a completely new car around this modification, because he still saw room for improvement for his 911 GT3. He already knew what the new model could be called, as the RS abbreviation for the air-cooled sports Porsche had so far been missing from the 996.

The first hurdle: the name Porsche 911 GT3 RS was reserved for racing cars in the current Porsche nomenclature. He therefore turned to Hartmut Kristen and Johannes Trost, both responsible for motorsport. He asked them to name their racing cars Porsche 911 GT3 RSR so that the RS would be free for his car. The plan worked, and the motorsport experts released the fast letters for a production car.

Preuninger consulted with a few confidants, including Roland Kussmaul, to plan the car. It was not just about the wheel mounts. The men improved the 911 GT3 in many areas that were relevant to motorsport. Above all, however, they were designing a tribute to the many, venerable 911 Carrera RSs of past model series.

Porsche's first road-legal 911 GT3 RS was developed with motorsport in mind. First and foremost, the car was a homologation vehicle designed to race better than before. The means were the same as those that had already brought success to its RS predecessors—less weight and complexity, sophisticated aerodynamics, and a more powerful engine.

DESIGN WITHOUT A DESIGNER

Inspired by the classic look of the 911 Carrera RS 2.7 in white with lettering on the sides, Andreas Preuninger built a design

Porsche always painted the 911 GT3 RS in Carrera white. *Alcantara was used in the interior.*

Notably larger wing: rear spoiler with visible carbon fiber

QUICK APPROVAL ROUND FOR THE GT3 RS

When Lagaaij finally found the words, he was thrilled. He felt honored, he said. After all, he helped design the Carrera lettering for the original RS back then. He liked the new interpretation of the logo, as well as the car as a whole, which had to be built. Preuninger had his permission to present his car to the Management Board.

When it came to the appointment, Preuninger was unlucky with the weather. He showed the board his car outside on a rainy day. The cloth was wet on the sheet metal, and all the guests were in a bad mood due to the weather. After his presentation, Porsche boss Wendelin Wiedeking asked Preuninger whether Porsche would earn money with the car. Preuninger said yes. His business plan—with 200 planned vehicles—fulfilled the minimum requirements. That was enough for a yes from the boardroom. The 911 GT3 RS idea became an official project.

HANDY, LIGHT, AND FAST

The aim of this project was not only to homologate new parts, but also to achieve noticeably better handling than the 911 GT3. The new wheel mounts were the linchpin. Almost everything around them had changed. The body was lower, the springs and dampers were firmer, the wishbones were split all around, and the suspension could be adjusted in a variety of ways—ideal conditions for motorsport. And for sources of error, Preuninger knew that suspension components that were not precisely adjusted according to the manufacturer's specifications would very quickly have a negative effect on the drivability of the GT3 RS.

prototype of the new 911 GT3 RS. Without the knowledge of his superiors, he procured a white Porsche 911 and customized it according to his own ideas. This included rims with polished horns, a redesigned rear wing based on the current Cup car, and the internally named "Waves of the Danube" stickers for the sides of the vehicle.

Preuninger also designed these himself. A traditional Carrera lettering, analogous to its predecessors, was out of the question because the car was not a Carrera in the new Porsche nomenclature. Only the basic vehicles still bore this name. One night, Preuninger loaded all the necessary information into a graphics program. There he squeezed and pulled the "GT3 RS" lettering until the result fit the proportions of the car. He then added a strip and had the logo printed for his concept car.

When he was finished, Preuninger confessed to his superior and head of motorsport, Hartmut Kristen, what he had secretly done: "I've built a car. Can you take a look?" Kristen asked Preuninger to show the car to him and then to Porsche chief designer Harm Lagaaij. Preuninger felt uneasy because of the sudden involvement of those at the decision-making level. But he invited them over, prepared his car, and covered it with a cloth. At the meeting, Preuninger began his presentation by saying that motorsport needed new wheel mounts. He was of the opinion that this justified a special model. With the sentence "I think it should look like this," he pulled the cloth off the car. Kristen and Lagaaij stood motionless in front of the prototype. Lagaaij grimaced. Preuninger feared the worst.

The front end of the 911 GT3 RS clearly distinguished it the 911 GT3.

For the brakes, the most powerful 911 GT3 derivative used parts from the 911 GT3, but the engineers improved the ventilation of the front brakes. And, as with the 911 GT3, they adapted the optional ceramic brake. It weighed 18 kilograms (39 lbs.) less than the standard steel part and was resistant to fading. For optimum performance, however, higher temperatures were required compared to the standard brake.

In the RS tradition, the car should weigh less, especially since the 996 with its standard safety equipment was heavier than its predecessors anyway. Compared to a 911 GT3 with the Clubsport package, the 911 GT3 RS shed around 50 kilograms (110 lbs.).

It achieved this with modifications to the bodywork (14 kilograms, [31 lbs.]), a lightened single-mass flywheel including an adapted clutch (20 lbs.), a carbon-fiber front hood (17.5 lbs.), and a polycarbonate rear window (4.4 lbs.). During development, the engineers were not sure whether the lightweight rear window would be able to withstand the negative pressure created in the interior at top speed with the windows open. Roland Kussmaul tried it out and reported that it bulged "frighteningly," but withstood the pressure.

Air conditioning and radio were not fitted ex works but were available at no extra charge. And the 911 GT3 RS got a rear wing made of carbon fiber (weight savings of 4.4 lbs.), which was visually based on the spoiler of the Cup car. Preuninger was particularly pleased about this point. The 911 GT3 RS only showed the lightweight material on the outside on the large spoiler, on the wing mirrors, or when the trunk lid was open, since it has no color on the inside. The Porsche emblem on the nose is made of foil.

AN ENGINE FOR HOMOLOGATION

The engine of the 911 GT3 RS was important for the success of the car. According to the data sheet and press release, it was like that of the 911 GT3—in other words, it was still the Mezger engine with 964 and GT1 roots. However, being on a par with the 911 GT3 only existed in theory. For reasons of convenience, Porsche did not homologate the RS engine but entered the 911 GT3 output (381 hp) in the papers. In fact, all RS vehicles were noticeably more powerful. Their engines produced around 400 hp.

For the first time in a series-production car, Porsche had implemented ram-air technology. At high speeds, the airstream pushed so strongly into the intake tract that excess pressure was created, like a turbocharged engine. In addition to the extra air in the cylinder, Porsche injected more fuel. This resulted in more energetic combustion—performance increased at high speeds.

More powerful than stated: the engine of the 911 GT3 RS produced just 381 hp on paper. In reality, it was usually more than 400 hp.

The intake scoop on the rear hood was the result of an elaborate experiment.

Unique selling point: the rims of the 911 GT3 RS were polished and painted.

The Recaro bucket seats had fireproof coverings.

The front hood was made of carbon fiber but only showed this on the inside.

To force the air into the combustion chamber in this way, the aerodynamicists designed a ram pressure collector on the hood. Their approach was trial and error—just like their colleagues back then with the spoiler of the 911 Carrera RS 2.7. "We tinkered until we measured the right dynamic pressure. Then we knew it had to look like this," Preuninger remembered the work. On the other side of the engine, flow-optimized catalytic converters de-throttled the exhaust system. The single-mass flywheel improved the engine's response.

Porsche also gave the first 200 examples of the 911 GT3 RS a special feature: their cylinder heads had polished combustion chambers. This was not an advantage in series production, but Porsche was allowed to use these cylinder heads in motorsport. These combustion chambers can be gauged with enhanced precision. In racing cars, Porsche achieves even more power in combination with optimized ignition timing.

FACTORY SPECIFICATIONS UNDERCUT

Even in the standard car, there was a noticeable increase in performance. The large rear wing generated 35 kilograms (77 lbs.) of downforce at 200 kph (124 mph) but minimally reduced the drag coefficient (911 GT3: 0.29; 911 GT3 RS: 0.30). But with its optimized engine and lighter body, it sprinted faster to 100 kph (4.4 seconds) and to 200 kph (14.0 seconds). In the *Sport Auto* test, it even undercut its factory specifications. The testers measured 4.2 seconds for the standard sprint and 13.5 seconds for acceleration to 200 kph. In both disciplines, it was significantly faster than the 911 GT3—and it even outpaced the more powerful 911 Turbo.

In addition to weight and power, the tires of the 911 GT3 RS were also responsible for its performance, especially on the racetrack. It was fitted with 235/40ZR18 and 295/30ZR18 Pirelli P Zero Corsa tires as standard. These were sports tires (ultra-high-performance tires), which came very close to real racing tires in terms of their properties. They offered enormous advantages on dry roads but were at a disadvantage in the wet.

The standard roll bar increased safety. A bolted extension, which turned the bar into a cage, was included for use in motorsport. And bucket seats with flame-retardant upholstery complied with FIA regulations.

FORM FOLLOWS FUNCTION

Some aspects of the development of the first 911 GT3 RS were rather casual. At one point or another, function took precedence over design. For example, the exhaust air routing from the radiator was taken from the Cup car. To channel the warm air through the fender, the supplier sawed three cut-outs in the component and glued a grille in front of it—and the air outlet was ready. In later models, Porsche constructed thermodynamic works of art for this purpose.

Approval of the rear spoiler was similarly rudimentary. Porsche wanted to offer its customers a setting for the racetrack; however, the TÜV did not want to permit it for the road. The solution: the cars were delivered with additional red wedges. To fit them, customers had to loosen their spoilers, insert the wedges, and screw the spoilers back on again. The color difference was to ensure that they were not used in road traffic.

THE SALES HURDLE

History repeated itself. The Porsche sales department had feared that the 1972 911 Carrera RS 2.7 would be a failure. It was a similar story with the 911 GT3 RS from 2003. The sales team regarded the car as obscene and predicted only minimal interest worldwide. They estimated that only 195 vehicles could be sold. Nevertheless, Preuninger's business case worked with this figure. When the car went into series production, it was a success.

The design of the GT3 RS was not the only detail that annoyed the sales department. Too late, it was noticed that Preuninger's lettering on the sides of the vehicle, in its distorted form, did not follow the manufacturer's specifications at all. And the logo on the front hood was a sticker from the Porsche Selection. It shouldn't have been there, since the "Stuttgart" lettering above the rearing horse is black on some vehicles, not gold. Porsche was therefore inadvertently producing vehicles with an incorrect logo.

Porsche was one of the first manufacturers to offer such tires for a production vehicle.

INDIVIDUAL LOOK

Visually, the 911 GT3 RS was also intended to be very different from all other 911 derivatives. Porsche achieved this, on the one hand, by painting the vehicle exclusively in Carrara White, supplemented by the side lettering in blue or red. The carbon spoiler also helped to distinguish it from the other models.

The wheel rims also played a certain part in this. As with the prototype, they were elaborately finished for the production car. First, their bed was polished and masked. Then the star was painted to match the "Waves of the Danube." Porsche only went to this effort for a better look.

For the interior, Preuninger would have liked to have seen suede on the steering wheel and gear knob. But initial tests revealed the disadvantages of this material. After a short time, the leather looked worn and unkempt. He took inspiration from the interiors of his Lancia Delta Integrale and opted for easy-to-care-for and durable Alcantara. The synthetic fiber—which, incidentally, has been on the market for as long as the RS models of the Porsche 911—now adorned the steering wheel, gearshift, and door pulls. Aside from a few individual parts, the interior of the 911 GT3 RS was similar to that of the 911 GT3 with the Clubsport package: three-point and six-point seat belts were designed in the respective contrasting colors. Pre-fitting for a battery master switch was on board.

THE 911 GT3 RALLY CAR

COMPETITION FROM BAVARIA

Even before the 911 GT3 RS was finished and on the market, it had competition. And it came, of all things, from a mid-class coupe. BMW launched a new model, the M3 CSL, in mid-2003, shortly before the market launch of the 911 GT3 RS that autumn. It was a lightweight version of the M3, equipped with particularly grippy Michelin tires (Pilot Sport Cup).

In the Auto Quartet disciplines, the BMW was still behind the 911 GT3 (acceleration, top speed). But it achieved impressive times on the racetrack. In the *Sport Auto* test, the M3 CSL was quicker around the Nordschleife than the 911 GT3. Preuninger's demand for the 911 GT3 RS was therefore that Porsche must build the faster car. He remembered with a smile, "And so it was. No problem!" The driver for the specialist magazine *Sport Auto* lapped the Nordschleife of the Nürburgring in the 911 GT3 RS in 7:47 minutes, taking three seconds off the BMW's time. Walter Röhrl even drove the 911 GT3 RS around the "Green Hell" in 7:43 minutes. No other road-legal 911 was faster at that time. The balance of power between the sportiest production cars was restored.

MORE INTEREST THAN TOOLS

In addition, the concerns of the sales department proved to be unfounded. Porsche built a total of 682 units of the 911 GT3 RS, 140 of them with right-hand drive. None of the cars made it

Porsche tried out the 911 GT3 in rallying back in 2001. Walter Röhrl and Christian Geistdörfer took part in the Deutschland Rally with the first production 911 GT3 (registration: S-GT 408). The only modifications to the yellow road car: retuned springs and dampers as well as a modified hub that moved the steering wheel lower into the interior.

The legendary duo and their GT3 were not part of the classification but were the lead drivers. Nevertheless, Röhrl drove dynamically. After a jump, the 911 GT3 touched down awkwardly, and a nozzle broke off the oil tank. Retirement was imminent. Roland Kussmaul had the car towed to the nearest farmer, where the nozzle was welded back on. A short time later, the team was back on the track and finished the stage.

As the organizer of the event, the ADAC used Röhrl's fame to stir up enthusiasm for rallying—with success. From 2002 on, Germany was the organizer of the WRC. Porsche later developed a rally car based on the 911 GT3 RS under the direction of Hartmut Kristen. It was prepared for professional rally use with Kevlar body parts, increased ground clearance, a higher wheel speed, and a robust bitumen layer on the underbody.

The car was called the 911 GT3 RS Road Challenge. It was created on the initiative of Belgian Gérard Magniette, owner of the Future World racing team. He wanted to sell the sports car as an all-around carefree package to wealthy rally fans. The project failed before it began. Financial miscalculations and a lack of interest led Magniette to withdraw. What remained were ten converted examples. They found customers—and became an investment. The Rallye 911 is rarer than the 911 R or 911 SC RS models.

to the USA and Canada through official channels. As with the original model from 1972, more than three times the originally planned quantity was produced. Proof for all the doubters that there was great interest in extreme road sports cars. The limiting factor for the fastest Porsche 996 was not customer interest, but the design of the tools at the suppliers who built the individual parts for the 911 GT3 RS. They were supposed to produce components for only two hundred vehicles. The tools were not designed for a significantly larger series, and Porsche began running out of parts for the car before the purchasing power of its customers ran out—a good omen for the successors.

Unsuccessful foray into rally sport: the 911 GT3 RS Road Challenge experiment failed because instigator Gérard Maginette miscalculated. There were no buyers and only ten cars were produced.

A one-off for the Porsche Club of America: By special request, Porsche created a 996 based on the GT3 Sport Classic. Delivery was scheduled for spring 2022.

The Classic Club Coupe came with wheels in the classic Fuchs design.

PORSCHE 911 CLASSIC CLUB COUPE

Some interesting derivatives of the Porsche 911 did not make it onto the US market. Nevertheless, the oldest and largest brand club exists there, the Porsche Club of America (PCA). It was founded in 1955 and had a total of 144,560 members on January 1, 2022. Porsche maintains close contact with the club, and it even produced a special vehicle for it in 2022.

UNIQUE CAR WITH A DUCKTAIL

Inspired by the 911 Sport Classic (997), representatives of the PCA and Alexander Fabig, head of Individualization and Classics at Porsche, came up with an idea: they sketched a unique 911 of the 996 series. It was to have the visual features of the modern example and the drivetrain of the 2003 911 GT3. The car was based on a 1998 911 Carrera, which traveled from the state of Virginia to Stuttgart for restoration and conversion. There, Porsche Classic dismantled the vehicle, refurbished the body, reinforced the chassis, and produced new components. With a double-domed roof, the rear spoiler in the style of the 911 Carrera RS 2.7 from 1972, 18-inch Fuchs

rims, and specially designed materials in the interior, the vehicle became unique. Porsche tested the new shapes on a test vehicle on test tracks at Weissach, Nardo, and Idiada. After these tests, the manufacturer dismantled the prototype so that only one vehicle of this type existed. The Porsche 911 Classic Club Coupe is painted in sport gray metallic and features various accents in club blue, the color of the PCA. Inside, Alcantara covers the headlining and pillars. Seats and door panels are covered in black and slate gray leather strips woven together in a Pepita pattern. Tom Gorsuch, President of the PCA, praised the result and the collaborative effort: "We wanted to create something unique together that would generate enthusiasm. The fact that the finished Porsche 911 Classic Club Coupe looks like a single piece is the incredible thing about this challenging project."

Unique: a double-domed roof and sport gray metallic paint finish

The wheels measured 18 inches in diameter.

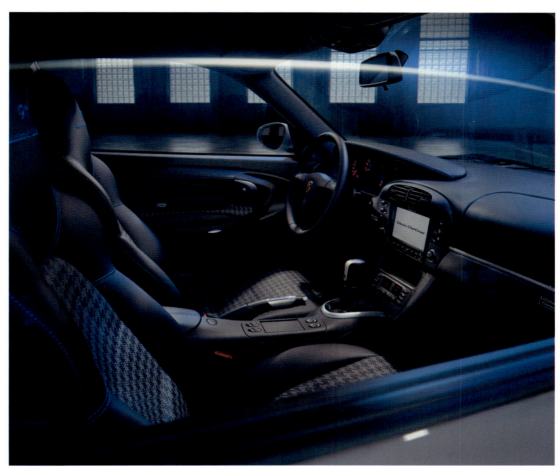

Mix of materials: Alcantara and leather, plus the classic pepita pattern

Porsche did not actually take up the ducktail again until the 997. This one-off was created for the PCA.

997

THE TYPE 997 BROUGHT THE CLASSIC 911 SHAPES BACK TO THE MODEL SERIES. APART FROM THE ROOF, EVERY VISIBLE BODY PART OF THE 997 DIFFERED FROM THOSE OF THE 996.

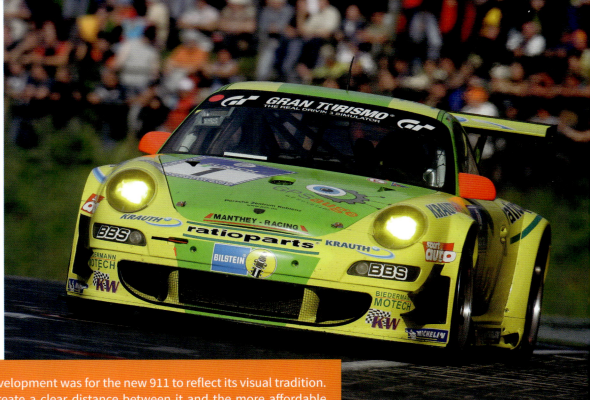

The basis for successful motorsport: with the 911 GT3 RSR, Porsche offered the perfect sports car for endurance racing.

One of the goals during development was for the new 911 to reflect its visual tradition. Porsche also wanted to create a clear distance between it and the more affordable Boxster. This differentiation succeeded. The cars were still similar in their structures, but you could no longer tell by looking at them. This visible lead was good for the perception of the 911.

Apparently, the sports car had hardly evolved technically. The new 911 was based on the old platform. It offered almost the same amount of space and very similar ergonomics. In addition, Porsche had hardly changed the still-young drivetrain—the gently modernized liquid-cooled boxers in the 911 Carrera and 911 Carrera S were only slightly more powerful than those of the previous model year. In fact, however, many innovations made it into the 911, including adaptive shock absorbers, a rear silencer with flap control, and a sport mode.

At the top end of the sporty range, Porsche was striving for a further lead: the 911 GT3 RS differed more than before from the base models. And for the first time, the GT department converted a 911 GT2 into an RS.

Visually, the 911 had evolved considerably since the model change.

Wide for the first time: the new 911 GT3 RS used the same body as the all-wheel-drive models of the 911. It was as wide as that of the Turbo version but dispensed with the air intakes on the rear wheel arches.

PORSCHE 911 GT3 RS

Porsche's GT boss Andreas Preuninger had concrete ideas early on about what the new top-of-the-range model should do better than its predecessor. The new 911 GT3 RS, once again positioned above the 911 GT3 and out of competition with the 911 Turbo, was to sound better. He compared the exhaust sound of the 996 series with that of two three-cylinder engines. The reason: one exhaust half processes the exhaust gases from one half of the engine (i.e., from three cylinders each). The characteristic sound of the vehicles previously came from the intake tract, explained Preuninger.

This was set to change with the successor. For the 997 GT3, he had in mind an exhaust system that combined the exhaust gases from both cylinder banks. Porsche had already implemented something similiar in the air-cooled 911. While journalists were testing the facelift of the 911 generation 996 around Venice for the first time, he consulted with engine developer Hans-Georg Breuer and Head of Motorsport Hartmut Kristen on the exhaust system of the 997.

They drew sketches for improvements on napkins. Kristen and Breuer feared that their ideas would cost millions for new tools. Nevertheless, the exhaust system of the successor model was created in this way. It was initially used in the Cup car, and later in the 911 GT3 and 911 GT3 RS production cars.

The complicated exhaust system consisted of two fan manifolds, two pre-silencers, catalytic converters, and a large, common main silencer. The tailpipes were arranged centrally in the rear apron. This feature was subsequently adopted by all future 911 GT3 and 911 GT3 RS cars. In addition to the new layout, the exhaust system had a flap control system, which fed the exhaust gases past the pre-silencers directly to the rear silencer—an innovation in the 911. When the flap was open, the exhaust back pressure was noticeably reduced. As a result, the torque increased between 2,000 and 4,000 rpm by 30 to 35 Nm (22 to 26 ft.-lbs.). In this mode, it became unpleasantly loud on the highway because the car roared under certain conditions. Customers could choose between power and comfort while driving. Porsche therefore coupled the exhaust flap to the Sport button, another innovation of the 997 generation.

For the first time with color: after its predecessor,
which was always Carrara white, Porsche painted the
new 911 GT3 RS in silver, black, orange, and green.
The rims and lettering were in a contrasting color.

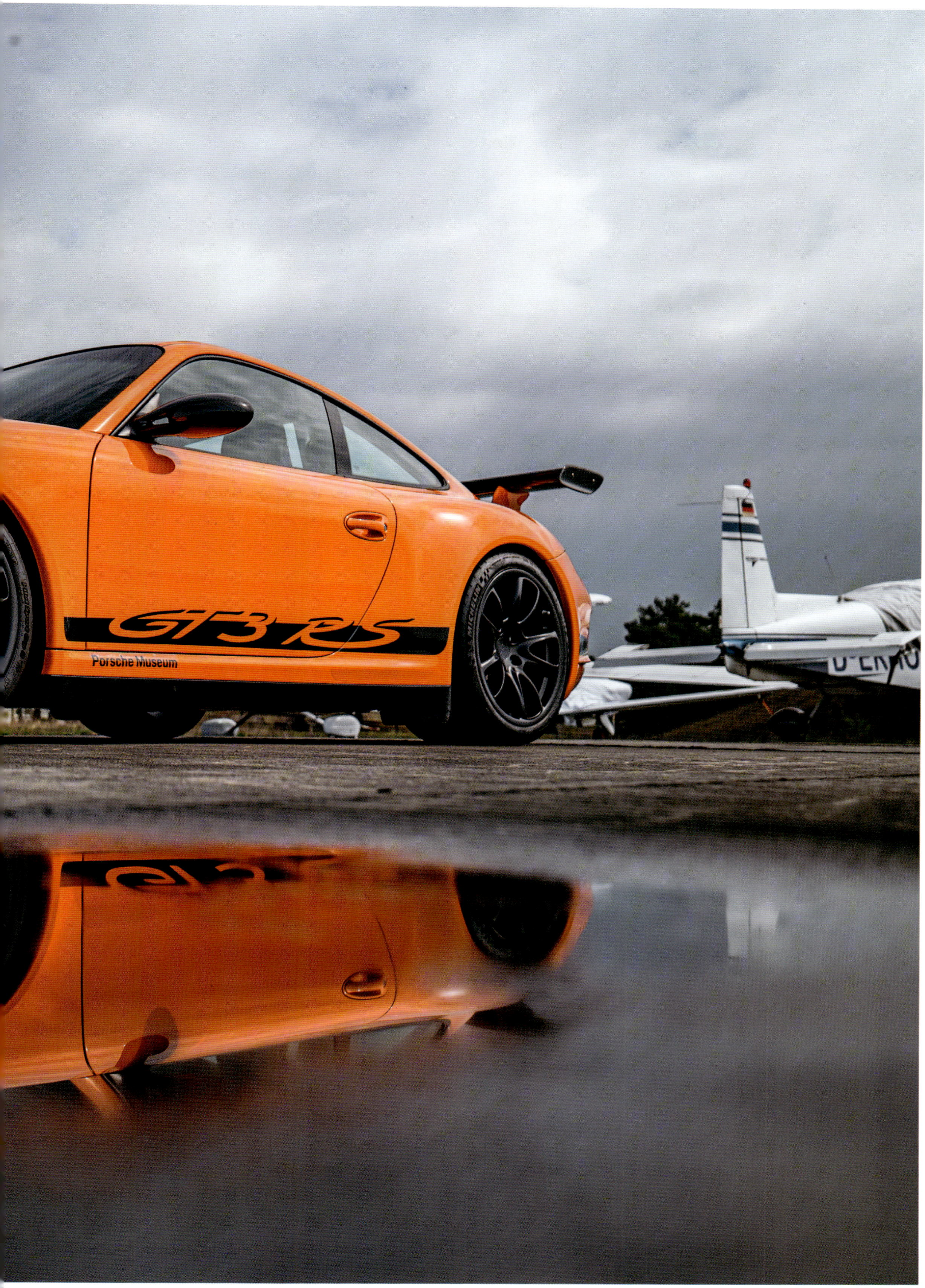
GT3 RS
Porsche Museum

A new exhaust system was used in the Type 997. It collected the exhaust gases from both cylinder banks in a rear silencer and therefore provided a new sound. It had a flap control system that was linked to the sports button in the interior.

THE COLORS OF THE GT3 RS

Another important change in the GT3 RS came at the customers' request. When Porsche put a water-cooled RS on the road for the first time with the 996, the choice of colors was limited. In memory of the 911 Carrera 2.7 from 1972, only red or blue accents on the white bodywork were possible. Other paint finishes were not available for money or good words. Not every customer liked that. In the 997, the manufacturer therefore broadened the palette. A total of four colors are available—two of them at no extra cost, two for an extra charge.

In addition to power delivery and sound, the Sport button also controlled the accelerator pedal characteristics and, for the first time, the adjustable dampers. Porsche introduced Porsche Active Traction Management (PASM) with the model change. In normal mode, the setup corresponds approximately to that of its predecessor. In Sport mode, the dampers of the 911 GT3 RS work harder.

The inspiration for one of the colors came from the USA. One sleepless night, Preuninger was watching a NASCAR race on television. He was impressed by a car whose basic color was silver, with orange accents. The next day, he had this combination shown to him on the 911 GT3 RS via virtual reality

The 911 GT3 RS weighed 20 kilograms less than the 911 GT3. What demanded a great deal of effort from the engineers was hardly noticeable on the racetrack in the lap times and handling.

In the 997 model series, the 911 GT3 RS had its exhaust tailpipes in the middle of the rear apron for the first time. Porsche retained this look from then on.

and immediately initiated the implementation. In addition to silver-orange, the black-orange option was also added.

The optional colors of green and orange, each with black stickers, had already been chosen at that point. The sales department had dispensed with descriptive names—the colors spoke for themselves. White paint with black or red accents was also available on special request.

Porsche painted the rims of the 911 GT3 RS orange (for the exterior colors of Arctic Silver Metallic and Black) or black (for the exterior colors Green or Orange). This made the 911 GT3 RS a trendsetter. Black rims on a production car were still a novelty at that time. Instead of the contrasting colors, the rims were also available in silver at no extra charge.

WITH A WIDE BODY

The fact that there would be a new 911 GT3 RS was almost a formality for the 997 generation. The sales figures of its predecessor had given Porsche's GT department a good deal of confidence among the management. Since the 911 GT3 of the 997 model also sold well, the decision was quickly made to produce a new RS version. This was to be more clearly differentiated from the less powerful 911s than before, both visually and technically.

The most important innovation in the new 911 GT3 RS: henceforth, it would be based on the wider body of the all-wheel-drive models. This added 44 millimeters (1.7 in.) to the rear of the vehicle. The space gained provided room for a wider track at the rear axle (plus 34 millimeters or 1.3 in.), implemented with a lower wheel offset (minus 17 millimeters, [0.67 in.] each). In this way, the developers minimized the tendency of the car to roll and enabled greater lateral acceleration. The gap between the GT3 RS and the GT3 was increased.

Another advantage of the new body: it permitted a wider spoiler. The test organizations determined how large this could be, based on the body dimensions. With more surface area for the airstream, it generated additional downforce. At the same time, the 911 GT3 RS achieved the drag coefficient of its predecessor (0.30).

LESS CARBON FIBER IN THE 911 GT3 RS

The production staff also wanted a less exclusive hood for the new model. The carbon-fiber part of the predecessor did not fit particularly well and meant additional work during assembly. This request also helped the project budget. The developers therefore agreed—the 997 GT3 RS would be one of a total of two models without a carbon-fiber hood.

Despite this, the top model weighed 20 kilograms (44 lbs.) less than the 911 GT3. A carbon-fiber wing, polycarbonate rear window, plastic engine hood (including air collector for the ram air system), and carbon-fiber bucket seats—taken from the Porsche Carrera GT super sports car—reduced the weight. Porsche also installed a single-mass flywheel again. Air conditioning and radio were only available on request, but at no extra charge.

For the first time, Porsche made unique skirts for the 911 GT3 models. They stood out clearly from those of the 911 Carrera and improved the airflow. The GT3 and GT3 RS were visually similar, but only apparently so. Since the top model comes with a wider rear end and a slightly longer front overhang, the components do differ.

TECHNICALLY CLOSE TO THE 911 GT3

Porsche was already using the revised wheel mounts on the front axle in the 911 GT3. However, there were still differences in the chassis. The 911 GT3 RS got modified wheel mounts and split wishbones on the rear axle. In addition, the rear track had been widened and the front axle had been adjusted; according to factory specifications, the 911 GT3 RS had 10 minutes more camber. The mechanical modifications allowed more room for maneuvering in the 911 RSR motorsport version.

The drivetrain was closer to the 911 GT3. A high-revving version of the new 911 engine did not yet exist at that time. The basic

features of the engine were therefore still taken from the 996 911 GT3 RS, but it had been extensively revised for its use in the new 911 GT3. A new, variable intake system increased performance. It adjusted the length of the air flow depending on the engine speed and thus optimized combustion.

In addition, the 3.6-liter Mezger engine had been given revised cylinder heads and a higher compression ratio. And in its new configuration, it revved up to 8,400 rpm, 200 rpm more than before. With a modified exhaust system, power output increased to 415 hp. In reality, this was usually more than stated on the spec sheet. In addition, there was the lighter single-mass flywheel, which was the special feature of the RS. *Sport Auto* found "in terms of spontaneity and revving pleasure, the engine has noticeably improved, at least subjectively."

HARDLY ANY FASTER IN THE TEST

All in all, technically the 911 GT3 RS largely corresponded to the 911 GT3. The wide rear end, more revving pleasure, a 20-kilogram (44 lb.) weight advantage, and modifications to the rear axle could only give it a slight lead, if any at all. Horst von Saurma lapped the Nordschleife of the Nürburgring in 7.48 minutes for Sport Auto in both cars. The differences were "fine adjustments" was the verdict.

However, the result did not mean a bad verdict for the 911 GT3 RS but was proof of the quality of the car on which it was based, the 911 GT3. "It already achieved the highest

Typical 911 GT3 RS: no rear seat, but a roll bar with reinforcing struts

Visually, the 911 GT3 RS differed significantly from the 911 GT3. Technically, there was scarcely any difference.

Carbon fiber was always an important design element in the 911 GT3.

*RS asceticism no longer
meant doing without:
unlike the original RS, the
Type 997 had five round
instruments.*

score ever awarded in the Supertest (77)," summarized von Saurma. The RS version was on a par. The 911 GT3 and 911 GT3 RS thus topped the specialist magazine's list of best cars, placing them ahead of super sports cars such as the Lamborghini Murciélago LP 640 and the Pagani Zonda F.

Walter Röhrl proved that the 911 GT3 RS was ultimately the faster car: he lapped the Nordschleife in the top sports model in 7:45 minutes, two seconds faster than in the 911 GT3. Small flaw: Röhrl was even faster in the predecessor.

DRIVING ASSISTANCE IN THE GT3 RS

For the first time in an RS model from Porsche, the driver was no longer left to his own devices. The GT3 vehicles were equipped with traction control in the 997 model. The developers adapted it from the Porsche Carrera GT super sports car. An affront for purists, but a real help for everyone else. The new system was intended to provide stability, especially on wet roads. Porsche once again equipped the 911 GT3 RS with sports tires (Michelin Pilot Cup Sport), which had a disadvantage in the wet compared to regular tires. The electronic assistant could partially compensate for this and prevent worse.

*In the Type 997, Porsche offered the sporty PASM (Porsche
Active Suspension Management) adjustable suspension
with 30 millimeters lowering for the first time. It came as
standard on the 911 GT3 RS. The setup was linked to the
vehicle's driving modes.*

New 911 GT3 RS, new design: the flags were designed by Cayenne illustrator Stephen Murkett.

PORSCHE 911 GT3 RS

After the conspicuous differentiation between the 911 GT3 and the 911 GT3 RS, as part of the facelift, Porsche also wanted to differentiate more clearly between the two models technically. Contributing to this decision was the fact that the top model had failed to register any best times on the Nordschleife—not even by the manufacturer.

MORE POWERFUL THAN THE 911 GT3

For the model update, the team around Andreas Preuninger carried out a thorough redesign of the GT3 RS. As of 2009, it differed clearly from the GT3. Many measures made the car faster. Some were visible at first glance—for example, the enlargement of the wheel arches in front and the wider tires. Others were hidden in the engine bay, in the chassis tuning, in the adjustment options, and in the air routing on the underside. The result caused Horst von Saurma of *Sport Auto* to speak of "a new chapter in the handling dynamics." In the press kit for the IAA 2009, Porsche itself called the car

The 3.8-liter boxer engine of the 911 GT3 RS produced 450 hp. This made it officially more powerful than the engine of the 911 GT3 for the first time.

shorter. The automatic dual-clutch transmission of the Carrera models was not yet ready for the RS models (and their fans) in the 997 model—it did not fit the Mezger engine due to the different flange position.

In addition to the displacement, the drivetrain benefited from further significant changes in both 911 GT3 engines. More revs (8,500 rpm), an increased compression ratio (12.2:1), and detailed work on the intake and exhaust system as well as the catalytic converters increased performance. The team also added a camphasing system on the exhaust side for the first time. Exhaust emission properties was now an important factor, since the standards were becoming ever stricter. The new GT3 RS already had to meet the Euro 5a specifications, which for the first time considered particulate emissions from petrol engines.

"We had to make sure that the thing burned properly," summarized Preuninger. What sounded simple was a real task for the engine developers around Hans-Georg Breuer. The complexity of the engine, which was still based on the design by Hans Mezger, was also increasing significantly. During development the double camphasing system, in particular, caused problems. During test drives, mechanisms came loose and led to engine damage. Special washers later fixed the components in the production version.

"the last level of a 911 for the road before a pure racecar for the circuit." It proved this categorization soon afterwards in an incomparable PR stunt: the manufacturer entered the production car in the most tradition-rich long-distance races (see page 156).

UPGRADE TO 3.8 LITERS DISPLACEMENT

Overall, the 911 GT3 RS had changed more than a facelift would suggest. Above all, it had been given a revised engine. It now delivered 450 hp from a displacement of 3.8 liters. The engineers achieved the advantage over the old 3.6-liter engine with a larger bore (102.7 millimeters or 4.04 in.) with the same stroke (76.4 millimeters or 3 in.).

The larger engine was already used in the new 911 GT3. However, it produced 15 hp less than in the top-of-the-range model. This was the first time that the GT3 RS differed from its base model in the specification sheet. Optimizations in the intake tract and an improved exhaust system provided the extra power.

There was also an additionally lightened single-mass flywheel. Compared to the part in the predecessor, it lost a further 1.4 kilograms (3 lbs.). In addition, the manual six-speed gearbox was more closely stepped for better traction. Gears 1 to 5 had an 11 percent shorter ratio, while sixth gear was 5 percent

SLIGHT WEIGHT ADVANTAGE

The revised GT3 RS underwent the traditional RS diet and received modern additions. A titanium rear silencer, carbon-fiber spoiler, plastic rear window, and lightweight door panels reduced weight. Optional halogen headlights and a lithium-ion starter battery shed further kilos. Compared to the 911 GT3, the 911 GT3 RS saved a total of 25 kilograms (55 lbs.). Equipped with a cage, it was still 9 kilograms (20 lbs.) lighter. It was only 100 kilograms (220 lbs.) heavier than the ascetic Cup car.

When the 911 GT3 RS was almost finished, another innovation was added to the project—its brake disks were to consist of an aluminum pot and a steel friction ring. This meant that the contact surface of the brake pads remained resilient, but the center of the component became lighter. The proposal came late from the brake development department. But this design saved weight. Preuninger pushed the idea through—and equipped the 911 GT3 RS with a unique brake for the first time.

DEMONSTRATION ON THE NÜRBURGRING

The endurance racing team for the production Porsche: motor journalist Chris Harris, DTM driver Roland Asch, Sport Auto editor-in-chief and racing driver Horst von Saurma, and professional racing driver and VLN/NLS commentator Patrick Simon.

Porsche entered a road-legal 911 GT3 RS in the 2010 edition of the 24-hour race at the Nürburgring to show how well its technology performed in racing. It only differed from the production version in those points that the FIA prescribed for all participants in the race. In addition, the car used in the race had increased camber.

Journalists Chris Harris and Horst von Saurma, DTM driver Roland Asch, and long-distance racing driver Patrick Simon took turns at the wheel of the production car. The four men steadily worked their way forward from forty-second on the grid. Their pit stops went according to plan; the car only needed fuel, brake discs and pads, and regularly a fresh driver. At dawn, Asch thanked Preuninger on the radio for the great car as he whizzed along the Döttinger Höhe—and sang as he overtook Cup cars, because the production car was faster on the straights. At the end of the race, they finished in thirteenth place overall. The highlight: the standard 911 GT3 RS with the registration number S-GO 2400 completed the route from Stuttgart to the Ring on its own wheels and made the return journey after the race slightly damaged, but also under its own power. Von Saurma drove his racing car back home on the highway. Strictly speaking, therefore, the RS had taken part in a 30-hour race.

The Porsche 911 GT3 RS was driven to the Ring on its own wheels, completed the 24-hour race there without any problems, and then drove back to Stuttgart. Thanks to the car's higher top speed, the company's internal competitors were often left behind on the high-speed passages of the Green Hell.

The production car worked its way up from forty-second on the grid to thirteenth overall in the 24-hour race at the Nürburgring.

THE MUCH FASTER CAR

However, the car made the greatest progress in the area of the chassis. Head of Development Karsten Schebsdat did not begin the optimizations on the rear axle as usual. Instead, he had Michelin develop front tires with better lateral control and tuned the rest of the car accordingly, right down to the active engine mounts.

With a special rubber compound, a wider contact patch (245s in front, 325s in the rear), a suspension tuned to this, optimized traction control, and further improved aerodynamics (160 kilograms, or 352 pounds, of downforce at top speed), the facelift of the 911 GT3 RS earned high praise from the specialist media. In the *Sport Auto* test, the RS lapped the Nordschleife 15 seconds faster than its predecessor from the same model series. The time of 7:33 minutes was achieved in normal mode.

In the British *Car Magazine*, Ben Pulman was also enthusiastic: "The feedback from the steering is superbly detailed, the ceramic brakes leave just as lasting an impression as the performance, and the Cup tires provide enormous grip. Every kilometer is exhilarating, and it's certainly one of the best cars of 2010." Pulman added: "There are things about Porsche that

you should hate (the Cayenne, for example), but [the 911 GT3 RS] is something to celebrate."

DECOR LIKE A SPEEDBOAT

Visually, the new 911 GT3 RS stood out clearly from its predecessor. Widened front fenders (26 millimeters, or 1 inch) accommodated the new, wider wheels. The front and rear aprons had been modified, the revised spoiler had an aluminum substructure, and the rims were bolted to the hubs with a central locking system. In addition to all these changes, Andreas Preuninger wanted to see further updates. He had had enough of the "GT3 RS" on the flank. He enlarged the lettering and moved it to the fenders—just as the Clubsport version of the G model once presented its logo in 1988. He had another idea for the free space on the side. One of his passions was speedboats, and at that time, they often had a stylized checkered flag on their outer skin.

He decided that the 911 GT3 RS should also have a checkered flag. Preuninger convinced Head of Development Wolfgang Dürheimer and asked Cayenne designer Stephen Murkett for a suggestion. Both men shared a passion for speedboats.

The 997 model series' facelift saw it receive new taillights— such as these for the 911 GT3 RS.

Carbon-fiber bucket seats, rims with central locking, and colorful accents in the interior: the 911 GT3 RS was all about the details, both technically and visually.

From the facelift on, the carbon spoiler had a substructure made of lightweight aluminum.

Murkett therefore knew exactly how best to implement the task. "After three or four hours of work with adhesive tape on the car, he was finished. And it looked exactly how I had imagined it," Preuninger recalled. Murkett's design went into series production. Six months after its presentation at the IAA at the Nürburgring, the 911 GT3 RS flew a real checkerboard flag when it passed the endurance test at the 24-hour race.

The front fenders of the 911 GT3 RS were now wider than those of the 911 GTS.

Porsche optimized the engine, chassis, and aerodynamics of the 911 GT3 RS. With more power and downforce, and a sensitive setup, it was significantly faster than its immediate predecessor.

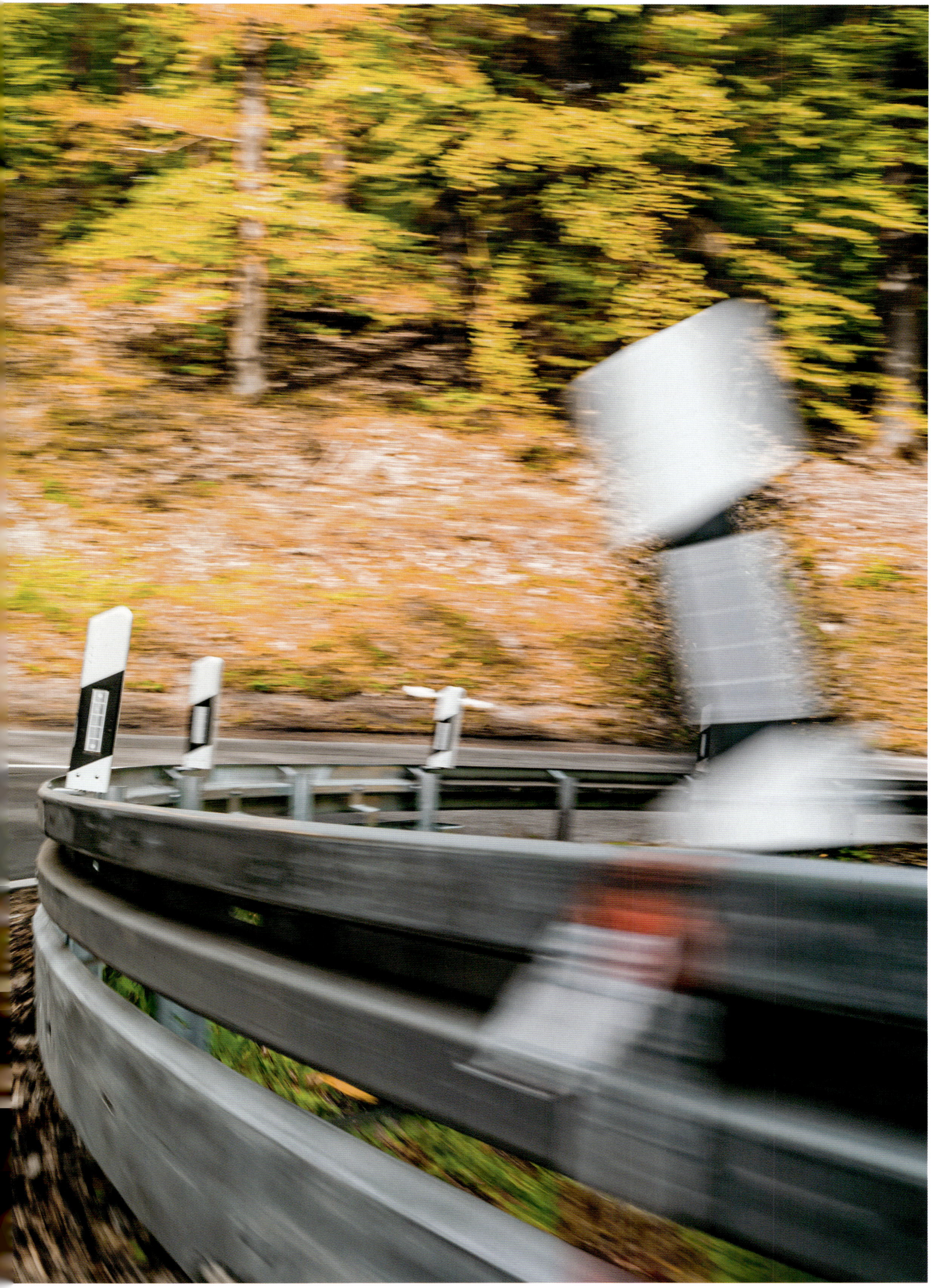

Walter Röhrl was involved in the development of the 911 GT2 RS.
The benchmark for the first 911 GT2 RS was the Carrera GT. It was
supposed to undercut it by one second on the Nordschleife—in the
end, it would be ten seconds.

PORSCHE 911 GT2 RS

Previously, Porsche had only built RS 911s with naturally aspirated engines. This was the case in the air-cooled era and would remain so in the water-cooled era. Since the 993 generation, however, there had been a sporty top model based on the 911 Turbo—the 911 GT2 was the turbocharged counterpart to the 911 GT3. Both derivatives excelled in the disciplines of weight, handling, and aerodynamics but used different drive systems.

THE FIRST 911 RS WITH TURBOCHARGERS

The idea of a GT2 RS first arose in 2007. Porsche's GT team was working simultaneously on the 911 GT2 and the 911 GT3 RS, both from the 997 model series. One night, during test drives in Estoril, a team mechanic thought aloud, "Imagine if we transferred everything we do with the GT3 RS to the GT2."

The GT2 was not the responsibility of Andreas Preuninger, but of Alan Lewin. But Preuninger liked the idea. "The GT2 wasn't quite as extreme as I would have made it. There was still enough room for an RS cure," he recalled. And he then implemented it in secret. The project began with a silver 911 GT2, which Preuninger optimized according to his ideas.

The most powerful manual Porsche 911: 620 hp and 700 Nm from 3.6 liters of displacement powered the 911 GT2 RS exclusively to the rear axle. The right-hand- drive model had a smaller fuel tank, with a capacity of 67 liters.

A SECRET 911 GT2 RS

On board was Karsten Schebsdat, the GT2's technical project manager, plus several dedicated engineers. Their mission: to take out everything that made the car heavy and put in everything that made it fast. The car was to be as light as possible, for the time being without regard to a potential production version.

The prototype was given the lightweight construction elements of the 911 GT3 RS, as well as widened fenders and a carbon-fiber front hood. In the same step, heavy insulating material was removed from the car until it weighed just 1,340 kilograms (2,954 lbs.). The 3.6-liter engine was given a power boost to around 580 hp, plus reinforced internals. At this stage, the developers still did not care about emissions standards.

It retained the manual transmission and rear-wheel drive. The prototype was called the "beast" because it felt about as rough as the sum of its parts suggested. When Walter Röhrl set the lap record at the Nürburgring in the "standard" 911 GT2 (7:32 minutes), the Beast was also on-site. After Röhrl's stint, Preuninger asked him to take to the track again. This time with the "beast."

Röhrl was surprised because the prototype already looked used. But he complied with Preuninger's request. And he drove the "beast" to a lap time of 7:29 minutes—while other vehicles were on the track. Röhrl seemed convinced and asked for a production version. Preuninger agreed, "The car was so much fun that we absolutely had to make it happen." The code name of the production vehicle was "Project 7:27." This was the target lap time for the finished car—one second faster than the Porsche Carrera GT. A special feature that the car shared with many of its RS siblings: the impetus for the car came from the GT department, not from marketing.

Röhrl remained closely involved with the project during the development of the 911 GT2 RS. One day, when he was driving a Ferrari 599 on the Nordschleife for a comparison time, he recognized another 599 on the track. Röhrl caught up with the car and eventually passed it when the other driver made a small mistake. After his lap, Röhrl drove onto the country road to cool the car down. His competitor followed his example and drove alongside him. Röhrl recognized Michael Schumacher at the wheel of the other car. However, this story is only known because Schumacher got upset about the experience in the presence of his mechanics. And the mechanics later laughed out loud about it. After that, everyone at the Ring knew about it.

CARBON FIBER FOR THE 911 GT2 RS

Because the model, with its enormous performance, was in a high price class anyway, the team could implement ideas that it had so far left out of the 911 GT3 RS. Yes, expensive cars have advantages, at least when it comes to development. A lot of carbon fiber was used. The widened fenders, front hood, and rear wing of the production model were made of this lightweight material, as were the door panels. As the most extreme road model in the 911 portfolio, the GT2 RS was intended to show off the material to demonstrate its motorsport genes. The hood at the front and the spoiler lip in the rear are finished in visible matte carbon fiber.

The hood, however, led to problems soon after the 911 GT2 RS hit the market. When the car arrived at dealerships, some of them wondered about the matte carbon fiber on the front hood—and promptly got out the buffing machine, because carbon fiber was usually shiny. Though their intentions were good, they ruined the expensive body parts. The polishing

The 911 GT2 RS was initially created in secret. The engineers had a free hand and designed a lightweight, powerful prototype with the nickname "Beast."

was irreparable. Even a large orange sticker on the windshield bearing an explanation did not help against such misinterpretations. Another problem when the car hit the market: when the 911 GT2 RS debuted, many customers accused Porsche of pure greed. They accused it of being a GT2 with parts from the GT3 RS that only existed for the company's margin. Malicious tongues called it the GT2 facelift. Preuninger dismissed the accusations: "Testing a car with this much power and rear-wheel drive is very time-consuming." The car had a good 700,000 kilometers (435,000 miles) of testing and more than 80,000 engineering hours.

A SPECIAL VEHICLE HANDOVER

Preuninger himself supported Porsche's communications department and gave presentations on the special features of his car. One of these presentations took place in a special setting. Porsche Cars North America organized major events in El Toro and West Palm Beach for deliveries in the USA. In February 2012, all US buyers who wished to attend the event would take delivery of their GT2 RSs at the same time.

After a comprehensive briefing with information about the car, all participants were led to an area that could not be seen. Employees rolled aside the privacy screen and presented the vehicles—forty in West Palm Beach, twenty in El Toro, each labeled in motorsport style with the names of their owners and their companions. As a supporting program, Porsche offered rides on the racetrack in the 911 GT3 Cup and in 911 GT2 RS cars that had already been driven. Motorsport legend Hurley Haywood would be among those driving the cars around the track. All buyers who were not present would receive their vehicles a few days later.

70 KILOGRAMS LIGHTER, WITH AN ADDED 90 HORSEPOWER

It is difficult to describe how fast the 911 GT2 RS is in practice, in part because there had been nothing like it previously. On the Nordschleife, it ran away from all the cars with regular MOT road approvals.

Visible matte carbon fiber on the hood led to misunderstandings on delivery: Porsche dealers polished the component—and ruined it in the process.

The standard fuel tank of the 911 GT2 RS had a capacity of 90 liters.

Porsche company driver Timo Kluck lapped the Green Hell in seven minutes, eighteen seconds—four seconds faster than the extreme Dodge Viper ACR. The Maserati MC12 and Paganzi Zonda F Clubsport were even further behind in the list of fastest cars.

In *Sport Auto*, Horst von Saurma found an understandable explanation for the car's format when he compared the recorded data with that for the 911 GT3 RS. "While the cornering speeds . . . are at roughly the same level, the Porsche 911 GT2 RS rushes past the Porsche 911 GT3 RS on the acceleration stages and the long straights with an excess of speed, as if the latter had been ordered to exercise tactical restraint by the director: at 275 kph (171 mph) at the Schwedenkreuz and 300 kph (186 mph) on the Döttinger Höhe. The GT3 RS: 258 and 276 kph (160 and 171 mph) respectively."

TO THE EXTREME

In fact, the production version of the 911 GT2 RS was noticeably lighter than the 911 GT3 RS. Despite the heavier engine technology, its standard weight was 1,370 kilograms (3,020 lbs.), five

The rear spoiler of the 911 GT2 RS was made of carbon fiber.

The carbon-fiber door panels saved a total of 700 grams of weight.

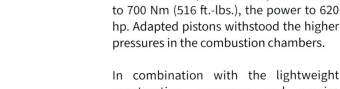

With 1.6 bar of boost pressure and many other modifications, the Turbo engine's output rose to 620 hp.

Weight reduction in detail: the 911 GT2 RS weighed less than the 911 GT3 RS.

kilograms (11 lbs.) less than the 911 GT3 RS with its naturally aspirated engine. It was a conglomeration of measures that squeezed every last ounce out of the car. These included the carbon fiber door panels (minus 700 grams, or 1.5 lbs.), the omitted cup holder (minus 1.5 kilograms, or 3.3 lbs.), and a special carpet with lighter insulation (minus 4 kilograms, or 8.8 lbs.). Air conditioning and radio were again only optional and free of charge. The new turbochargers, the increased boost pressure, and the larger intercoolers were largely responsible for the 90 hp increase compared to a 911 GT2. The two VTG turbochargers compressed the intake air in the RS model at 1.6 instead of 1.4 bar (23.2 instead of 20.3 psi). The torque increased to 700 Nm (516 ft.-lbs.), the power to 620 hp. Adapted pistons withstood the higher pressures in the combustion chambers.

In combination with the lightweight construction measures and precise Uniball bearings in the chassis, the result was an incomparable driving machine. In the British trade magazine *Autocar*, Andrew Frankel considered the GT2 RS to be "legalized madness." Car journalist Chris Harris wrote that, compared to a 911 Turbo, the 911 GT2 RS was from another world.

All-wheel drive was not an issue in Porsche's first 911 GT2 RS. A second drive axle would add too much weight to the car and thus reduce performance. Optimized aerodynamics were more important anyway. The top model generated 60 percent more downforce than a GT2. This did increase the drag coefficient, but this was not a problem in view of the performance.

Porsche limited the 911 GT2 RS of the 997 series to five hundred units. They sold out within a few months. The car remains the fastest and most powerful Porsche 911 with manual transmission.

The Porsche 911 GT3 RS 4.0 drew 500 hp from a displacement of 4.0 liters. For the jump from 3.8 to 4.0 liters, it received the crankshaft of the competition car.

Even years later, at Porsche the 911 GT3 RS 4.0 of the Type 997 was the benchmark for its successors.

PORSCHE 911 GT3 RS 4.0

For the 2010 motorsport season, Porsche was working on a successor to the 911 Cup S racing car. The special feature of the new 911 GT3 R was that it had a Mezger engine with a displacement of 4 liters. The boxer engine made a lasting impression on GT engine boss Hans-Georg Breuer. He raved to Andreas Preuninger about how great this engine worked. Preuninger came up with the idea of making the engine roadworthy and installing it in a test vehicle.

The order went to designer Helmut Schmid. He was about to retire and was able to round off his career with a special car. For the time being, nobody knew what he was doing behind the closed doors of the GT department. He was installing the first 4.0-liter road-going engine in an aqua blue 911 GT3.

When the prototype was finished, everyone who drove it was enthusiastic. Preuninger found, "We cannot keep this from our customers; we will make a special series out of it!" The proposal received the approval of the management board.

From the ideas of building a street car with a racing engine grew what was to be the ultimate Porsche 911. Preuninger's department put all the experience it had gained with the 997 and its extreme sports derivatives into the project—everything they had learned to date from three RS models.

FROM THE ENGINE TO THE TOTAL CONCEPT

The GT3 RS 4.0 project started with the engine. Preuninger was keen to see the largest expansion stage of the Mezger boxer engine in series production, because it felt much more powerful than the extra 200 cubic centimeters (12.2 cu. in.) of displacement would suggest. As with his first RS, the 911 GT3 RS from 2003, he enriched this basic idea with tasks for all the other disciplines. In chassis development the engineers replaced the standard rubber mounts with Uniball joints with significantly reduced play. This improved the precision of the car—and also helped on another level. "The rolling comfort in the super test Porsche 911 GT3 RS 4.0, contrary to a premature assumption, was not worse, but better," marveled Horst von Saurma in *Sport Auto*.

New suspension springs with increased coil spacing saved weight compared to the 911 GT3 RS. The team used them in combination with so-called helper springs. They ensured that the main springs were continuously preloaded. The adaptive shock absorbers had also been given a new setup. They were now better adapted to the conditions of the Nürburgring-Nordschleife in sporty driving mode.

DOWNFORCE AND PERFORMANCE

Meanwhile, the aerodynamicists focused on downforce and balance. Small air deflectors on the front apron, known as flics, increased downforce on the front axle by 15 percent. Together with the revised front lip, they were the counterpart to the fixed rear wing, which was now more exposed to the wind. *Drive* moderator Chris Harris joked that you couldn't put your tea down on it as well as you could on the wing of an RS 3.8.

Overall, the car generated 190 kilograms (419 lbs.) of downforce at maximum speed. Despite the increased engine power, this remained at 310 kph (192 mph). This meant little on the racetrack. The GT3 RS 4.0 lapped the Nürburgring in 7 minutes and 27 seconds.

The drivetrain was based on the 3.8-liter engine of its predecessor. It was given the crankshaft of the race car. Stroke was increased to 80.4 millimeters (3.2 in.), which resulted in a displacement of 3,996 cubic centimeters (243.9 cu. in.). With forged pistons, titanium connecting rods, a slightly increased compression ratio of 12.6:1, and a revised intake tract (including air filter from the 911 GT3 R Hybrid), as well as new manifolds, the engine produced 500 hp. This made the GT3 RS 4.0 as powerful as a 911 Turbo. Equally impressive was the torque of 460 Nm (339 ft.-lbs.) at 5,750 rpm.

CARBON FIBER YOU CAN'T SEE

The RS 4.0 used all available lightweight construction methods—for example, side windows made of plastic, plus a hood, rear spoiler, and fenders made of carbon fiber. However, it did not show the material but hid it under paint. There were several reasons for this. First, Preuninger preferred a discreet look for the model. Second, the components weighed less this way. Several heavy layers of material were required to give the carbon an aesthetic finish. All these measures ensured that

The 4.0-liter engine originated largely from the competition vehicle.

Simple straps on the doors and a twelve o'clock marking on the steering wheel in the interior of the 911 GT3 RS 4.0

For the last time, an RS model was available exclusively with a manual transmission.

dry weight was only 70 kilograms (154 lbs.) greater than that of the Cup 911. Porsche listed a DIN weight (with operating materials) of 1,360 kilograms (3,998 lbs.) in the spec sheet.

Visually, Preuninger generally had no desire to follow fashion but instead realized his own ideas. The 4.0 was painted white with silver accents and white rims. The wheels initially met with resistance internally. Nevertheless, they went into series production. Preuninger added a black version as a counterpoint to this innocent exterior. Its internal nickname: Darth Vader.

PREREQUISITE: POWER

During internal test drives, the robust tuning of the gear lever and clutch was particularly noticeable. August Achleitner, responsible for the 911 model series, was enthusiastic about the car but criticized the stiff levers. Preuninger's answer: it feels right on the racetrack.

Von Saurma agreed: "When it comes to fast shifting maneuvers, it can hardly be surpassed in terms of precision. The gears slip in with such smoothness that it is a real pleasure to be able to operate a conventional gear stick. The precise engagement and disengagement mechanism of the clutch also allows you to feel the connection between the engine and gearbox with your foot—a welcome feature, especially after a quick downshift at the start of a corner."

Wolfgang König's assessment of the Super 911 in Auto Bild was similarly enthusiastic. "It is unbelievable how dryly and precisely this 500 hp beast responds to the driver's input. How confidence-inspiring, and all without ruining the suspension comfort. Perfect. And definitely another 911 classic." An accurate prediction: a good ten years after its market launch, the small series limited to six hundred units is one of the most sought-after 911 derivatives.

Matt Farah, moderator of the You Tube channel *The Smoking Tire*, summed it up: "Everything about this car is precise. The gearshift is precise. The engine is hyper-precise. The steering positions the

Additional air ducts: the small vanes on the front apron were called flics. They were being used for the first time on a production Porsche.

Porsche sold the 911 GT3
RS 4.0 exclusively in black
or white. There were no
other color choices.

car with millimeter precision." He was particularly impressed by the traction coming out of corners.

FOUR-POINT-ZERO AS A BENCHMARK

The GT3 RS 4.0 from the 997 model series was also particularly valuable for Porsche. The 2011 model would continue to serve as a benchmark for successors in certain areas in the 2020s. Andreas Preuninger still has an example at his disposal against which new vehicles must measure themselves. He appreciates it above all for its steering precision—and because the car drives so wonderfully directly.

During his presentation, Preuninger described the RS 4.0 as "bulletproof." One anecdote describes particularly well just how durable and reliable it is: as one of his frequently used test vehicles, a 911 GT3 RS 4.0 had clocked more than 120,000 kilometers, was a comparison vehicle in the development of the 911 R, and was rarely spared.

Once, the engineers in Calabria had to open a plastic window with a borrowed hand drill because they had locked the key inside. Preuninger's conclusion about this car: "It drives like new. It doesn't rattle, it hasn't had any unscheduled stops, it's simply a great car." High praise for a model from such a top segment—especially from its developer.

*The final, largest expansion stage of the
Mezger engine continues to delight fans of
the brand. It is regarded as one of the best
powerplants used by the Porsche 911.*

The 911 GT3 RS 4.0 shone on the racetrack: it lapped the Nürburgring Nordschleife in 7:27 minutes. This time was once the development target for the much more powerful 911 GT2 RS with its 620 hp engine.

The return of the ducktail: Porsche brought the legendary rear spoiler back in a small special series. The car sold out immediately.

PORSCHE 911 SPORT CLASSIC

In 2009, Porsche took up the charismatic spoiler of the 911 Carrera RS 2.7 from 1972. For a small series of 250 vehicles, the Porsche Exclusives department responsible for special requests modeled a similarly shaped rear hood for the 911 of the 997 model series. The name of this special series: Porsche 911 Sport Classic.

RETRO SPOILER

This car is not about maximum downforce. The manufacturer's current RS models show what that looks like. The Sport Classic focuses on iconic design. In addition to the newly invented rear end, it has a double-domed roof, a special wheel in Fuchs design, its own color (Sport Classic Grey), and individual seat covers made of woven leather.

The engine of the 911 Sport Classic was basically the same as that of the 911 Carrera S. With an optimized intake tract, its output increased by 23 hp to 408 hp. Porsche mated the engine to a manual six-speed transmission with mechanical rear axle lock. Ceramic brakes (PCCB) and the adjustable sports suspension (PASM) with two centimeters lowering were included as standard.

Porsche's main aim with this model was to demonstrate the possibilities of Porsche Exclusive Manufacture. The manufacturer obviously hit a nerve with this. The special model, which costs 201,682 euros, was sold out after just 48 hours.

991

WITH THE 991 GENERATION, PORSCHE FUNDAMENTALLY CHANGED THE 911 FOR THE SECOND TIME. THE NEWLY DEVELOPED PLATFORM ENABLED THE CLASSIC SPORTS CAR TO HAVE A COMPOSITE CONSTRUCTION FOR THE BODY SHELL, WHICH WAS NOW MADE OF ALUMINUM AND STEEL.

The great effort paid off. Although the sports car had grown significantly once again, it was lighter. Its body weighs 80 kilograms less than that of its predecessor, a big step in view of the increase in size. The complete, thoroughly modernized car with many additional control units was 40 kilograms lighter than the old 911.

The change from the 997 to the 991 brought a lot of additional technology. However, the most drastic change did not come until the facelift: beginning in 2015, the engines of the 911 were generally equipped with turbochargers—a concession to fleet consumption. Only the 911 GT3 and its derivatives were allowed to retain naturally aspirated engines. Nevertheless, there were also fundamental changes to the hottest variants of the new 911.

Several anniversaries fell within the 991's construction period, which Porsche honored accordingly. In 2013, Porsche was celebrating the fiftieth birthday of the 911, among other things with a special model limited to 1,963 units. This number stood for the year of the model series' birth. Another Porsche anniversary: on May 11, 2017, the plant in Zuffenhausen completed its one millionth model. It was a 911 Carrera S in Irish Green, with many attractive details reminiscent of its predecessors. Meanwhile, Porsche was rethinking old traditions with the GT3 RS—all in the spirit of even more speed.

The end of the manual transmission: the new 911 GT3 RS was equipped exclusively with a fast-shifting dual-clutch transmission (PDK).

PORSCHE 911 GT3 RS

Hitherto, the 911 GT3 RS had traditionally served two target groups. Racing drivers and purists alike loved it as a street-legal sports car that put performance center stage. Its engine did not have to accelerate unnecessary weight; its chassis did not have to heave luxurious fat pads around the curves. It was the automotive version of a defined athlete. The fact that modern driver assistance systems were on board was not a problem, because they could be switched off.

The switch to the 991 model series opened up new possibilities for the 911. Technology was now being introduced that was previously not available in the 911. This was of interest for the 911 GT3 RS if it also made it faster—even if this meant that it became heavier or that the developers had more work to do. Many additional control units increased the effort involved in designing the model. The electronics engineers treated the lightweight construction claim with great respect.

Porsche had so far justified the fact that no 911 RS had been equipped with a dual-clutch transmission with the additional weight of the automatic transmission. This reason now seemed to have been forgotten, since the new 911 GT3 RS was only available with the seven-speed, dual-clutch transmission (PDK). In addition, its rear axle steered a few degrees at high speeds to increase stability. Both technologies made the car quicker, but it annoyed purists. What they did not know at this time: Porsche was planning the limited 911 R with manual transmission for them. And if they did not like it, there was always the manual Cayman GT4.

SCOOPS ON THE WHEEL ARCHES

The base 911 grew with the change to the 991 generation; thus the GT3 RS also grew larger. It was eleven centimeters longer than its predecessor. At the same time, its wheelbase was stretched by an additional ten centimeters (four inches). With the body of the new 911 Turbo, it was almost four centimeters (1.6 in.) wider than the 997 RS. Within the generation, the base car and GT3 RS were separated by 7.2 centimeters (2.83 in.) in width.

An important difference compared to its predecessor: the 911 Turbo now had a wider body than the all-wheel-drive models. To be able to drive the maximum possible track width on the rear axle, the 911 GT3 RS had to adopt the turbo body— including its air scoops in the rear wheel arches. The GT team tried to find a purpose for them because GT boss Andreas Preuninger did not want to simply cover them: "That would not be our style."

One idea was suggested during the development phase: a cleverly designed air duct could increase downforce by acting as a sort of integrated spoiler—an interesting technique that Aston Martin, for example, used to avoid large wings. Porsche, however, chose a different path. The aerodynamic characteristics of the turbo body ensured that there was excess pressure at the openings at high speeds—enough to achieve an even better ram-air effect than over the hood. The airstream pushes into the intake tract in such a way that overpressure is created—similar to turbocharging or supercharging. It therefore made sense to tap the fresh air for the engine at the wheel arches.

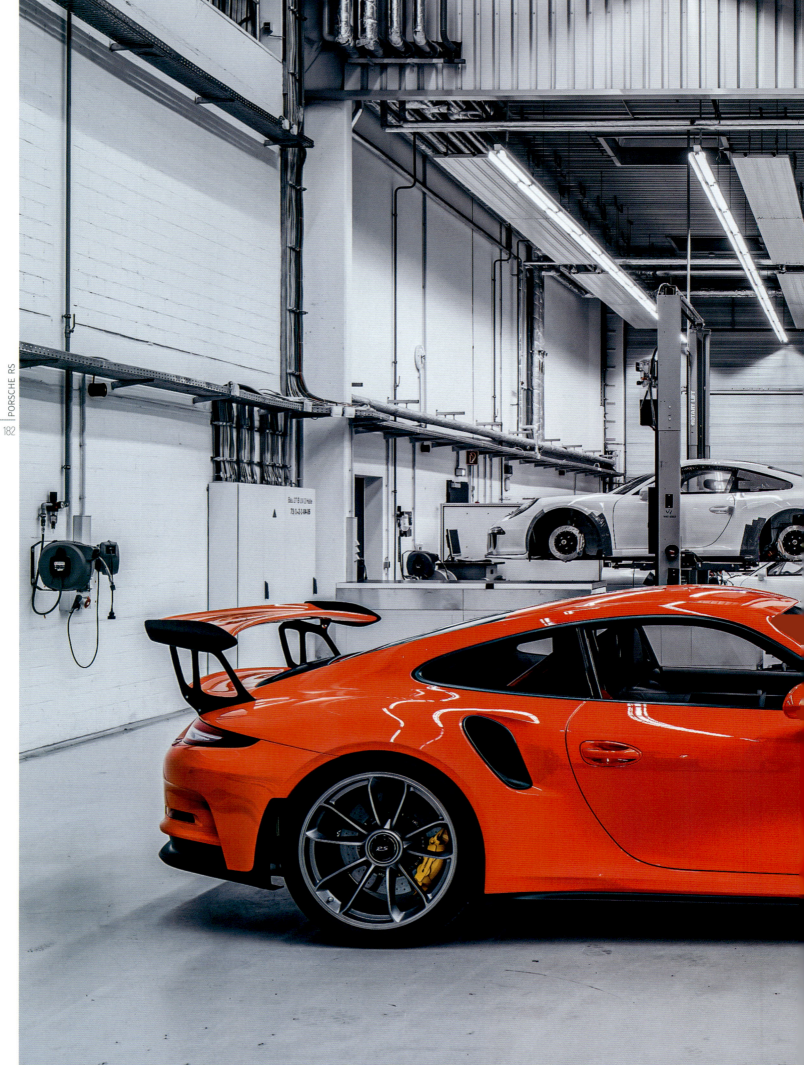

New scoops and a large wing moved the 911 GT3 RS visually a good deal closer to the racetrack. That was a good thing because it was what customers wanted.

The 911 GT3 RS's impressive aerodynamics generated a total of 345 kilograms of downforce at a speed of 310 kph.

This entailed structural measures for further air routing, because the body was actually designed to guide the air to the intercoolers of the 911 Turbo. These were located behind the rear tires. The developers worked closely with production to develop a body passage. Together, they found a solution. This measure fit in with the specifications, since customers wanted a more racing look. The wide body with the additional scoops helped here. In addition, according to Preuninger, the intake could now be heard better from the driver's seat.

345 KILOGRAMS OF DOWNFORCE

There were now also scoops on the carbon fiber front fenders, which had been widened by 4.5 centimeters (1.8 in.). They were intended to ventilate rather than aerate. They no longer allowed the airstream to flow from the wheel arches under the car to generate lift. It now flowed out of the wheel arches upward and away to the rear, a crucial detail that was difficult to homologate for a road car. However, with honeycombs and a grille underneath, approval was still possible.

These aerodynamic measures generated a downforce in the 911 GT3 RS that put all its predecessors in the shade. In this discipline, the car even rivaled the Porsche 918 Spyder hyper sports car from 2013. At top speed (310 kph, 192 mph), it generated 345 kilograms (760 lbs.) of downforce. The Cup

car outperformed it by another 20 percent. What the GT3 RS 4.0 from the previous model series achieved at 300 kph (186 mph), the new car managed at 200 kph (124 mph).

WITHOUT MEZGER FOR THE FIRST TIME

The 991 generation of the 911 GT3 RS was the first not to be powered by the legendary Mezger engine. Although it shone with its durability, it was limited in certain areas. These included internal friction and the injection system. The costs and emissions also no longer really fit the times. It was therefore replaced by a further development of the 3.8-liter six-cylinder boxer from the current 911 Carrera S.

Porsche was already converting the power unit into a high-revving engine for the 911 GT3. It was fitted with forged aluminum pistons, titanium connecting rods, and valve control via lightweight rocker arms. All that remained of the original Carrera engine was the engine block, the timing chain, and auxiliary units such as the alternator.

The engineers designed a new crankshaft for the 911 GT3 RS. It was made from the same steel alloy as that of the 919 Hybrid Le Mans prototype. It also had a stroke of 81.7 millimeters (3.2 in.), four millimeters (0.16 in.) more than the 911 GT3. This increased the displacement to 4.0 liters (244 cu. in.). To keep the piston speeds within limits, Porsche reduced the maximum speed to 8,800 rpm. Only a symbolic deficit, said Andreas Preuniger. "In the application of the engine, 9,000 rpm would not have brought any significant advantage."

Specific connecting rods, pistons, camshaft profiles, valve springs, and cylinder heads had also been added, as well as an adapted oil system. The new engine delivered 500 hp and 460 Nm (339 ft.-lbs.) of torque—conservatively stated. Nevertheless, on paper it was just as powerful as the 4.0-liter engine in the 997 GT3 RS 4.0. Was the GT3 RS stagnating?

Not at all, because the engineers' development was not necessarily about increasing performance. Preuninger called the power-to-weight ratio in the 911 GT3 RS a "sweet spot." Even without an increase in power, the car was significantly faster than all its predecessors. Expressed in the most important currency of the 911 GT3 RS: the car lapped the Nürburgring-Nordschleife in 7:20 minutes. To date, only the 620 hp 911 GT2 RS had been faster there at Porsche. Its lead was two seconds.

TECHNOLOGICAL LEAP

The 911 GT3 RS achieved these driving figures with a combination of many measures. Chistian Gebhardt summarized in *Sport Auto* after the test: "On the Nordschleife, the Porsche 911 GT3 RS shines thanks to its aerodynamics, the wider track, and the larger wheel/tire combination. . . . The turn-in behavior is like poetry. The chassis setup of the test car was very agile. As a result, it reacts noticeably to load changes, but these remain easy to control. Traction under load is fantastic thanks to the combination of the PTV Plus torque vectoring function and electronically controlled rear axle lock. The ceramic brakes impressed with their high deceleration and stability."

With the fast shift times of the newly tuned, specially applied dual-clutch transmission, the added agility thanks to steering rear wheels, the long wheelbase that calmed the body, and new, wider tires on larger rims (265/35ZR20 at the front, 325/30ZR21 at the rear), the new GT3 RS clearly outperformed its equally powerful pre-

With a wider track, longer wheelbase, and rear-axle steering, the handling of the 911 GT3 RS was significantly improved compared to its predecessor.

decessor. This was not only felt by Ring racers, but even by the Auto Quartet players: the new car sprinted to 100 kph half a second faster than the 911 GT3 RS 4.0.

At the press presentation of the car at Bilster Berg, Rally legend and Porsche ambassador Walter Röhrl categorized the characteristics: "Longitudinal dynamics and top speed are not an issue for us; that's not interesting. Where do you want to drive faster than 300 kph today?" For him, the important thing was what happened "when you drive around the corner." Röhrl described the many measures in the 911 GT3 RS as "pieces of a mosaic" that together formed a coherent picture. Porsche was particularly careful in fine-tuning the assistance systems. "They are not intended to patronize the customer, but to make the car faster," summarized Preuninger. Röhrl joked in his well-known clever way: "The only disadvantage is that even less experienced drivers can drive these cars fast. It used to be easier to stand out as a good driver."

ADDED WEIGHT AND LIGHTWEIGHT CONSTRUCTION

Contrary to the previous RS maxim, the new 911 GT3 RS now had to be heavier in order to be faster. The new wheel set, the gearbox, the rear-axle steering, the electronics—all this added weight to the car. It felt like the defined athlete of the 997 model series had to bulk up in order to perform better. The weight gain was only a disadvantage on paper. Preuninger said, "It's only annoying until you drive it. All things considered, you don't feel the extra weight."

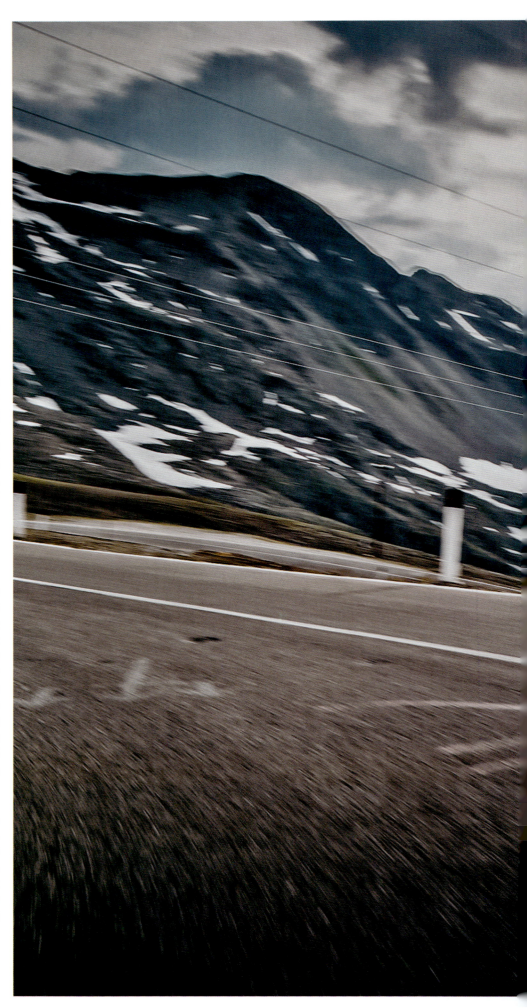

According to the standard, the 911 GT3 RS weighed 1,495 kilograms (3,295 lbs.) with driver and fuel. This was 10 kilograms (22 lbs.) less than the 911 GT3 of the same model generation, but 60 kilograms (132 lbs.) more than the old 911 GT3 RS 4.0. To achieve this weight despite the additional technology and mechanics, Porsche slimmed down the base car with old and new tricks.

The hood and fenders were made of carbon, the rear windows of plastic, and the exhaust system muffler of titanium. For the first time, Porsche had given the 911 GT3 RS a magnesium roof with a 30-centimeter-wide (11.8-in.) embossing as a reminder of the air-cooled models. The seats came from the Porsche 918 Spyder. Optional extras included ceramic brakes, a lithium-ion battery, and the elimination of the radio and air conditioning.

TIME SETS LIMITS

The new 911 GT3 RS showed how important the extreme road sports car was for Porsche—even more than its predecessors. Preuninger's team doubled in size because so many innovations were introduced into the car at the same time. A particular challenge: all the modifications had to fit into the production line of the 911—from the openings for the air ducts to the delicate fenders and the tires, which would probably not fit into the production line of many other manufacturers.

The 911 GT3 RS was a prestige project, but it also had to earn money. And it did. Porsche sold a total of 6,128 units of the car. This is not an artificial limitation, but rather the limited capacities in vehicle construction. Porsche simply did not have the time to build any more 911 GT3 RSs.

The car for purists: a slim body and no rear wing on the 911 R.

The 911 R came with a newly developed manual transmission

A slightly modified GT3 RS engine powered the 911 R.

THE ALMOST-RS FOR PURISTS

There was a plan behind this because Porsche noticed the reservations early on. During the development of the 911 GT3 and 911 GT3 RS, Preuninger himself had countless discussions about the transmission. Fans thought that only a manual transmission would suit the top-of-the-range cars. He wanted to avoid such comments in the second half of the model cycle. That is why he was having a suitable manual transmission developed for the special 911 R model. With this component on the shelf, he wanted to offer an alternative for purists in the 911 GT3 in the future. However, the 911 R idea almost went wrong. The car was presented quite spontaneously and unprepared at a board meeting. With little time and no warning, the managers were not enthusiastic about the car. Only in the weeks that followed was Preuninger able to convince the decision-makers.

The 911 R did not have a (full) RS in its name, but it was powered by an RS engine. At its rear was the 4.0-liter boxer from the GT3 RS, with 500 hp. The technology package (including rear-axle steering) was fitted into a narrow body. The plastic windows were also taken from the RS. With the manual transmission and without wings, it even weighed 70 kilograms (154 lbs.) less. The only drawback: the R "only" revved up to 8,500 rpm because its large flywheel would otherwise put too much strain on the crankshaft bearings.

Peter R. Fischer wrote in *Auto Bild* after his first drive in the 911 R that "the 911 R is exactly the driving machine that purists have wanted for so long. Agile, greedy, and always ready to set off mechanical fireworks. This 911 is the highlight of the model series." And he pleaded with customers, presumably

PORSCHE 911 R

Not everyone was happy about the new capabilities of the 911 GT3 RS. Purists criticized the automatic transmission in particular. While many a friend of raw locomotion squeezed an oil-smeared tear out of the corner of one eye, the GT team around Andreas Preuninger had long been working on a consolation. Shortly before the 911 facelift, the special 911 R model was launched, a car with a manual transmission for gentleman drivers.

Under load, the 911 GT2 RS showed its glowing red catalytic converters through the open exhaust flaps.

unsuccessfully, "Please don't put it away," because the limitation of the special model to 991 units makes the car an immediate object of speculation.

PORSCHE 911 GT2 RS

The new Porsche 911 GT2 RS made its first appearance digitally. In mid-June 2017, the racing game Forza Motorsport 7 made its debut at the E3 electronics trade fair in Los Angeles—and with it the fast 911, since it adorned the box cover of the game. It was already racing virtually during the presentation. Meanwhile, Porsche itself was still keeping quiet about the car.

700 HP AT THE REAR AXLE

The real 911 GT2 RS would not be unveiled by the manufacturer until a good two weeks later, at the Goodwood Festival of Speed. The car demonstrated its sound, speed, and traction on the 1.86-kilometer (1.16-mile) racetrack on the Earl of March's estate. Several drivers, including rally legend Walter Röhrl, demonstrated the fastest road-legal Porsche so far to the spectators.

Porsche saved itself the detour of a 911 GT2 without RS with the 991 generation. The GT2 RS was the only car that the manufacturer had positioned above the 911 Turbo S in the performance spectrum. With an output of 580 hp (607 hp in the 911 Turbo S Exclusive), there was not enough room for two more powerful GT vehicles.

WATER INJECTION FOR THE INTERCOOLERS

During the two-and-a-half-year development of the new 911 GT2 RS—nicknamed King Kong—it was initially unclear whether it would even be able to keep an appropriate distance from the 911 Turbo S. Jörg Kerner, Head of Powertrain Development, gave a sobering outlook early in the project: 620 hp, perhaps 640 hp, was possible. This would hardly make the new GT2 RS more powerful than the old one, if at all. In initial test drives, the earlier model was even faster.

Andreas Preuninger, Head of GT Vehicles, still wanted more power in his new car. He thought it should have 700 hp. The limiting factor was not the stability of the engine, but the amount of cold, oxygen-rich air available. After all, the engine could only produce such high power if there was enough oxygen in the combustion chambers. In practice, however, it was not possible to guarantee a constant supply for 700 hp in the planned application. Particularly at high outside temperatures, performance dropped under continuous load.

"King Kong" on the Nürburgring: the 911 GT2 RS topped all previous best times.

An old Lancia provided the solution to the problem: the Lancia Delta Integrale Evoluzione 16V had a special intercooling system. Preuninger's team opted for the same approach. When the air in the intake manifold was warmer than 50°C (122°F), the engine was revving faster than 3,000 rpm, and the accelerator pedal was depressed more than 90 percent, a water spray system cooled the intercoolers and thus the intake air of the 911 GT2 RS. This trick ensured that sufficient oxygen reached the combustion chambers again. The result: 700 hp was available at all temperatures.

LARGE TURBOCHARGER IN THE 911 GT2 RS

The most powerful 911 engine was based on the 3.8-liter unit of the current 911 Turbo. A lot of brainpower had gone into the engine, and not just because of the unusual intercooler. "This is anything but a chipped turbo," explained Preuninger at the press presentation of the car on the racetrack at Portimão, Portugal. Much more than simply adapting the software was required to achieve the performance level.

The engine team adapted one turbocharger per cylinder bank from the 718 Boxster or Cayman S. These are large turbochargers with variable turbine geometry for better response. The boost pressure increased from 1.3 bar (911 Turbo) to 1.55 bar or 22.5 psi (911 GT2 RS). Special pistons reduced the compression ratio from 9.5:1 to 9.0:1 to prepare the engine for the additional loads. With a view to stability, performance, and character, GT boss Preuninger proudly said, "This is one of the best GT engines we have ever made."

Preuninger had further requirements for the engine. He did not want his car to surf on a wave of torque like a turbo. It should rev up explosively and reward additional revs with even more power. The torque curve was correspondingly unusual. It described a real curve with only a short plateau. Martin Urbanke enthused after testing the car for *Autozeitung*, "The characteristics of the 700 hp power plant are similar to those of a free-breathing naturally aspirated engine—only with much, much more thrust in all positions."

SOUNDS LIKE A 930

In addition, the sporty 911 top model should not sound like a current 911 Turbo. Preuninger would prefer the sound of the legendary 930, the first 911 Turbo from 1974. To achieve this, he tried something unusual: he had a prototype driven without a muffler. The exhaust system consisted only of manifolds, turbos, catalytic converters, and tailpipes. "Not much was missing," smiled Preuninger, looking back. However, this design was a little too loud for the noise pollution laws.

The production car was therefore fitted with a lightweight titanium muffler, in part to eliminate unwanted droning in certain load ranges. However, the muffler had a flap circuit that created an exhaust gas routing based on the sound prototype. You could even see it. With the exhaust flaps open, the view of the catalytic converters was unobstructed. Under heavy use, they glowed bright red through the tailpipes.

To ensure that the 3.8-liter biturbo boxer delivered its output of 700 hp in all situations, Porsche introduced a water spray system for the intercoolers.

Limited space: the manifold, turbocharger, catalytic converter, and rear muffler were in a very confined space between the engine and rear apron.

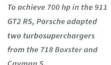

To achieve 700 hp in the 911 GT2 RS, Porsche adapted two turbosuperchargers from the 718 Boxster and Cayman S.

The 911 GT2 RS took the air outlets in the fenders from the 911 GT3 RS.

Unlike its predecessor, there was no manual gearbox in the new car. The development team had adapted the seven-speed, dual-clutch gearbox (PDK) from the Carrera models, just as it had done for the 911 GT3 RS. As there, the team implemented the "paddle-neutral" function familiar from other manufacturers. If the driver pulled both shift paddles on the steering wheel at the same time, both clutches opened. This moved the automatic a step closer to a manual transmission—and even allowed mischief if the driver so wished.

NO ALL-WHEEL DRIVE IN THE GT2 RS

In view of the enormous engine power, Porsche discussed internally the possibility of equipping the car with all-wheel drive. Preuninger rejected this idea. He wanted a light and purist car; weight was more important than outstanding traction. Chassis and tire developers agreed because they could tune a vehicle with rear-wheel drive more precisely. In addition, calculations showed that a second drive axle did not make the GT2 RS any faster. The rear-wheel-drive car did not even show any real deficits when sprinting. Porsche stated that the

911 GT2 RS accelerated to 100 kph in 2.8 seconds. *Auto Bild* even measured a tenth of a second less for the standard sprint in the test. The specially manufactured tires called Michelin Cup 2 R, fitted in the sizes 265/35ZR20 and 325/30ZR21, played a large part in these values.

Only Uniball bearings were used in the chassis. These allowed less play and made the handling more precise. Many suspension components came from the 911 GT3 RS, including the rear axle steering. Height, camber, toe, and stabilizer bars could be adjusted. New were lightweight springs, supplemented by helper springs for constant preload. A lightweight ceramic brake system was included as standard. In the press kit, Porsche described the design of the 911 GT2 RS: "The spring rates of the coil and torsion springs are designed as in motorsport. What the driver loses in comfort, he gains several times over in lateral stability."

CONTACT PRESSURE AND LIGHTWEIGHT CONSTRUCTION

The 911 GT2 RS also largely adopted aerodynamic and lightweight construction elements from the 911 GT3 RS from 2015, although the GT team had optimized it in some respects. For example, it had a larger rear wing. Scoops in the front hood guided cooling air to the front axle brakes without impairing the drag coefficient. Wider side skirts increased the surface area of the underbody. This created greater negative pressure under the car.

In the road setting, the 911 GT2 RS generated 340 kilograms (749 lbs.) of downforce at 340 kph (211 mph). With the spoilers in motorsport mode, the downforce was even 450 kilograms (992 lbs.) at top speed. Thanks to the enormous torque of 750 Nm (553 ft.-lbs.), it barely slowed down on the straights.

The roof was made of magnesium; the fenders, hood, air scoops, and many small parts in the interior were made of carbon fiber. Porsche built the front and rear panels from lightweight polyurethane. The manufacturer used lightweight glass for the rear and side windows. This weighed about as much as polycarbonate but was more resistant to scratches and breakage. The sound system and air conditioning could be left off if desired, to save even more weight. Ideally, the car weighed 1,470 kilograms (3,240 lbs.) without the driver.

The 911 GT2 RS only achieved its optimum weight for an extra charge. The Weissach package, already an option in the Porsche 918 Spyder, reduced the weight of the car by a further 30 kilograms (66 lbs.). The package included magnesium rims (minus 11.5 kilograms, or 25 lbs.) and a titanium roll bar (minus 9.5 kilograms, or 21 lbs.). In addition, the front hood, roof, stabilizers, coupling rods, and interior parts were made of carbon fiber, and it had lighter carpeting. The surcharge: 29,750 euros.

RECORD ON THE NORDSCHLEIFE

Equipped like this, the 911 GT2 RS broke the record for road cars on the Nordschleife of the Nürburgring. Porsche works driver Lars Kern drove the 20.6-kilometer comparative distance in 6:47.3 minutes on September 20, 2017. He even beat the best time set by his colleague Marc Lieb in the Porsche 918 Spyder in 2013 (6:57 minutes).

In the *Sport Auto* test report, Christian Gebhardt described the behavior of the 911 GT2 RS on the legendary Eifel circuit: "The phenomenal lap time is primarily due to the good drivability of the Biturbo RS. The suspension setup with high mechanical grip and the aerodynamic concept with plenty of downforce give the powerful 911 largely neutral handling. The very good control setup of the rear axle steering, the electronically controlled rear axle differential lock, the ABS, and not least the traction control are also responsible for the good drivability." The editor's lap time: 6:57 minutes.

The strong competition repeatedly challenged the 911 GT2 RS. First Lamborghini undercut it with the Aventador SVJ LP770-4 (6:44.97 minutes), then Mercedes with the AMG GT Black Series (6:43.62 minutes). Porsche reclaimed the title—together with the Manthey-Racing racing team, the 911 GT2 RS MR was created with modifications to the aerodynamics and chassis. Lars Kern improved his time to 6:38.84 minutes with this car in June 2021. On October 28, 2022, professional racing driver Maro Engel set a fabulous new time with a 1,000 hp Mercedes-AMG One: 6:30.705 minutes. However, to achieve this lead of just over eight seconds, Mercedes built a road-legal Formula 1 racer. Its list price: 3.27 million euros—ten times the price of a 911 GT2 RS with a Manthey upgrade.

The most powerful 911 felt much rawer than the less powerful derivatives.

The optional Weissach package eliminated 30 kilograms, in part with a titanium roll bar.

THE RETURN OF "MOBY DICK"

A very special car was being created based on the 911 GT2 RS. In 2018, Porsche was redesigning it in the style of the 1970s racing cars. Specifically, its shape was reminiscent of the Porsche 935/78, which fans of the time affectionately referred to as "Moby Dick" due to its elongated shape, imposing widening, and white bodywork.

Porsche presented itself and its fans with the new 935 to mark the big sports car anniversary. On June 8, 1948, Porsche 356 No. 1 received its operating license. A good seventy years later, the manufacturer celebrated the milestone birthday with a limited special edition. Curious: this car of all cars did not receive a license.

The new Porsche 935 was a club sports car without road approval or homologation. It did not follow any motorsport rules. It was therefore only suitable for club sport events or racetrack training—if it was driven at all. It could not be driven on the road or even in an endurance race. Strictly speaking, it was therefore a car without a purpose. But that did not detract from its fascination.

With it, Porsche cited the important milestones in its own motorsport history. From the wooden-look gear knob (909 Bergspyder, 917) to titanium tailpipes (908), narrow LED brake lights (919 Spyder), and aerodynamically clad rims (935), to the carbon steering wheel (911 R), it had several details on board that belonged to the brand.

The 935 took over many parts of the chassis and the drivetrain from the 911 GT2 RS. With a welded-in cage, carbon-fiber add-on parts, a steel brake system with racing pads, and wide 18-inch rims, Porsche made the car fit for the racetrack. A white base coat came as standard, with Martini decor as an option. Porsche limited production of the 935 to seventy-seven units. In Germany, the car cost 835,318.12 euros.

While Porsche established turbochargers in the 911 base models, the 911 GT3 RS got a more powerful naturally aspirated engine.

For safety: the roll bar was standard on board in Europe. The car could be had without it at no extra charge.

PORSCHE 911 GT3 RS

A number sequence steeped in history almost made it into the facelifted 911. Porsche tested boxer engines with a displacement of 2.7 liters before the car went into series production. In 1972, this marked the sporting peak of the 911 Carrera RS 2.7. A little later, it became the standard in the 911. The benchmark almost returned in the new 911 Carrera; however, the developers opted for engines with a displacement of 3.0 liters. For the first time in 911 history, they were also equipped with turbochargers below the 911 Turbo.

9,000 RPM

While Porsche had made the biggest technical change to the 911 base models since the introduction of water cooling, the 911 GT3 RS appeared to

No record, but a reason to celebrate: the 911 GT3 RS raced around the Nürburgring Nordschleife in less than seven minutes.

keep much the same. The new model remained true to the high-revving, naturally aspirated engine. Nevertheless, the car had changed significantly for the facelift. In the spec sheet, this can be seen in one figure in particular: the engine's maximum speed was now 9,000 rpm. This figure is highly symbolic, especially in communication. The fact that the new 4.0-liter, naturally aspirated engine of the GT3 RS revved so high would delight any motorsport fan. But just like top speed (312 kph) and acceleration (3.2 seconds to 100 kph), it was only a pleasant side effect, not the development goal—because that was efficiency.

AN ALMOST NEW ENGINE

Porsche achieved the high engine speed with a design innovation. The engine had a fixed valve train. Hydraulic valve lash adjustment was no longer required. In this way, Porsche simplified the valve train enormously. Unlike in the past, the valve lash in the new 911 GT3 RS did not have to be

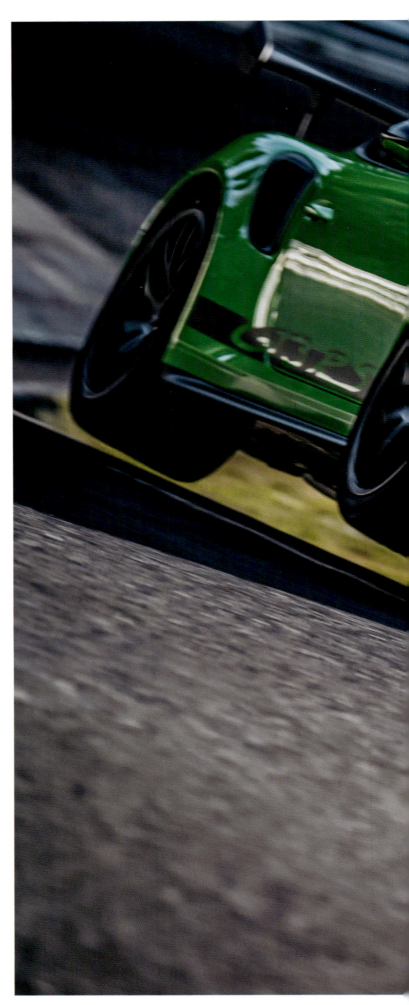

adjusted manually on a regular basis. The factory setting was good for 300,000 kilometers (186,000 miles)—virtually for life.

The engineers had thus eliminated the biggest disadvantage of a fixed valve train, making it possible to benefit from its advantages. This was because the lightweight rocker arms allowed more speed. And the engine required much less oil in the cylinder heads. This resulted in reduced oil volumes and reduced oil pressure. The oil pump had to work less.

To implement this modification, Porsche built new cylinder heads. They had the familiar combustion chambers and valves, but modifications to the valve train and oil circuit. In addition, narrower piston rings and a new coating on the cylinder liners were used. All these measures reduced internal friction enormously. Andreas Preuninger, Head of GT Vehicles, summarized: "Everything about the engine is easier. We have de-throttled it, which means we have significantly reduced the frictional power and internal resistance." The engine's higher cutoff speed enabled more power in combination with new camshafts. The 4.0-liter, naturally aspirated engine now delivered 520 hp and 470 Nm (346 ft.-lbs.). Preuninger added, "There was a lot of racing technology in it, which was incredibly noticeable in the engine. Although we only had a nominal 20 hp more, the car drove completely differently."

FINE-TUNING OF THE AERODYNAMICS, CHASSIS, AND TRANSMISSION

Three years after the first 911 GT3 RS of the Type 991, Preuninger's team had gathered a lot of experience with the 991. The new car had the large rear wing of the 911 GT2 RS and its new air ducting at the front. Scoops in the front hood supplied the front axle brakes with fresh air. All air intakes in the front section now worked for the aerodynamics. At top speed, the car generated a total of almost 500 kilograms of downforce. Porsche had also adapted the chassis from the 911 GT2 RS. In contrast to its direct predecessor, elasto-kinematic bearings were no longer used, but only Uniball bearings. These measures ensured "even greater precision." The surcharge list also included Michelin Cup 2 R tires.

Programming was now also part of the 911 GT3 RS's fine-tuning. The new edition had been given a revised steering characteristic and shorter shift times in the seven-speed,

dual-clutch transmission. "We have gained 10 to 15 percent in many areas. All in all, that added up to quite a lot," said Preuninger, describing the development of the car.

IMPRESSIVE REVIEWS

Porsche proved just how much the car had changed with these modifications in April 2018. Racing driver Kévin Estre lapped the Nordschleife of the Nürburgring in 6:56.4 minutes—twenty-four seconds faster than its direct predecessor, and one minute faster than the 911 GT3 from 1999. "The GT3 RS is incredibly close to our GT3 R racing car, especially in the fast corners and under braking," said Estre after his record lap. For the *Sport Auto* test, Christian Gebhardt drove around the Nordschleife in the new 911 GT3 RS hardly any slower. His lap time was 7:05 minutes. Gebhardt summarized: "The level of driving dynamics perfection that the cornering hero 911 GT3 RS has now achieved is simply sensational. The drivability on the racetrack is fantastic. A lot of detailed work has gone into this, which deserves the highest praise for the developers. One example of this is the ABS setup. This is not the only area where Porsche's GT team is now far ahead of the competition."

In the *Autozeitung* test, Paul Englert emphasized the stress on the driver: "The Porsche 911 GT3 RS Type 991.2 is the most dynamic and at the same time most balanced super sports car I have ever tested. Porsche's development department has managed to compose such a harmonious ensemble from the complex systems of steering, chassis, aerodynamics, and drivetrain that there is basically no way to improve on it. The real highlight of this test, however, is the Michelin Pilot Sport Cup 2 R, which takes the 911 to a higher level of driving dynamics. After almost 15 racetrack laps, I can only admit: This thing really kills you!"

WITH THE WEISSACH PACKAGE FOR THE FIRST TIME

The 911 GT3 RS achieved its best performance in its lightest form. As with the 918 Spyder and 911 GT2 RS, this was now

available as an extra. The Weissach package contained lightweight construction elements that were not included as standard. With a total weight savings of 30 kilograms (66 lbs.), it made the car even more suitable for use on the racetrack. The scope of the package was the same as that of the GT2 RS. In return for a surcharge of 17,850 euros, the 911 GT3 RS weighed just 1,430 kilograms (3,152 lbs.).

As before, Porsche offered the Clubsport package in the 911 GT3 RS at no extra charge. It included a steel roll bar, a fire extinguisher, a pre-installation for a battery isolator, and a six-point seat belt for the driver.

GREEN FROM THE G SERIES

The new 911 GT3 RS made its public debut at the Geneva Motor Show in Lizard Green. Designer Barbara Sika explained the tactic behind the eye-catching color to Porsche magazine *Christophorus*: "The lizard green 911 GT3 RS should catch people's eyes and draw them into the showroom."

The fact that the car wore this color was due to a coincidence. In 2015, Andreas Preuninger attended the "Rennsport Reunion," an event organized by Porsche at Laguna Seca. There, he noticed a visitor's Porsche 911 G in the parking lot. The car was painted yellow-green, and the color inspired him so much that he took a photo of it and sent it to the design department. There, this inspiration became the communication color for the 911 GT3 RS. It appeared in lizard green at every opportunity. Alternatively, Porsche sold the car in white, black, Indian red, racing yellow, GT silver metallic, chalk, Miami blue, and lava orange.

The 911 GT3 RS took its rear wing from the GT2 RS. Its new engine produced 20 hp more than its predecessor.

992

PORSCHE PREPARED THE 911 SERIES FOR THE FUTURE. WITH THE MODEL CHANGE FROM TYPE 991 TO 992, THE SPORTS CAR RETAINED ITS BASIC ARCHITECTURE.

A present for a milestone birthday: to mark the fiftieth anniversary of the 911 Carrera RS 2.7, the 911 GT3 RS model 992 made its debut in a classic color scheme.

Nevertheless, the car was changing. A newly developed eight-speed, dual-clutch gearbox was able to accommodate an electric motor. Double floors in the body created space for batteries. The 911 had been hybrid-capable since 2019, but not hybridized for the time being.

The dimensions of the 911 hardly changed with the model change. Its front section was two centimeters longer than its predecessor so that the car could keep pace in terms of pedestrian protection and assistance. The new gadgets included a night vision system and an automatic wet mode. All the sheet metal parts of the 992 were new, even if they did not look it. Its headlights were slightly steeper, and the rear lights were flatter. The narrow rear-wheel-drive body had been dropped; the 911 Carrera already had wide all-wheel-drive hips.

The interior of the 911 became digital. Only the rev counter, which was still centrally positioned, was analog. Displays around it take over the tasks of the instruments. The 911 adopted the infotainment system from the front-engined Panamera and Cayenne. In this context, many buttons disappeared from the interior. Their functions were now hidden in menus.

Extensive changes to the familiar engines reduced particulate emissions and improved the spontaneity of throttle response. The basic engine of the 992 generation now delivered 385 hp. With 650 hp, the 911 Turbo S almost reached the level of the discontinued 911 GT2 RS. And the GT department was working on new, extreme RS models.

PORSCHE 911 GT3 RS

The 911 GT3 RS occupies a special position in the Porsche portfolio. Performance is more important to it than comfort. It has been without a rear seat since its first edition. In the 992 generation, the developers went one step further—the GT team eliminated the small trunk under the front hood.

SPEED BEFORE LUGGAGE COMPARTMENT

Whereas normal 911s could at least transport hand luggage, a large radiator in the new 911 GT3 RS kept the operating fluids at the right temperature. No great loss in an RS model, but a major change in the concept of the vehicle. This conversion was the first component in a complicated aerodynamic mosaic that made the model probably the sportiest road-legal Porsche ever built.

Up to now, Porsche had distributed three radiators behind the front apron in all road-legal 911s. In the 911 GT3 RS, however, even such constants were up for debate because, to set itself apart from its predecessors, the car had to change. Aerodynamics was once again an important anchor point. "We spent a good 250 hours in the wind tunnel, more than twice as long as the predecessor," reported Porsche's GT Director Andreas Preuninger.

860 KILOGRAMS OF DOWNFORCE

The new GT3 RS directed the airstream more precisely than any of its predecessors. Scoops in the front hood channeled the warm radiator exhaust air to the sides of the vehicle. Fins on the roof edges ensured that it did not get into the intake tract but flowed past the car. Instead, the engine breathed in cold, fresh air.

The Type 992 took up an idea that emerged during the development of

Part of the ingenious aerodynamics: the single radiator concept with S-shaped air flow through the front end (S-duct layout).

For the first time, the rear spoiler of a production Porsche towered above the roof of the car.

The air scoops in the side panels no longer collected the process air in the Type 992. Instead, they improved the aerodynamics.

Every opening on the body of the 911 GT3 RS had a function. The only exception: two blind covers at the rear of the vehicle. Porsche labeled them "No Vent."

Fifty years of difference: 911 Carrera RS 2.7 (1972) and 911 GT3 RS (2022) were the aerodynamic flagship cars of their time. While at the beginning of the Porsche 911's RS history, a small ducktail at the rear was sufficient, this top model had active air guidance systems and extensive conversion measures for ideal airflow.

the GT3 RS (991.1). The car once again used the body of the 911 Turbo, including the side inlets. However, these no longer collected the intake air for the engine but instead channeled it around the wheel arches to the rear. In this way, they contributed to the car's downforce. Preuninger explained the division of tasks: "The aerodynamics come from the motorsport department, which also develops the GT racing cars. You notice this on every meter; the GT3 RS drives extremely precisely."

The center radiator concept came directly from the 911 RSR and 911 GT3 R racing cars. With a large radiator under the front hood, there was space in the front of the vehicle for optimized airflow. In combination with the new rear wing, which for the first time extended beyond the vehicle roof, a downforce of 409 kilograms (901 lbs.) was generated at 200 kph (124 mph). At a speed of 285 kph (177 mph), the car even generated 860 kilograms (1,895 lbs.) of downforce. Preuninger drew an abstractive comparison: "Then there are two horses on the roof."

DRAG REDUCTION FROM FORMULA 1

The enormous downforce resulted in a deficit on long straights. Porsche had therefore designed a way of temporarily reducing downforce for the 911 GT3 RS. Active aerodynamic elements behind the front apron and on the rear wing could be moved into a position that reduced drag at the touch of a button—making the car more streamlined. This was a so-called Drag Reduction System (DRS), as used in Formula 1 and the DTM. The system also had an important function. "The DRS regulates and synchronizes the wings in a third of a second for permanent, optimal aero balance," explained Preuninger. "The aerodynamic balance of 70 percent at the rear and 30 percent at the front always remains constant, completely whether accelerating, braking, or cornering. This means that the GT3 RS drives like it's on rails and is very close to the RSR."

The active aerodynamics automatically supported emergency braking with an air brake function. This reduced the braking distance from 200 kph (124 mph) by 2.5 meters (8.2 ft.). With the airflow in a streamlined position, the car accelerated faster. "Drivers can control the system by using the DRS switch on the steering wheel. Or the system can also regulate itself automatically if required," summarized Preuninger.

The customers and fans of the 911 GT3 RS always wanted more visual proximity to motorsport. That is why every opening, every grille, and every hood on the body of the new 911 GT3 RS had a function. With one exception: there is a blind opening on the outside of the rear bumper. The words "No Vent" are written on it. Even in the uncompromising sports Porsche, there is room for a little Easter Egg.

The spoiler system of the new 911 GT3 RS produced up to 860 kilograms of downforce.

New buttons on the steering wheel of the 911 GT3 RS adjusted important parameters. These included . . .

. . . rebound and compression damping of the suspension as well as the setting of the traction control.

DIRECT SUSPENSION ADJUSTMENT

In addition to the aerodynamics, other elements of the 911 GT3 RS could be adjusted from the driver's seat. New rotary wheels on the steering wheel controlled important functions that influenced handling. These included the adjustment of the rebound and compression stages of the shock absorbers, separately for the front and rear axles. Such adjustments were usually made mechanically on the shock absorbers. The transverse lock (separately for load and push mode), traction control, and ESP could also be adjusted at the steering wheel.

Porsche also optimized the suspension itself. The wishbones on the front axle were designed in a teardrop shape to contribute to downforce. In addition, the car dips less under braking than its predecessor. To achieve this, the chassis engineers moved the front ball joint of the lower trailing arm farther down and adjusted the rear axle suspension. This improved the vehicle balance.

ONLY SLOWER ON THE STRAIGHTS

A new 911 GT3 RS did not necessarily have to outperform its predecessor on the spec sheet. But it had to better it on the racetrack. The development goal was always a more drivable car. Ego-relevant dimensions such as top speed and acceleration hardly counted. That was why no customer would be disappointed that the 992 model 911 GT3 RS had a top speed of 296 kph, 16 kph slower than the previous model. After all, a few more kilometers per hour at the top end of the scale are of little use on the racetrack. A lot of downforce in the corners and more traction when accelerating, on the other hand, help a lot. This is why Porsche preferred to opt for extreme aerodynamics and a short ratio of the seven-speed, dual-clutch transmission, which is adapted from that of the predecessor.

The engine of the 911 GT3 RS was still based on that of its predecessor. It now produced 525 hp, almost 1 percent more than before. In its current form, it had optimized camshaft profiles and an improved individual throttle system and continued to have a fixed valve train. As before, it revved up to a maximum of 9,000 rpm. The car could not comply with emissions regulations at higher revs.

CARBON-FIBER DOORS FOR THE FIRST TIME

Lightweight construction remained an important topic for the 911 GT3 RS. Like its predecessors, the new model relied on carbon fiber. In addition to the front fenders, the hood, and the roof, the doors were also made of this lightweight material for the first time. What sounded like a logical step was not particularly trivial. "It was an incredible challenge to use carbon-fiber doors in a legally approved road car. It has been around in motorsport for a long time, but there we also drive with a rigid roll cage with cross struts in front of the doors. We do not have that in a production car, which means the door must withstand a side

Despite its 525hp engine, the 911 GT3 RS of the Type 992 could not reach 300 kph, but it did shine with its unique aerodynamics.

crash and be designed differently," explained Preuninger. This was achieved in the 911 GT3 RS with struts that were integrated into the door. The sporty top model did without the folding door handles of the other 992 derivatives.

As in the predecessor, the Weissach package brought further lightweight elements into the car on request (surcharge: 35,992 euros). Stabilizer bars and roll bars were then made of carbon fiber, the rims optionally of magnesium. The package also included shift buttons with magnetic operation and visible carbon on the bodywork. The total weight saving was 19.4 kilograms (42.75 lbs.).

Stefan Helmreich described the shift feel with the new paddle shifters in *Sport Auto*: "A minor detail? Allegedly. Because the effect is enormous: the defined pressure point creates an imaginary connection to the gears; the metallic click refines the short-and-painless shifting process into a sensual act."

IMPRESSIVE ON THE NORDSCHLEIFE

Unlike on its predecessors, the air conditioning and infotainment system in the 992 generation 911 GT3 RS could not be removed. The components were too integrated into the vehicle to justify the weight savings logistically. They were therefore included as standard. With a lot of new technology on board, the vehicle weight increased by 20 kilograms (44 lbs.) to 1,450 kilograms (3,196 lbs.) compared to its predecessor (plus 1.4 percent). However, this was not the first time in RS history that a heavier car achieved best times on the racetrack without much extra power.

The reference track for Porsche's fastest road cars is the Nordschleife of the Nürburgring—Porsche brand ambassador Jörg Bergmeister lapped the "Green Hell" in the 911 GT3 RS in 6:49.328 minutes on October 5, 2022. Despite driving into the wind on the Döttinger Höhe and competing on cold asphalt, he beat his predecessor's best time by 11.5 seconds. He was a good ten seconds off the current fastest Porsche, the 911 GT2 RS (991.2).

Bergmeister praised the car after his lap: "The 911 GT3 RS is in a league of its own, especially in the fast sections. Here, the car is at a level that is otherwise only known from high-class racing cars. The car also sets new standards in braking. It makes fast runs on the Nordschleife so much fun."

After the first test drive on the racetrack at Silverstone, Helmreich confirmed this description. "The GT3 RS is a driving dynamics sensation that remains a toy despite the seriousness of its intentions—thanks to the many setting options for the chassis and drive," he wrote in *Sport Auto*. British journalist Chris Harris took the same opportunity to state succinctly and bluntly, "It feels like a bloody racing car to me!"

Matt Saunders went into more detail in the British magazine *Autocar*: "The GT3 RS is clearly a more serious and purposeful track tool than any of its predecessors. But it's also cleverer and more adaptable." It therefore brought the RS concept from 1972 into the modern age—even if this contradicted the car's original simplicity.

The 992 911 Sport Classic was based on the 911 Turbo. Unlike its base, it had a manual transmission.

PORSCHE 911 SPORT CLASSIC

What the wind tunnel shaped in 1972, the Porsche design department still found chic in 2022. To mark the anniversary of the 911 Carrera RS 2.7, Porsche gave itself a new 911 with a duck tail. It bore the name 911 Sport Classic. And, much like its ancestor from 2009 (997), in addition to the traditional spoilers, it also had a double-domed roof, a special gray color, and Fuchs-designed rims.

What was new, however, was the wide turbo body—and the turbo engine. Porsche reduced the output of the 3.8-liter engine, which normally produced at least 580 hp, to 550 hp for the special model. Now unusual: the manufacturer combined the engine with a manual seven-speed gearbox including intermediate throttle function. This made the Sport Classic the most powerful manual 911 in the 992 model series.

The special model also took the sports suspension with adjustable dampers (PASM) and the braking system from the Turbo. The rear-wheel drive saved weight. Nevertheless, the 911 Sport Classic was not about lap or sprint times, but about driving experience and history. The anniversary car cost at least 281,758 euros. Porsche limited the model to 1,250 units—five times as many as its predecessor from 2009.

THE OTHER RS MODELS

THE RS ABBREVIATION HAS EXISTED AT PORSCHE LONGER THAN THE 911. BUT IT'S THE FLAGSHIP SPORTS CAR THAT SUSTAINABLY CARRIES THE LETTERS. EVERY GENERATION OF THE 911 GETS AT LEAST ONE RS MODEL.

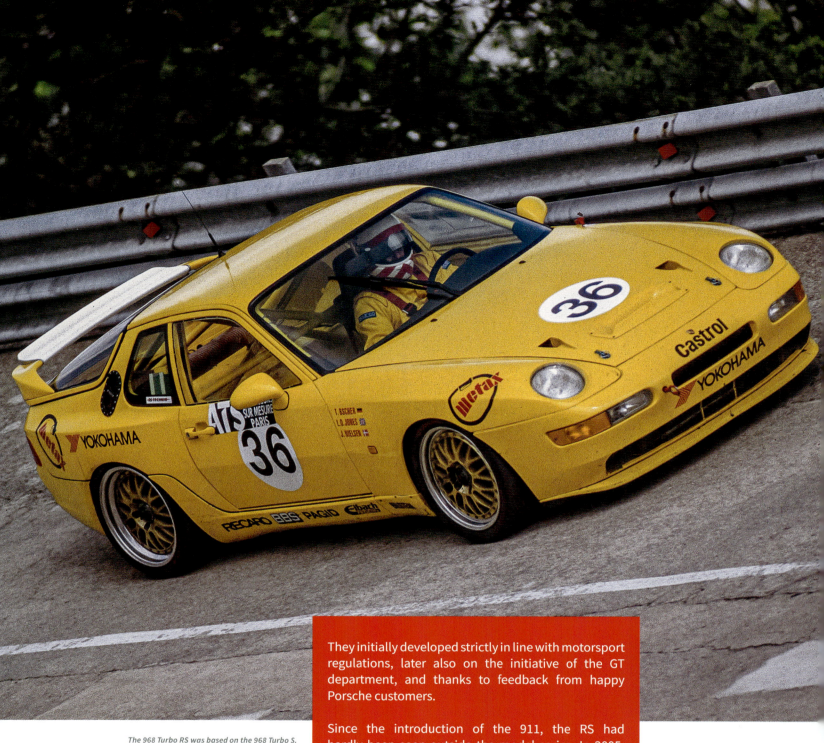

The 968 Turbo RS was based on the 968 Turbo S. Porsche built it for private teams for competition in the new GT class. The German team Seikel Motorsport with the driver trio of John Nielsen / Thomas Bscher / Lindsay Owen-Jones contested the thirteenth 1,000 km Race of Paris at the Autodrome de Linas-Montlhéry on May 29, 1994, with the vehicle shown here. However, retirement prevented a countable result in this fourth race of the BPR Global GT Series that year.

They initially developed strictly in line with motorsport regulations, later also on the initiative of the GT department, and thanks to feedback from happy Porsche customers.

Since the introduction of the 911, the RS had hardly been seen outside the model series. In 2005, Porsche presented the Spyder RS, an LMP2 vehicle for endurance racing without any connection to production cars. In 2008, a special Boxster model bore the name RS 60 Spyder to honor the 718 RS 60 Spyder from 1960. In neither case was it an RS model in the classic sense.

But they did exist, the RS models outside Porsche's rear-engine bubble. Porsche only produced them in homeopathic doses. Their rarity holds a fascination all its own.

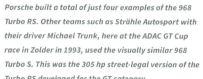
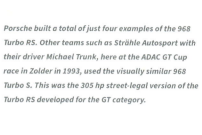

Porsche built a total of just four examples of the 968 Turbo RS. Other teams such as Strähle Autosport with their driver Michael Trunk, here at the ADAC GT Cup race in Zolder in 1993, used the visually similar 968 Turbo S. This was the 305 hp street-legal version of the Turbo RS developed for the GT category.

Porsche had no plans for series production: the 968 Turbo RS was a thoroughbred racing car.

The car did take part in the ADAC GT Cup, which would be held in Germany from 1993, with guest starts in Belgium (Zolder), the Netherlands (Zandvoort), and Austria (Salzburg).

PORSCHE 968 TURBO RS

FOUR WITH FOUR

When Group C ended in 1992, Porsche adapted its portfolio. The manufacturer developed a racing version of the Porsche 968, based on the 968 Turbo S, for the ADAC GT Cup, introduced in 1993. The model series was threatened with extinction due to a lack of success. An appearance in motorsport was intended to improve its reputation and sales figures.

Porsche called the race car the 968 Turbo RS. There were no plans for factory use. Instead, private teams were to win with it in the new GT class and in endurance races. To this end, the manufacturer retuned the springs and dampers, installed a racing clutch and a cage, fit 9.5 x 18 and 11 x 18-inch rims, and reduced the car's weight to 1,200 kilograms. With modifications to the turbocharger, intake tract, and exhaust system, the 3.0-liter four-cylinder engine, with 305 hp in the production model, now produced 350 hp.

The ADAC GT Cup stipulated a minimum weight of 1,350 kilograms (2,976 lbs.). For this purpose, ballast was added to the car. In addition, the regulations stipulated a power-to-weight ratio of 4 kilograms (8.8 lbs.) per horsepower to ensure equal opportunities. For this purpose, Porsche reduced engine output to 337.5 hp.

In its first race on the Avus in Berlin, the opening event of the newly created ADAC GT Cup, a 968 Turbo RS (Team Joest, driver Manuel Reuter, starting number 34, here at Zolder) finished fourth—the highlight of its career.

NO SUCCESS IN MOTORSPORT

The motorsport history of the 968 Turbo RS got off to a slow start. Porsche loaned the first 968 Turbo RS—the test and photo vehicle based on a Turbo S—to the Joest racing team because their car was not ready in time. This allowed Manuel Reuter to take part in the first GT races on the AVUS and in Zolder for Joest in the new racing Porsche.

In Berlin, Reuter was able to take the lead from third place at the start. He finished the race in fourth place—the highlight of the 968 Turbo RS's racing history. In Belgium, the 968 retired with a technical defect. A short time later, Joest received the car he had ordered and raced it at the Nürburgring. The car crashed shortly after the start.

In total, only four examples of the 968 Turbo RS were built, including the prototype with Turbo S chassis. There was little interest in the car, in part because Porsche already offered an established endurance car in the form of the 911. The brief motorsport intermezzo could not save the 968. It was discontinued with the 1995 model year.

In private hands, the vehicles built continued to take part in races, including at Le Mans and Spa. One example was subsequently given a road license. The 968 remained Porsche's only RS model with a transaxle chassis. And it became the rarest Porsche RS ever.

2021

2021

The first mid-engine RS of the modern era: Porsche's GT department optimized the 718 Cayman.

PORSCHE 718 CAYMAN GT4 RS

PORSCHE 718 CAYMAN GT4 RS

It took almost fifty years for Porsche to convert a production car other than the 911 into an RS model. The basis for this RS exotic was the compact and lightweight Porsche 718 Cayman. This was already available as the purist 718 Cayman GT4, as well as the 718 Cayman GT4 Clubsport for the racetrack. In November 2021, Porsche would unveil the wiry and powerful 718 Cayman GT4 RS as the top model in the series.

MID-ENGINE SPORTS CAR

The fast Cayman took its engine from the Porsche 911 GT3 (992). It was the 4.0-liter, naturally aspirated boxer engine that also powered the 911 GT3 Cup racing car in

The 718 Cayman GT4 RS was powered by the 4.0-liter boxer engine, producing 500 hp.

almost identical form. It had a fixed valve train and revved to a maximum of 9,000 rpm. In the Cayman GT4 RS, it delivered 500 hp and a maximum torque of 450 Nm (331 ft.-lbs.).

In the 911 derivatives, the engine was in the rear of the vehicle. For use in the Cayman mid-engined car, it was rotated by 180 degrees and modified at various points. These mainly concerned the oil circuit as well as the intake air and exhaust gas routing. A longer exhaust system increased the back pressure and reduced performance. The fact that the engine in the Cayman GT4 RS delivered 10 hp less than in the 911 GT3 was not a stable order to maintain the hierarchy, but a design-related consequence.

A manual gearbox was not an option during development. On the one hand, it cost time on the racetrack despite its lower weight. On the other hand, Porsche did not have a suitable gearbox in its range. The manual transmission of the 718 Cayman GT4 was not designed for the torque and speed of the RS engine.

THE FIRST AND MODERN 718

The 718 Cayman GT4 underwent an RS makeover that only the Porsche 911 could match. Lightweight construction, optimized suspension and brakes, grippy tires, and different aerodynamics with a focus on downforce improved its racetrack capabilities enormously. The GT4 RS lapped the Nordschleife of the Nürburgring in 7:04.511 minutes—23.6 seconds faster than the 718 GT4 without RS.

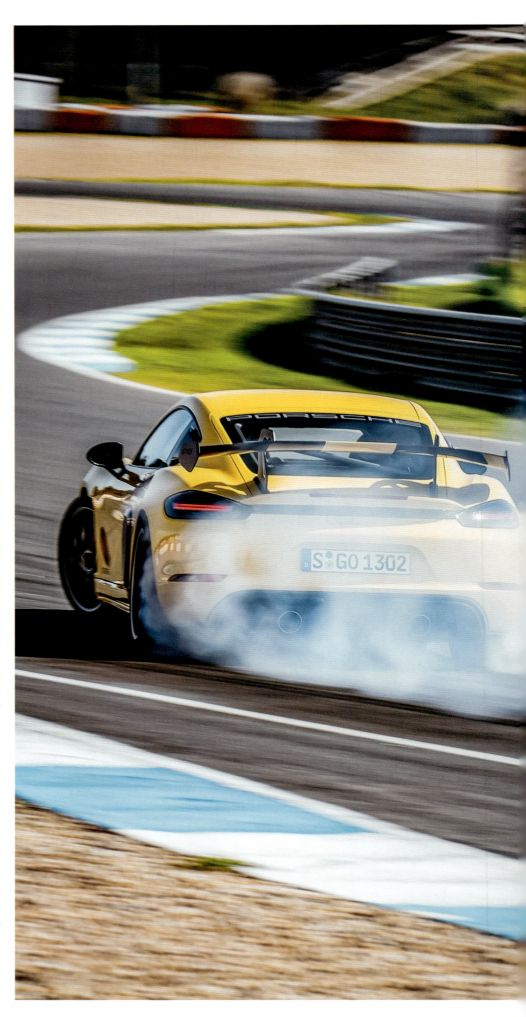

Porsche tuned the 718 Cayman GT4 RS precisely—but it still drove wildly.

The 718 Cayman GT4 RS drew in its process air directly behind the side windows—very close to the passengers' ears.

One of the last of its kind: Porsche installed a naturally aspirated engine in the 718 Cayman GT4 RS. As of 2025, the new generation of the model will be all electric.

Optionally, the audio system and air conditioning can be left off the Cayman GT4 RS.

As in the larger RS models: a strap for opening the door . . .

. . . and a twelve o'clock mark on the steering wheel.

For this time, Porsche adapted the front axle of the 911 GT3 RS (991.2 generation), including helper springs, gentle lowering, and adjustment options for toe, camber, and stabilizer bars. Uniball bearings increased precision, while a wider track reduced body roll. It came with adaptive dampers, a mechanical limited slip differential, and a brake system with discs made from an aluminum-gray cast iron composite as standard. Ceramic discs and magnesium rims were available as an option.

A rear wing with gooseneck, fenders with front wheel arch ventilation, and a new front lip increased downforce by 25 percent compared to the GT4. Carbon elements, reduced insulation, fewer trim parts, and thin glass panels reduced the weight by 35 kilograms. With the optional Weissach package and the omission of air conditioning and audio system, the weight was further reduced to 1,415 kilograms (3,119 lbs.). This made the Cayman lighter than a 911 GT3 RS. An open-top version based on the 718 Boxster, called the 718 Spyder RS, was launched in 2023.

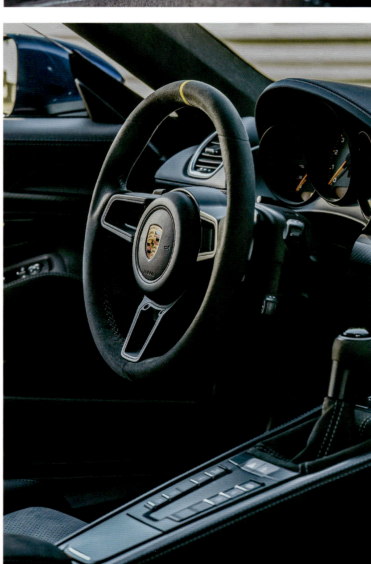

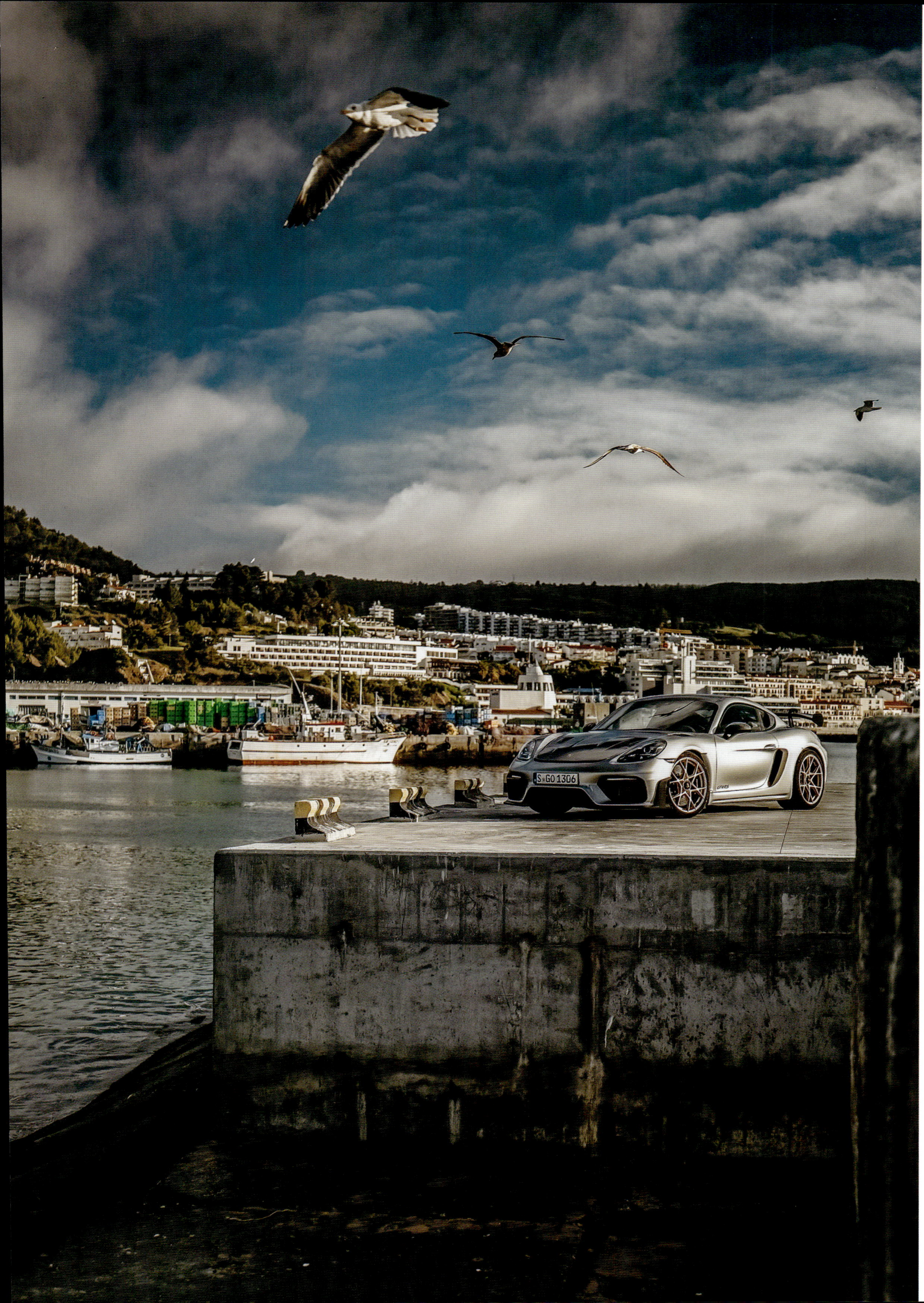

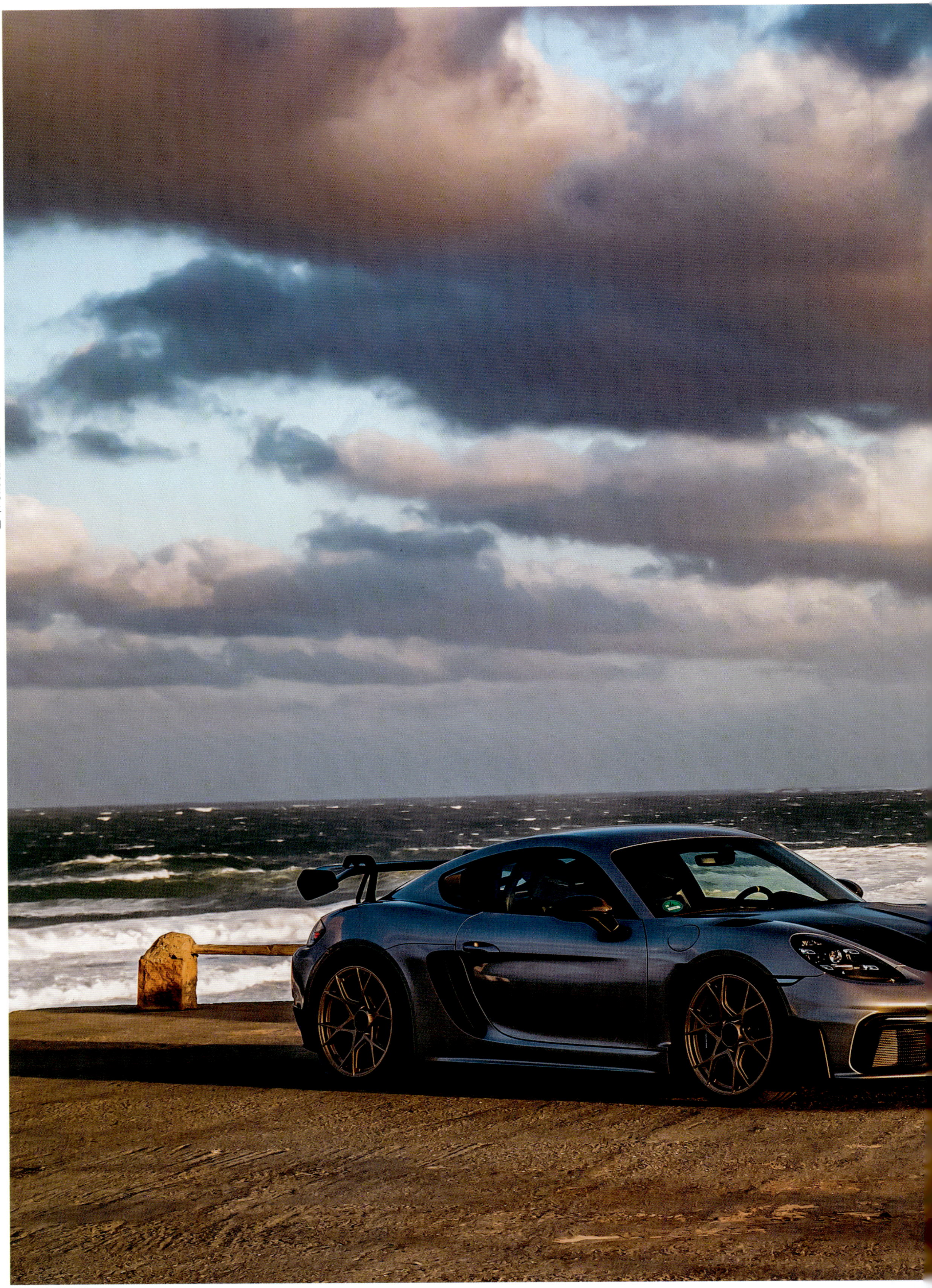

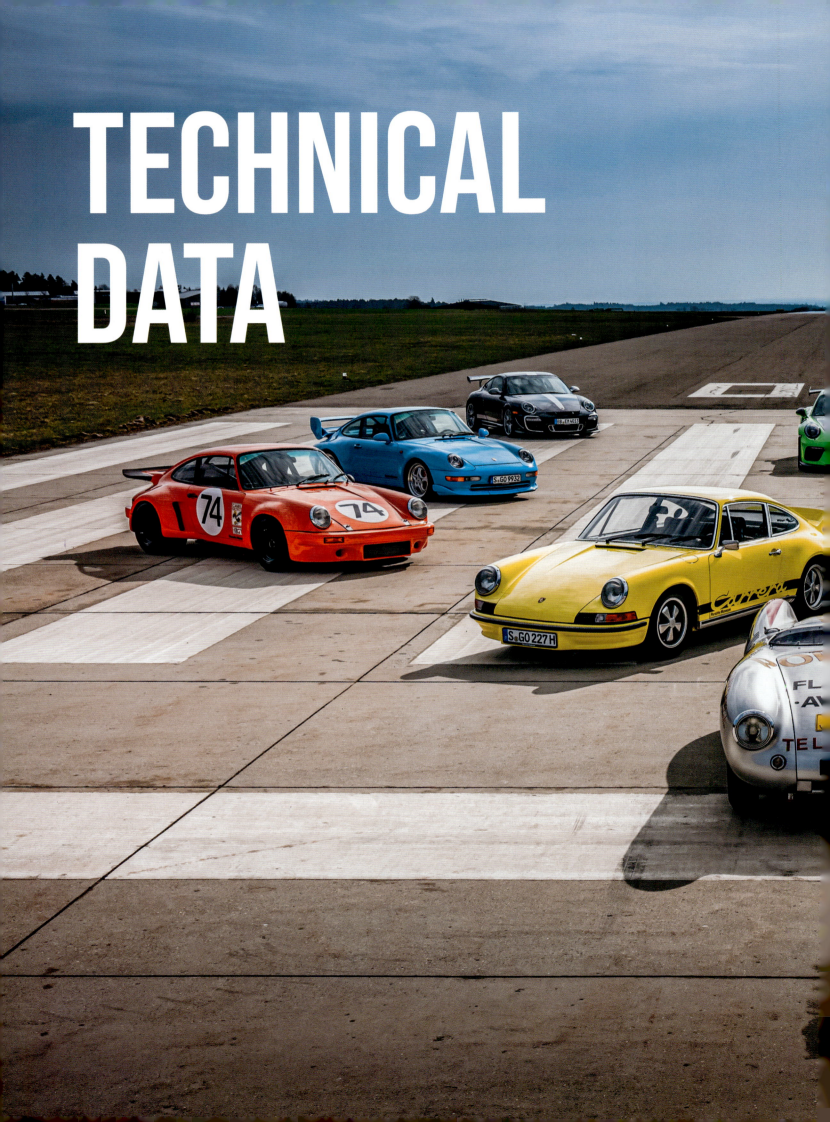

TECHNICAL DATA

911 CARRERA RS 2.7 SPORT

	Series	911 F Model
Model	Sales designation	911 Carrera RS 2.7 Sport (M471)
	Production period	1972–1973
Engine	Type	Air-cooled, six-cylinder boxer engine
	Displacement	164 cu. in.
	Bore x stroke in inches	3.5 x 2.8
	Output in hp / kW	210 / 154 at 6,300 rpm
	Torque	188 ft.-lbs. at 5,100 rpm
	Valve control	OHC via double chain, two valves per cylinder
	Mixture preparation	Mechanical Bosch double-row injection pump
	Compression ratio	8.5:1
Power Transfer	Transmission	Model 915/08 five-speed manual transmission
	Gear ratio, 1st gear	3.182
	Gear ratio, 2nd gear	1.834
	Gear ratio, 3rd gear	1.261
	Gear ratio, 4th gear	0.925
	Gear ratio, 5th gear	0.724
	Gear ratio, 6th gear	
	Gear ratio, 7th gear	
	Gear ratio, reverse gear	3.325
	Axle ratio	4.429
	Locking effect in %	80
	Drive	Rear-wheel drive
Body and Suspension	Front-wheel suspension	Independent suspension on spring struts and wishbones, one round torsion bar per wheel in longitudinal direction, double-acting hydraulic shock absorbers, stabilizer bar
	Rear-wheel suspension	Independent suspension on trailing arms, one round torsion bar per wheel in transverse direction, double-acting hydraulic shock absorbers, stabilizer bar
	Steering	Rack and pinion
	Turning circle	35 ft.
	Brake system	Hydraulic system, internally ventilated discs all around, two-piston aluminum fixed calipers at the front, two-piston cast iron fixed calipers at the rear
	Brake discs in inches	11.1 x 0.8 front, 11.4 x 0.8 rear
	Rim sizes in inches	6 x 15 / 7 x 15
	Tire sizes	185/70VR15 / 215/60VR15
Dimensions and Weights	Length / width / height in inches	161.5 / 65 /52
	Wheelbase	89.4 in.
	Front and rear track in inches	54 / 54.9
	Empty weight in lbs.	2,116
	Trunk volume	7 cu. ft., front
	Fuel tank contents in gal.	22.5, including 2.4 in reserve
Performance	Maximum speed	152 mph
	Time from 0 to 62 mph	5.8 sec.
	Fuel consumption	21.8 mpg
Other	Total made	217 (200 plus 17 homologation vehicles)
	Price at market launch	34,000 marks; with M471, 36,500 marks

911 CARRERA RS 2.7 TOURING

Model	Series	911 F Model
	Sales designation	911 Carrera RS 2.7 Touring (M472)
	Production period	1972–1973
Engine	Type	Air-cooled, six-cylinder boxer engine
	Displacement	164 cu. in.
	Bore x stroke in inches	3.5 x 2.8
	Output in hp / kW	210 / 154 at 6,300 rpm
	Torque	188 ft.-lbs. at 5,100 rpm
	Valve control	OHC via double chain, two valves per cylinder
	Mixture preparation	Mechanical Bosch double-row injection pump
	Compression ratio	8.5:1
Power Transfer	Transmission	Model 915/08 five-speed manual transmission
	Gear ratio, 1st gear	3.182
	Gear ratio, 2nd gear	1.834
	Gear ratio, 3rd gear	1.261
	Gear ratio, 4th gear	0.925
	Gear ratio, 5th gear	0.724
	Gear ratio, 6th gear	
	Gear ratio, 7th gear	
	Gear ratio, reverse gear	3.325
	Axle ratio	4.429
	Locking effect in %	80
	Drive	Rear-wheel drive
Body and Suspension	Front-wheel suspension	Independent suspension on spring struts and wishbones, one round torsion bar per wheel in longitudinal direction, double-acting hydraulic shock absorbers, stabilizer bar
	Rear-wheel suspension	Independent suspension on trailing arms, one round torsion bar per wheel in transverse direction, double-acting hydraulic shock absorbers, stabilizer bar
	Steering	Rack and pinion
	Turning circle	35 ft.
	Brake system	Independent suspension on trailing arms, one round torsion bar per wheel in transverse direction, double-acting hydraulic shock absorbers, stabilizer bar
	Brake discs in inches	11.1 x 0.8 front, 11.4 x 0.8 rear
	Rim sizes in inches	6 x 15 / 7 x 15
	Tire sizes	185/70VR15 / 215/60VR15
Dimensions and Weights	Length / width / height in inches	163.25 / 65 / 52
	Wheelbase	89.4 in.
	Front and rear track in inches	54 / 54.9
	Empty weight in lbs.	2,370
	Trunk volume	7 cu. ft., front
	Fuel tank contents in gal.	22.5, including 2.4 in reserve
Performance	Maximum speed	149 mph
	Time from 0 to 62 mph	5.8 sec.
	Fuel consumption	21.8 mpg
Other	Total made	1308
	Price at market launch	34,000 marks; with M471, 36,500 marks

911 CARRERA RSR 2.8

Model	Series	911 F Model
	Sales designation	911 RSR 2.8 (M491)
	Production period	1973
Engine	Type	Air-cooled, six-cylinder boxer engine
	Displacement	171 cu. in.
	Bore x stroke in inches	3.6 x 2.8
	Output in hp / kW	285 / 209 at 8,000 rpm (up to 300 hp)
	Torque	210.2 ft.-lbs. at 6,500 rpm
	Valve control	OHC via double chain, two valves per cylinder
	Mixture preparation	Mechanical Bosch double-row injection pump / mechanical intake manifold injection
	Compression ratio	10.3:1
Power Transfer	Transmission	Manual five-speed transmission, depending on use Model 915 with separate oil cooling
	Gear ratio, 1st gear	3.182
	Gear ratio, 2nd gear	1.834
	Gear ratio, 3rd gear	1.261
	Gear ratio, 4th gear	0.925
	Gear ratio, 5th gear	0.724
	Gear ratio, 6th gear	
	Gear ratio, 7th gear	
	Gear ratio, reverse gear	3.325
	Axle ratio	4.429
	Locking effect in %	80
	Drive	Rear-wheel drive
Body and Suspension	Front-wheel suspension	Independent suspension on spring struts and wishbones, one round torsion bar per wheel in longitudinal direction, double-acting hydraulic shock absorbers, stabilizer bar, additional progressive coil springs
	Rear-wheel suspension	Independent suspension on trailing arms, one round torsion bar per wheel in transverse direction, double-acting hydraulic shock absorbers, stabilizer bar, stabilizer bar, additional progressive coil springs
	Steering	Rack and pinion
	Turning circle	35 ft.
	Brake system	Perforated brake discs, four-piston brake caliper from the 917 shorttail
	Brake discs in inches	
	Rim sizes in inches	9 x 15 / 11 x 15
	Tire sizes	230/300-15 CR 88 356 / 260/300-15 CR 88 356
Dimensions and Weights	Length / width / height in inches	163.25 / 69 /51.2
	Wheelbase	89.4 in.
	Front and rear track in inches	54 / 54.9
	Empty weight in lbs.	2,021
	Trunk volume	
	Fuel tank contents in gal.	29
Performance	Maximum speed	161.5 mph
	Time from 0 to 62 mph	
	Fuel consumption	
Other	Total made	55
	Price at market launch	34,000 marks; with M491, 59,000 marks

911 CARRERA RS 3.0

Model	Series	911 G Model
	Sales designation	911 Carrera RS 3.0
	Production period	1974
Engine	Type	Air-cooled, six-cylinder boxer engine
	Displacement	182.7 cu. in.
	Bore x stroke in inches	3.74 x 2.77
	Output in hp / kW	230 / 169 at 6,200 rpm
	Torque	202 ft.-lbs.
	Valve control	OHC via double chain, two valves per cylinder
	Mixture preparation	Mechanical Bosch double-row injection pump / mechanical intake manifold injection
	Compression ratio	10.3:1
Power Transfer	Transmission	Mechanical Bosch intake manifold injection with 6-piston double row pump
	Gear ratio, 1st gear	3.182
	Gear ratio, 2nd gear	1.833
	Gear ratio, 3rd gear	1.261
	Gear ratio, 4th gear	0.926
	Gear ratio, 5th gear	0.724
	Gear ratio, 6th gear	
	Gear ratio, 7th gear	
	Gear ratio, reverse gear	3.325
	Axle ratio	4.429
	Locking effect in %	80
	Drive	Rear-wheel drive
Body and Suspension	Front-wheel suspension	Independent suspension on spring struts and wishbones, one round torsion bar per wheel in longitudinal direction, hydraulic telescopic shock absorbers, stabilizer bar
	Rear-wheel suspension	Independent wheel suspension on trailing arms, one round torsion bar transversely mounted per wheel, hydraulic telescopic shock absorbers, stabilizer bar
	Steering	Rack and pinion
	Turning circle	35 ft.
	Brake system	Hydraulic system, internally ventilated and perforated discs all around, four-piston aluminum fixed calipers from the 917 shorttail
	Brake discs in inches	11.8 x 1.10 front and rear
	Rim sizes in inches	8 x 15 / 9 x 15
	Tire sizes	215/60VR15 / 235/60VR15
Dimensions and Weights	Length / width / height in inches	166.7 / 69.9 / 52
	Wheelbase	89.4 in.
	Front and rear track in inches	56.6 / 57.6
	Empty weight in lbs.	2,337
	Trunk volume	7.1 cu. ft.
	Fuel tank contents in gal.	21.1, including 2.1 in reserve
Performance	Maximum speed	152 mph
	Time from 0 to 62 mph	5.3 sec.
	Fuel consumption	13.8 mpg
Other	Total made	110
	Price at market launch	64,980 marks

911 SC CARRERA RS

Model	**Series**	**911 G Model**
	Sales designation	911 Carrera RS 3.0
	Production period	1984
Engine	Type	Air-cooled, six-cylinder boxer engine
	Displacement	182.7 cu. in.
	Bore x stroke in inches	3.74 x 2.77
	Output in hp / kW	250 / 184 at 7,000 rpm
	Torque	184 ft.-lbs.
	Valve control	OHC via double chain, two valves per cylinder
	Mixture preparation	Mechanical injection
	Compression ratio	10.3:1
Power Transfer	Transmission	Model 915/71 five-speed manual transmission
	Gear ratio, 1st gear	3.182
	Gear ratio, 2nd gear	1.83
	Gear ratio, 3rd gear	2
	Gear ratio, 4th gear	1.381
	Gear ratio, 5th gear	1.08
	Gear ratio, 6th gear	
	Gear ratio, 7th gear	
	Gear ratio, reverse gear	3.325
	Axle ratio	3.875
	Locking effect in %	40
	Drive	Rear-wheel drive
Body and Suspension	Front-wheel suspension	Independent suspension on spring struts and wishbones, one round torsion bar per wheel in longitudinal direction, twin-tube gas pressure shock absorbers, stabilizer bar
	Rear-wheel suspension	Independent wheel suspension on light alloy semi-trailing arms, one round torsion bar per wheel in transverse direction, twin-tube gas pressure shock absorbers, stabilizer bar
	Steering	Rack and pinion
	Turning circle	
	Brake system	Hydraulic system, internally ventilated and perforated discs all around, black four-piston aluminum fixed calipers
	Brake discs in inches	11.8 x 1.10 front and rear
	Rim sizes in inches	12 x 1.25 front, 12.2 x 1.10 rear
	Tire sizes	205/55VR16 / 225/50VR15
Dimensions and Weights	Length / width / height in inches	166.7 / 69.9 / 50.8
	Wheelbase	89.4 in.
	Front and rear track in inches	53.4 / 59.1
	Empty weight in lbs.	2,330
	Trunk volume	4.6 cu. ft.
	Fuel tank contents in gal.	21.1, including 2.1 in reserve
Performance	Maximum speed	158.5 mph
	Time from 0 to 62 mph	5.3 sec.
	Fuel consumption	11.8 mpg
Other	Total made	20
	Price at market launch	188,100 marks

911 CARRERA RS

Model	Series	964
	Sales designation	911 Carrera RS Coupe
	Production period	1992
Engine	Type	Air-cooled, six-cylinder boxer engine
	Displacement	220 cu. In.
	Bore x stroke in inches	3.93 x 3.0
	Output in hp / kW	260 / 191 at 6,100 rpm
	Torque	239.7 ft.-lbs.
	Valve control	OHC via double chain, two valves per cylinder
	Mixture preparation	Sequential Bosch injection
	Compression ratio	11.3:1
Power Transfer	Transmission	Model G50/10 five-speed manual transmission
	Gear ratio, 1st gear	3.154
	Gear ratio, 2nd gear	1.895
	Gear ratio, 3rd gear	1.407
	Gear ratio, 4th gear	1.086
	Gear ratio, 5th gear	0.868
	Gear ratio, 6th gear	
	Gear ratio, 7th gear	
	Gear ratio, reverse gear	2.857
	Axle ratio	3.444
	Locking effect in %	20 / 100
	Drive	Rear-wheel drive
Body and Suspension	Front-wheel suspension	Independent suspension on McPherson struts and light alloy wishbones with negative rolling radius, coil springs, twin-tube gas pressure shock absorbers, stabilizer bar
	Rear-wheel suspension	Independent suspension on light alloy struts and semi-trailing arms, coil springs, twin-tube gas pressure shock absorbers, stabilizer bar
	Steering	Rack and pinion
	Turning circle	35 ft.
	Brake system	Internally ventilated and perforated brake discs, four-piston fixed calipers
	Brake discs in inches	12.7 x 1.26 front, 11.8 x 0.9 rear
	Rim sizes in inches	7.5 x 17 / 9 x 17
	Tire sizes	205/50ZR17 / 255/40ZR17
Dimensions and Weights	Length / width / height in inches	168.3 / 65 / 50
	Wheelbase	89.4 in.
	Front and rear track in inches	54.29 / 54.33
	Empty weight in lbs.	2,689.60
	Trunk volume	3.11 cubic ft.
	Fuel tank contents in gal.	20.3
Performance	Maximum speed	165 mph
	Time from 0 to 62 mph	5.3 sec.
	Fuel consumption	21.4 mpg
Other	Total made	2,282
	Price at market launch	145,500 marks

911 CARRERA RS N/GT

Model	Series	964
	Sales designation	911 Carrera RS Coupe N/GT
	Production period	1992
Engine	Type	Air-cooled, six-cylinder boxer engine
	Displacement	220 cu. In.
	Bore x stroke in inches	3.93 x 3.0
	Output in hp / kW	260 / 191 at 6,100 rpm
	Torque	239.7 ft.-lbs.
	Valve control	OHC via double chain, two valves per cylinder
	Mixture preparation	Sequential Bosch injection
	Compression ratio	11.3:1
Power Transfer	Transmission	Model G50/10 five-speed manual transmission
	Gear ratio, 1st gear	3.154
	Gear ratio, 2nd gear	1.895
	Gear ratio, 3rd gear	1.407
	Gear ratio, 4th gear	1.086
	Gear ratio, 5th gear	0.868
	Gear ratio, 6th gear	
	Gear ratio, 7th gear	
	Gear ratio, reverse gear	2.857
	Axle ratio	3.444
	Locking effect in %	20 / 100
	Drive	Rear-wheel drive
Body and Suspension	Front-wheel suspension	Independent suspension on McPherson struts and light alloy wishbones with negative rolling radius, coil springs, twin-tube gas pressure shock absorbers, stabilizer bar
	Rear-wheel suspension	Independent suspension on light alloy struts and semi-trailing arms, coil springs, twin-tube gas pressure shock absorbers, stabilizer bar
	Steering	Rack and pinion
	Turning circle	35 ft.
	Brake system	Internally ventilated and perforated brake discs, four-piston fixed calipers
	Brake discs in inches	12.7 x 1.26 front, 11.8 x 0.9 rear
	Rim sizes in inches	7.5 x 17 / 9 x 17
	Tire sizes	205/50ZR17 / 255/40ZR17
Dimensions and Weights	Length / width / height in inches	168.3 / 65 / 50
	Wheelbase	89.4 in.
	Front and rear track in inches	54.29 / 54.33
	Empty weight in lbs.	2,689.00
	Trunk volume	3.11 cu. ft.
	Fuel tank contents in gal.	20.3
Performance	Maximum speed	161.5 mph
	Time from 0 to 62 mph	5.3 sec.
	Fuel consumption	21.4 mpg
Other	Total made	290
	Price at market launch	160,000 marks

911 CARRERA RS AMERICA

Model	Series	964
	Sales designation	911 Carrera RS America Coupe
	Production period	1993
Engine	Type	Air-cooled, six-cylinder boxer engine
	Displacement	220 cu. In.
	Bore x stroke in inches	3.93 x 3.0
	Output in hp / kW	247 / 182 at 6,500 rpm
	Torque	239.7 ft.-lbs.
	Valve control	OHC via double chain, two valves per cylinder
	Mixture preparation	Sequential Bosch injection
	Compression ratio	11.5:1
Power Transfer	Transmission	Model G50/10 five-speed manual transmission
	Gear ratio, 1st gear	3.5
	Gear ratio, 2nd gear	2.059
	Gear ratio, 3rd gear	1.407
	Gear ratio, 4th gear	1.086
	Gear ratio, 5th gear	0.868
	Gear ratio, 6th gear	
	Gear ratio, 7th gear	
	Gear ratio, reverse gear	2.857
	Axle ratio	3.333
	Locking effect in %	
	Drive	Rear-wheel drive
Body and Suspension	Front-wheel suspension	Independent suspension on McPherson struts and light alloy wishbones with negative rolling radius, coil springs, twin-tube gas pressure shock absorbers, stabilizer bar
	Rear-wheel suspension	Independent suspension on light alloy struts and semi-trailing arms, coil springs, twin-tube gas pressure shock absorbers, stabilizer bar
	Steering	Rack and pinion
	Turning circle	35 ft.
	Brake system	Internally ventilated and perforated brake discs, four-piston fixed calipers
	Brake discs in inches	11.73 x 1.1 front, 11.77 x 0.94 rear
	Rim sizes in inches	7 x 17 / 8 x 17
	Tire sizes	205/50ZR17 / 255/40ZR17
Dimensions and Weights	Length / width / height in inches	168.3 / 65 / 51.6
	Wheelbase	89.4 in.
	Front and rear track in inches	54 / 53.85
	Empty weight in lbs.	2,954
	Trunk volume	3.11 cu. ft.
	Fuel tank contents in gal.	20.3
Performance	Maximum speed	161.5 mph
	Time from 0 to 62 mph	5.6 sec.
	Fuel consumption	20.5 mpg
Other	Total made	701
	Price at market launch	53,900 US dollars

911 CARRERA RS 3.8

Model	Series	964
	Sales designation	911 Carrera RS 3.8 Coupe
	Production period	1993
Engine	Type	Air-cooled, six-cylinder boxer engine
	Displacement	228.6 cu. in.
	Bore x stroke in inches	4 x 3
	Output in hp / kW	300 / 221 at 6,500 rpm
	Torque	265.5 ft.-lbs.
	Valve control	OHC via double chain, two valves per cylinder
	Mixture preparation	Sequential Bosch injection
	Compression ratio	11.0:1
Power Transfer	Transmission	Model G50/10 five-speed manual transmission
	Gear ratio, 1st gear	3.154
	Gear ratio, 2nd gear	1.895
	Gear ratio, 3rd gear	1.407
	Gear ratio, 4th gear	1.086
	Gear ratio, 5th gear	0.868
	Gear ratio, 6th gear	
	Gear ratio, 7th gear	
	Gear ratio, reverse gear	2.857
	Axle ratio	3.444
	Locking effect in %	20 / 100
	Drive	Rear-wheel drive
Body and Suspension	Front-wheel suspension	Independent suspension on McPherson struts and light alloy wishbones with negative rolling radius, coil springs, twin-tube gas pressure shock absorbers, stabilizer bar
	Rear-wheel suspension	Independent suspension on light alloy struts and semi-trailing arms, coil springs, twin-tube gas pressure shock absorbers, stabilizer bar
	Steering	Rack and pinion
	Turning circle	35 ft.
	Brake system	Internally ventilated and perforated brake discs, four-piston fixed calipers
	Brake discs in inches	12.7 x 1.3 front, 11.8 x 1.1 rear
	Rim sizes in inches	9 x 18 / 11 x 18
	Tire sizes	235/40ZR18 / 285/35ZR18
Dimensions and Weights	Length / width / height in inches	168.3 / 70 / 50
	Wheelbase	89.4 in.
	Front and rear track in inches	56.7 / 58.3
	Empty weight in lbs.	2,667
	Trunk volume	3.11 cu. ft.
	Fuel tank contents in gal.	24.3
Performance	Maximum speed	168 mph
	Time from 0 to 62 mph	4.8 sec.
	Fuel consumption	21.4 mpg
Other	Total made	90
	Price at market launch	225,000 marks

911 CARRERA RS

Model	Series	993
	Sales designation	911 Carrera RS Coupe
	Production period	1995–1996
Engine	Type	Air-cooled, six-cylinder boxer engine
	Displacement	228.6 cu. in.
	Bore x stroke in inches	4 x 3
	Output in hp / kW	300 / 221 at 6,500 rpm
	Torque	261.8 ft.-lbs.
	Valve control	OHC via double chain, two valves per cylinder
	Mixture preparation	Sequential Bosch injection
	Compression ratio	11.3:1
Power Transfer	Transmission	Model G50/31 six-speed manual transmission
	Gear ratio, 1st gear	3.154
	Gear ratio, 2nd gear	2
	Gear ratio, 3rd gear	1.522
	Gear ratio, 4th gear	1.242
	Gear ratio, 5th gear	1.024
	Gear ratio, 6th gear	0.821
	Gear ratio, 7th gear	
	Gear ratio, reverse gear	2.857
	Axle ratio	3.444
	Locking effect in %	40 / 65
	Drive	Rear-wheel drive
Body and Suspension	Front-wheel suspension	Independent suspension on McPherson struts and light alloy wishbones with negative rolling radius, coil springs, twin-tube gas pressure shock absorbers, stabilizer bar
	Rear-wheel suspension	Independent wheel suspension on four control arms each with LSA system and light alloy suspension stool, coil springs, twin-tube gas pressure shock absorbers, stabilizer bar
	Steering	Rack and pinion
	Turning circle	35 ft.
	Brake system	Internally ventilated and perforated brake discs, four-piston fixed calipers
	Brake discs in inches	19.6 x 1.95 front, 19.6 x 1.70 rear
	Rim sizes in inches	8 x 18 / 10 x 18
	Tire sizes	225/40ZR18 / 265/35ZR18
Dimensions and Weights	Length / width / height in inches	167 / 68.3 / 50
	Wheelbase	89.4 in.
	Front and rear track in inches	55.6 / 57.2
	Empty weight in lbs.	2,800
	Trunk volume	3.3 cu. ft.
	Fuel tank contents in gal.	24.3
Performance	Maximum speed	172 mph
	Time from 0 to 62 mph	5 sec.
	Fuel consumption	17 mpg
Other	Total made	1,014
	Price at market launch	147,900 marks; with Clubsport package, 164,700 marks

911 CARRERA RS CLUBSPORT

Model	Series	993
	Sales designation	911 Carrera RS Coupé Clubsport
	Production period	1995–1996
Engine	Type	Air-cooled, six-cylinder boxer engine
	Displacement	228.6 cu. in.
	Bore x stroke in inches	4.01 x 3
	Output in hp / kW	300 / 221 at 6,500 rpm
	Torque	261.8 ft.-lbs.
	Valve control	OHC via double chain, two valves per cylinder
	Mixture preparation	Sequential Bosch injection
	Compression ratio	11.3:1
Power Transfer	Transmission	Model G50/30 six-speed manual transmission
	Gear ratio, 1st gear	3.154
	Gear ratio, 2nd gear	2
	Gear ratio, 3rd gear	1.522
	Gear ratio, 4th gear	1.241
	Gear ratio, 5th gear	1.031
	Gear ratio, 6th gear	0.829
	Gear ratio, 7th gear	
	Gear ratio, reverse gear	2.857
	Axle ratio	3.444
	Locking effect in %	40 / 65
	Drive	Rear-wheel drive
Body and Suspension	Front-wheel suspension	Independent suspension on McPherson struts and light alloy wishbones with negative rolling radius, coil springs, twin-tube gas pressure shock absorbers, stabilizer bar
	Rear-wheel suspension	Independent wheel suspension on four control arms each with LSA system and light alloy suspension stool, coil springs, twin-tube gas pressure shock absorbers, stabilizer bar
	Steering	Rack and pinion
	Turning circle	35 ft.
	Brake system	Internally ventilated and perforated brake discs, four-piston fixed calipers
	Brake discs in inches	19.6 x 1.95 front, 19.6 x 1.70 rear
	Rim sizes in inches	8 x 18 / 10 x 18
	Tire sizes	225/40ZR18 / 265/35ZR18
Dimensions and Weights	Length / width / height in inches	167 / 68.3 / 50
	Wheelbase	89.4 in.
	Front and rear track in inches	55.6 / 57.1
	Empty weight in lbs.	2,800
	Trunk volume	3.3 cu. ft.
	Fuel tank contents in gal.	24.3
Performance	Maximum speed	172 mph
	Time from 0 to 62 mph	5 sec.
	Fuel consumption	17 mpg
Other	Total made	227
	Price at market launch	164,700 marks

911 GT3

Model	Series	911 996.1
	Sales designation	911 GT3
	Production period	1999–2001
Engine	Type	Liquid-cooled, six-cylinder boxer
	Displacement	219.7 cu. in.
	Bore x stroke in inches	3.93 x 3.0
	Output in hp / kW	360 / 265 at 7,200 rpm
	Torque	370 at 5,000 rpm
	Valve control	DOHC with variable valve timing (VarioCam) on the intake side and hydraulic valve lash adjustment, four valves per cylinder
	Mixture preparation	Intake manifold injection
	Compression ratio	11.7:1
Power Transfer	Transmission	Model G96/90 six-speed manual transmission
	Gear ratio, 1st gear	3.82
	Gear ratio, 2nd gear	2.15
	Gear ratio, 3rd gear	1.56
	Gear ratio, 4th gear	1.21
	Gear ratio, 5th gear	0.97
	Gear ratio, 6th gear	0.82
	Gear ratio, 7th gear	
	Gear ratio, reverse gear	2.86
	Axle ratio	3.44
	Locking effect in %	40 / 60
	Drive	Rear-wheel drive
Body and Suspension	Front-wheel suspension	Independent suspension on McPherson struts, transverse and trailing arms, split wishbones, uniball support bearings
	Rear-wheel suspension	Wheels individually guided on five control arms
	Steering	Hydraulically assisted rack and pinion
	Turning circle	35 ft.
	Brake system	Hydraulic system, perforated and internally ventilated discs, four-piston aluminum monoblock calipers
	Brake discs in inches	13 x 1.33 front, 13 x 1.10 rear
	Rim sizes in inches	8 x 18 / 10 x 18
	Tire sizes	225/40ZR18 / 285/35ZR18
Dimensions and Weights	Length / width / height in inches	174.4 / 64.5 / 50
	Wheelbase	92.5 in.
	Front and rear track in inches	58 / 58.9
	Empty weight in lbs.	2,976
	Trunk volume	3.9 cu. ft.
	Fuel tank contents in gal.	25.5 (right-hand-steering version: 16.9)
Performance	Maximum speed	187 mph
	Time from 0 to 62 mph	4.8 sec.
	Fuel consumption	18.2 mpg
Other	Total made	1,868
	Price at market launch	179,500 marks

911 GT3

Model	Series	911 996.2
	Sales designation	911 GT3
	Production period	2003–2005
Engine	Type	Liquid-cooled, six-cylinder boxer
	Displacement	219.7 cu. in.
	Bore x stroke in inches	3.93 x 3.0
	Output in hp / kW	381 / 280 at 7,400 rpm
	Torque	284 ft. lbs. at 5,000 rpm
	Valve control	DOHC with variable valve timing (VarioCam) on the intake side and hydraulic valve lash adjustment, four valves per cylinder
	Mixture preparation	Intake manifold injection
	Compression ratio	11.7:1
Power Transfer	Transmission	Model G96/96 six-speed manual transmission
	Gear ratio, 1st gear	3.82
	Gear ratio, 2nd gear	2.15
	Gear ratio, 3rd gear	1.56
	Gear ratio, 4th gear	1.21
	Gear ratio, 5th gear	1
	Gear ratio, 6th gear	0.85
	Gear ratio, 7th gear	
	Gear ratio, reverse gear	2.86
	Axle ratio	3.44
	Locking effect in %	40 / 60
	Drive	Rear-wheel drive
Body and Suspension	Front-wheel suspension	Independent suspension on McPherson struts, transverse and longitudinal control arms, split wishbones, uniball support bearings
	Rear-wheel suspension	Wheels individually guided on five control arms
	Steering	Hydraulically assisted rack and pinion
	Turning circle	34.75 ft.
	Brake system	Hydraulic system, perforated and internally ventilated discs, six-piston aluminum monoblock calipers at the front, four-piston aluminum monoblock calipers at the rear
	Brake discs in inches	13.8 x 1.3 front; 13 x 1.1 rear
	Rim sizes in inches	8½ x 18 / 11 x 18
	Tire sizes	234/40ZR18 / 295/30ZR18
Dimensions and Weights	Length / width / height in inches	174.6 / 70 / 50.2
	Wheelbase	92.7 in.
	Front and rear track in inches	58.6 / 58.6
	Empty weight in lbs.	3,042
	Trunk volume	3.9 cu. ft.
	Fuel tank contents in gal.	23.5 (right-hand-steering version: 16.9)
Performance	Maximum speed	187.7 mph
	Time from 0 to 62 mph	4.8 sec.
	Fuel consumption	18.2 mpg
Other	Total made	2,589
	Price at market launch	102,112 euros

911 GT3 RS

Model	Series	911 996.2
	Sales designation	911 GT3 RS
	Production period	2003–2004
Engine	Type	Liquid-cooled, six-cylinder boxer
	Displacement	219.7 cu. in.
	Bore x stroke in inches	3.93 x 3.0
	Output in hp / kW	381 / 280 at 7,400 rpm
	Torque	283 ft.-lbs. at 5,000 rpm
	Valve control	DOHC with variable valve timing (VarioCam) on the intake side and hydraulic valve lash adjustment, four valves per cylinder
	Mixture preparation	Intake manifold injection
	Compression ratio	11.7:1
Power Transfer	Transmission	Model G96/96 six-speed manual transmission
	Gear ratio, 1st gear	3.82
	Gear ratio, 2nd gear	2.15
	Gear ratio, 3rd gear	1.56
	Gear ratio, 4th gear	1.21
	Gear ratio, 5th gear	1
	Gear ratio, 6th gear	0.85
	Gear ratio, 7th gear	
	Gear ratio, reverse gear	2.86
	Axle ratio	3.44
	Locking effect in %	40 / 60
	Drive	Rear-wheel drive
Body and Suspension	Front-wheel suspension	Independent suspension on McPherson struts, transverse and trailing arms, split wishbones, uniball support bearings
	Rear-wheel suspension	Wheels individually guided on five control arms, split wishbones, actively controlled monotube gas pressure shock absorbers (PASM)
	Steering	Hydraulically assisted rack and pinion
	Turning circle	35 ft.
	Brake system	Hydraulic system, perforated and internally ventilated discs, six-piston aluminum monoblock calipers at the front, four-piston aluminum monoblock calipers at the rear
	Brake discs in inches	13.8 x 1.33 front; 13 x 1.1 rear
	Rim sizes in inches	9½ x 18 / 11 x 18
	Tire sizes	235/40ZR18 / 295/30ZR18
Dimensions and Weights	Length / width / height in inches	174.6 / 70 / 50.2
	Wheelbase	92.7 in.
	Front and rear track in inches	58.5 / 58.85
	Empty weight in lbs.	2,998
	Trunk volume	3.9 cu. ft.
	Fuel tank contents in gal.	23.5 (right-hand-steering version: 16.9)
Performance	Maximum speed	190 mph
	Time from 0 to 62 mph	4.4 sec.
	Fuel consumption	18.2 mpg
Other	Total made	682
	Price at market launch	120,788 euros

911 GT3 RS

Model	Series	911 997.1
	Sales designation	911 GT3 RS
	Production period	2005–2008
Engine	Type	Liquid-cooled, six-cylinder boxer
	Displacement	219.7 cu. in.
	Bore x stroke in inches	3.93 x 3.0
	Output in hp / kW	415 / 305 at 7,600 rpm
	Torque	298.7 ft. lbs. at 5,500 rpm
	Valve control	DOHC with variable valve timing (VarioCam) and hydraulic valve lash adjustment, four valves per cylinder
	Mixture preparation	Intake manifold injection
	Compression ratio	12.0:1
Power Transfer	Transmission	Model M97/77 or M97/77R six-speed manual transmission
	Gear ratio, 1st gear	3.82
	Gear ratio, 2nd gear	2.26
	Gear ratio, 3rd gear	1.64
	Gear ratio, 4th gear	1.29
	Gear ratio, 5th gear	1.06
	Gear ratio, 6th gear	0.92
	Gear ratio, 7th gear	
	Gear ratio, reverse gear	2.86
	Axle ratio	3.44
	Locking effect in %	28 / 40
	Drive	Rear-wheel drive
Body and Suspension	Front-wheel suspension	Independent suspension on McPherson struts, transverse and longitudinal control arms, split wishbones, actively controlled twin-tube gas pressure shock absorbers (PASM)
	Rear-wheel suspension	Wheels individually guided on five control arms, split wishbones, actively controlled monotube gas pressure shock absorbers (PASM)
	Steering	Hydraulically assisted rack and pinion
	Turning circle	35.76 ft.
	Brake system	Hydraulic system, perforated and internally ventilated discs, six-piston aluminum monoblock calipers at the front, four-piston aluminum monoblock calipers at the rear
	Brake discs in inches	13.8 x 1.3 front; 13 x 1.3 rear
	Rim sizes in inches	8.5 x 19 / 12 x 19
	Tire sizes	235/35ZR19 / 305/30ZR19
Dimensions and Weights	Length / width / height in inches	175.6 / 72.9 / 50.4
	Wheelbase	92.9 in.
	Front and rear track in inches	58.9 / 61.3
	Empty weight in lbs.	3,031
	Trunk volume	3.7 cu. ft.
	Fuel tank contents in gal.	23.8
Performance	Maximum speed	192 mph
	Time from 0 to 62 mph	4.2 sec.
	Fuel consumption	18.4 mpg
Other	Total made	1,909
	Price at market launch	133,012 euros

911 GT3 RS

Model	Series	911 997.2
	Sales designation	911 GT3 RS
	Production period	2009–2011
Engine	Type	Liquid-cooled, six-cylinder boxer
	Displacement	231.7 cu. in.
	Bore x stroke in inches	4 x 3
	Output in hp / kW	450 / 331 at 7,900 rpm
	Torque	317 ft.-lbs.
	Valve control	DOHC with variable timing and valve lift. switching (VarioCam Plus) as well as hydraulic valve lash adjustment, four valves per cylinder
	Mixture preparation	Intake manifold injection
	Compression ratio	12.2:1
Power Transfer	Transmission	Model M97/77 or M97/77R six-speed manual transmission
	Gear ratio, 1st gear	3.82
	Gear ratio, 2nd gear	2.26
	Gear ratio, 3rd gear	1.64
	Gear ratio, 4th gear	1.29
	Gear ratio, 5th gear	1.06
	Gear ratio, 6th gear	0.88
	Gear ratio, 7th gear	
	Gear ratio, reverse gear	2.86
	Axle ratio	3.89
	Locking effect in %	28 / 40
	Drive	Rear-wheel drive
Body and Suspension	Front-wheel suspension	Independent suspension on McPherson struts, transverse and longitudinal control arms, forged control arms, Uniball support bearings, actively controlled twin-tube gas pressure shock absorbers (PASM)
	Rear-wheel suspension	Wheels individually guided on five control arms, split wishbones, actively controlled monotube gas pressure dampers (PASM)
	Steering	Hydraulically assisted rack and pinion
	Turning circle	35.75 ft.
	Brake system	Hydraulic system, perforated and internally ventilated discs, six-piston aluminum monoblock calipers at the front, four-piston aluminum monoblock calipers at the rear
	Brake discs in inches	15 x 1.3 front; 13.8 x 1.1 rear
	Rim sizes in inches	9 x 19 / 12 x 19
	Tire sizes	245/35ZR19 / 325/30ZR19
Dimensions and Weights	Length / width / height in inches	175.6 / 72.9 / 50.4
	Wheelbase	92.7 in.
	Front and rear track in inches	59.4 / 61.2
	Empty weight in lbs.	3,020
	Trunk volume	3.7 cu. ft.
	Fuel tank contents in gal.	17.7 (optional: 23.8)
Performance	Maximum speed	192 mph
	Time from 0 to 62 mph	4 sec.
	Fuel consumption	17.8 mpg
Other	Total made	1,619
	Price at market launch	145,871 euros

911 GT3 RS 4.0

Model	Series	911 997.2
	Sales designation	911 GT3 RS 4.0
	Production period	2011
Engine	Type	Liquid-cooled, six-cylinder boxer
	Displacement	243.9 cu. in.
	Bore x stroke in inches	4 x 3.2
	Output in hp / kW	500 / 368 at 8,250 rpm
	Torque	339 ft.-lbs.
	Valve control	DOHC with variable intake and exhaust timing (VarioCam) and hydraulic valve lash adjustment, four valves per cylinder
	Mixture preparation	Intake manifold injection
	Compression ratio	12.6:1
Power Transfer	Transmission	Model M97/74 six-speed manual transmission
	Gear ratio, 1st gear	3.82
	Gear ratio, 2nd gear	2.26
	Gear ratio, 3rd gear	1.64
	Gear ratio, 4th gear	1.29
	Gear ratio, 5th gear	1.06
	Gear ratio, 6th gear	0.88
	Gear ratio, 7th gear	
	Gear ratio, reverse gear	2.86
	Axle ratio	3.89
	Locking effect in %	28 / 40
	Drive	Rear-wheel drive
Body and Suspension	Front-wheel suspension	Independent suspension on McPherson struts, transverse and longitudinal control arms, forged control arms, Uniball support bearings, actively controlled twin-tube gas pressure shock absorbers (PASM)
	Rear-wheel suspension	Wheels individually guided on five control arms, split wishbones, actively controlled monotube gas pressure dampers (PASM)
	Steering	Hydraulically assisted rack and pinion
	Turning circle	35.75 ft.
	Brake system	Hydraulic system, perforated and internally ventilated discs, Six-piston aluminum monoblock calipers at the front, four-piston aluminum monoblock calipers at the rear
	Brake discs in inches	15 x 1.3 front; 13.8 x 1.1 rear
	Rim sizes in inches	9 x 19 / 12 x 19
	Tire sizes	245/35ZR19 / 325/30ZR19
Dimensions and Weights	Length / width / height in inches	175.6 / 72.9 / 50.4
	Wheelbase	92.7 in.
	Front and rear track in inches	59.4 / 61.2
	Empty weight in lbs.	2,998
	Trunk volume	3.7 cu. ft.
	Fuel tank contents in gal.	17.7 (optional: 23.8)
Performance	Maximum speed	192.6 mph
	Time from 0 to 62 mph	3.9 sec.
	Fuel consumption	17 mpg
Other	Total made	613
	Price at market launch	178,596 euros

911 GT2 RS

Model	Series	911 997.2
	Sales designation	911 GT2 RS
	Production period	2010–2011
Engine	Type	Liquid-cooled, six-cylinder boxer
	Displacement	219.7 cu. in.
	Bore x stroke in inches	3.9 x 3
	Output in hp / kW	620 / 456 at 6,500 rpm
	Torque	516 ft.-lbs.
	Valve control	DOHC with variable intake-side timing and valve lift. Switching (VarioCam Plus) and hydraulic valve lash adjustment, four valves per cylinder
	Mixture preparation	Biturbo charging with two VTG turbochargers, expansion intake system, intake manifold injection
	Compression ratio	9.0:1
Power Transfer	Transmission	Model M97/705 six-speed manual transmission
	Gear ratio, 1st gear	3.15
	Gear ratio, 2nd gear	1.89
	Gear ratio, 3rd gear	1.4
	Gear ratio, 4th gear	1.09
	Gear ratio, 5th gear	0.89
	Gear ratio, 6th gear	0.73
	Gear ratio, 7th gear	
	Gear ratio, reverse gear	2.86
	Axle ratio	3.44
	Locking effect in %	28 / 40
	Drive	Rear-wheel drive
Body and Suspension	Front-wheel suspension	Independent suspension on McPherson struts, transverse and longitudinal control arms, split wishbones, coil springs with helper springs, uniball support bearings, actively controlled twin-tube gas pressure shock absorbers (PASM)
	Rear-wheel suspension	Wheels individually guided on five control arms, split wishbones, coil springs with helper springs, actively controlled monotube gas pressure shock absorbers (PASM)
	Steering	Hydraulically assisted rack and pinion
	Turning circle	35.75 ft.
	Brake system	Hydraulic system, perforated and internally ventilated carbon-ceramic discs (PCCB) with aluminum brake pot, six-piston aluminum monoblock calipers at the front, four-piston aluminum monoblock calipers at the rear
	Brake discs in inches	15 x 1.3 front; 13.8 x 1.1 rear
	Rim sizes in inches	9 x 19 / 12 x 19
	Tire sizes	245/35ZR19 / 325/30ZR19
Dimensions and Weights	Length / width / height in inches	176 / 73 / 50.6
	Wheelbase	92.5 in.
	Front and rear track in inches	59.4 / 61.2
	Empty weight in lbs.	3,020
	Trunk volume	3.7 cu. ft.
	Fuel tank contents in gal.	23.8
Performance	Maximum speed	205 mph
	Time from 0 to 62 mph	3.5 sec.
	Fuel consumption	19.75 mpg
Other	Total made	519
	Price at market launch	237,578 euros

911 GT3 RS

Model	Series	911 991.1
	Sales designation	911 GT3 RS
	Production period	2015–2016
Engine	Type	Liquid-cooled six-cylinder boxer
	Displacement	243.9 cu. in.
	Bore x stroke in inches	4 x 3.2
	Output in hp / kW	500 / 368 at 8,250 rpm
	Torque	339 ft.-lbs. at 6,250 rpm
	Valve control	DOHC with variable timing (VarioCam) on intake and exhaust side and hydraulic valve lash adjustment, four valves per cylinder
	Mixture preparation	Direct fuel injection
	Compression ratio	12.9:1
Power Transfer	Transmission	Seven-speed, dual-clutch transmission (PDK)
	Gear ratio, 1st gear	3.75
	Gear ratio, 2nd gear	2.38
	Gear ratio, 3rd gear	1.72
	Gear ratio, 4th gear	1.34
	Gear ratio, 5th gear	1.11
	Gear ratio, 6th gear	0.96
	Gear ratio, 7th gear	0.84
	Gear ratio, reverse gear	3.42
	Axle ratio	4.19
	Locking effect in %	Regulated rear axle transverse lock
	Drive	Rear-wheel drive
Body and Suspension	Front-wheel suspension	Independent suspension on McPherson struts, transverse and longitudinal control arms, actively controlled twin-tube gas pressure shock absorbers (PASM)
	Rear-wheel suspension	Wheels individually guided on five control arms, split wishbones, actively controlled monotube gas pressure shock absorbers (PASM)
	Steering	Electromechanical power steering with variable steering ratio, rear axle steering
	Turning circle	36.4 ft.
	Brake system	Hydraulic system, perforated and internally ventilated discs all round, six-piston aluminum monoblock calipers at the front, four-piston aluminum monoblock calipers at the rear
	Brake discs in inches	15 x 1.3 front; 15 x 1.2 rear
	Rim sizes in inches	9.5 x 20 / 12.5 x 21
	Tire sizes	265/35ZR20 / 325/30ZR21
Dimensions and Weights	Length / width / height in inches	189 / 74 / 50.8
	Wheelbase	96.7 in.
	Front and rear track in inches	62.5 / 61.3
	Empty weight in lbs.	3,130
	Trunk volume	4.4 cu. ft. front, 9.2 rear
	Fuel tank contents in gal.	16.9 (optional: 23.8)
Performance	Maximum speed	192.6 mph
	Time from 0 to 62 mph	3.3 sec.
	Fuel consumption	18.5 mpg
Other	Total made	6,128
	Price at market launch	181,690 euros

911 GT3 RS

Model	Series	911 991.2
	Sales designation	911 GT3 RS
	Production period	2018–2019
Engine	Type	Liquid-cooled, six-cylinder boxer
	Displacement	243.8 cu. in.
	Bore x stroke in inches	4 x 3.2
	Output in hp / kW	520 / 383 at 8,400 rpm
	Torque	346 ft.-lbs. at 6,250 rpm
	Valve control	DOHC with variable timing (VarioCam) on intake and exhaust side and fixed valve train, four valves per cylinder
	Mixture preparation	Direct fuel injection
	Compression ratio	13.3:1
Power Transfer	Transmission	Seven-speed, dual-clutch transmission (PDK)
	Gear ratio, 1st gear	3.75
	Gear ratio, 2nd gear	2.38
	Gear ratio, 3rd gear	1.72
	Gear ratio, 4th gear	1.34
	Gear ratio, 5th gear	1.11
	Gear ratio, 6th gear	0.96
	Gear ratio, 7th gear	0.84
	Gear ratio, reverse gear	3.42
	Axle ratio	4.19
	Locking effect in %	Regulated rear axle transverse lock
	Drive	Rear-wheel drive
Body and Suspension	Front-wheel suspension	Independent suspension on McPherson struts, transverse and longitudinal control arms, uniball bearings, actively controlled twin-tube gas pressure shock absorbers (PASM)
	Rear-wheel suspension	Wheels individually guided on five control arms, split wishbones, uniball bearings, actively controlled monotube gas pressure shock absorbers (PASM)
	Steering	Electromechanical power steering with variable steering ratio, rear axle steering
	Turning circle	36.4 ft.
	Brake system	Hydraulic system, perforated and internally ventilated discs all round, six-piston aluminum monoblock calipers at the front, four-piston aluminum monoblock calipers at the rear
	Brake discs in inches	15 x 1.33 front; 15 x 1.2 rear
	Rim sizes in inches	9.5 x 20 / 12.5 x 21
	Tire sizes	265/35ZR20 / 325/30ZR21
Dimensions and Weights	Length / width / height in inches	179.4 / 74 / 50.4
	Wheelbase	96.6 in.
	Front and rear track in inches	62.5 / 61.3
	Empty weight in lbs.	3,141
	Trunk volume	4.4 cu. ft.
	Fuel tank contents in gal.	17.7 (optional: 23.8)
Performance	Maximum speed	193.8 mph
	Time from 0 to 62 mph	3.2 sec.
	Fuel consumption	17.8 mpg
Other	Total made	5,517
	Price at market launch	195,137 euros

911 GT2 RS

Model	Series	911 991.2
	Sales designation	911 GT2 RS
	Production period	2017–2018
Engine	Type	Liquid-cooled, six-cylinder boxer
	Displacement	231.9 cu. in.
	Bore x stroke in inches	4 x 3.05
	Output in hp / kW	700 / 515 at 7,000 rpm
	Torque	553 ft.-lbs. at 2,500–4,500 rpm
	Valve control	DOHC with variable intake-side timing and valve lift. Switching (VarioCam Plus) and hydraulic valve lash adjustment, four valves per cylinder
	Mixture preparation	Biturbo charging with two VTG turbochargers, direct injection
	Compression ratio	9.0:1
Power Transfer	Transmission	Seven-speed, dual-clutch transmission (PDK)
	Gear ratio, 1st gear	3.91
	Gear ratio, 2nd gear	2.29
	Gear ratio, 3rd gear	1.58
	Gear ratio, 4th gear	1.18
	Gear ratio, 5th gear	0.94
	Gear ratio, 6th gear	0.79
	Gear ratio, 7th gear	0.67
	Gear ratio, reverse gear	3.55
	Axle ratio	3.96
	Locking effect in %	Regulated rear axle transverse lock
	Drive	Rear-wheel drive
Body and Suspension	Front-wheel suspension	Independent suspension on McPherson struts, transverse and longitudinal control arms, uniball bearings, actively controlled twin-tube gas pressure shock absorbers (PASM)
	Rear-wheel suspension	Wheels individually guided on five control arms, split wishbones, uniball bearings; actively controlled monotube gas pressure shock absorbers (PASM)
	Steering	Electromechanical power steering with variable steering ratio, rear axle steering
	Turning circle	36.4 ft.
	Brake system	Hydraulic system, perforated and internally ventilated carbon-ceramic discs (PCCB) with aluminum brake pot, six-piston aluminum monoblock calipers at the front, four-piston aluminum monoblock calipers at the rear
	Brake discs in inches	16.14 x 1.4 front, 15.35 x 1.3 rear
	Rim sizes in inches	9.5 x 20 / 12.5 x 21
	Tire sizes	265/35ZR20 / 325/30ZR21
Dimensions and Weights	Length / width / height in inches	179 / 74 / 51
	Wheelbase	95.87 in.
	Front and rear track in inches	62.5 / 61.3
	Empty weight in lbs.	3,240
	Trunk volume	4.06 cu. ft.
	Fuel tank contents in gal.	16.9 (optional: 23.8)
Performance	Maximum speed	211 mph
	Time from 0 to 62 mph	2.8 sec.
	Fuel consumption	19.9 mpg
Other	Total made	4,094
	Price at market launch	285,220 euros

911 GT3 RS

Model	Series	911 992
	Sales designation	911 GT3 RS
	Production period	From 2022
Engine	Type	Liquid-cooled, six-cylinder boxer
	Displacement	243.8 cu. in.
	Bore x stroke in inches	4 x 3.20
	Output in hp / kW	525 / 386 at 8,500 rpm
	Torque	343 ft.-lbs.
	Valve control	DOHC with variable timing (VarioCam) on intake and exhaust side and fixed valve train, four valves per cylinder
	Mixture preparation	Biturbo charging with two VTG turbochargers, direct injection
	Compression ratio	9.0:1
Power Transfer	Transmission	Direct fuel injection
	Gear ratio, 1st gear	3.75
	Gear ratio, 2nd gear	2.38
	Gear ratio, 3rd gear	1.72
	Gear ratio, 4th gear	1.34
	Gear ratio, 5th gear	1.11
	Gear ratio, 6th gear	0.96
	Gear ratio, 7th gear	0.84
	Gear ratio, reverse gear	3.42
	Axle ratio	4.27
	Locking effect in %	Controlled rear axle transverse lock
	Drive	Rear-wheel drive
Body and Suspension	Front-wheel suspension	Independent suspension on double wishbones, drop-shaped wishbones, all bearings with Uniball, actively controlled shock absorbers (PASM)
	Rear-wheel suspension	Wheels individually guided on five control arms, split wishbones, all suspension bearings with Uniball; active controlled monotube gas pressure dampers (PASM)
	Steering	Electromechanical power steering with variable steering ratio, rear axle steering
	Turning circle	34.4 ft.
	Brake system	Hydraulic system, perforated and internally ventilated discs all around, six-piston aluminum monoblock calipers at the front, four-piston aluminum monoblock calipers at the rear
	Brake discs in inches	16 x 1.4 front; 15 x 1.2 rear
	Rim sizes in inches	10 x 20 / 13 x 21
	Tire sizes	275/35ZR20 / 335/30ZR21
Dimensions and Weights	Length / width / height in inches	180 / 74.8 / 52
	Wheelbase	96.7 in.
	Front and rear track in inches	64.2 / 62.3
	Empty weight in lbs.	3,196
	Trunk volume	
	Fuel tank contents in gal.	16.9 (optional: 23.8)
Performance	Maximum speed	184 mph
	Time from 0 to 62 mph	3.2 sec.
	Fuel consumption	17.6 mpg
Other	Total made	
	Price at market launch	229,517 euros

PORSCHE